Autobiography

14

Editor: William Buford
Assistant Editor: Diane Speakman
Managing Editor: Tracy Shaw
Associate Editor: Graham Coster
Executive Editor: Pete de Bolla
Design: Chris Hyde
Editorial and Office Assistant: Emily Dening
Editorial Assistants: Michael Comeau, Margaret Costa, Michael Hofmann, Alicja Kobiernicka, Piers Spence
Editorial Board: Malcolm Bradbury, Elaine Feinstein, Ian Hamilton, Leonard Michaels
US Editor: Jonathan Levi, 325 Riverside Drive, Apartment 81, New York, New York 10025

Editorial and Subscription Correspondence: Granta, 44a Hobson Street, Cambridge CB1 1NL. (0223) 315290.
All manuscripts are welcome but must be accompanied by a stamped, self-addressed envelope or they cannot be returned.

Subscriptions: £12.00 for four issues.

Back Issues: £3.50 each. *Granta* 1, 2, 3, 4 and 9 are no longer available. All prices include postage.

Granta is set by Lindonprint Typesetters, Cambridge, and is printed by Hazell Watson and Viney Ltd, Aylesbury, Bucks.

Granta is published by Granta Publications Ltd and distributed by Penguin Books Ltd, Harmondsworth, Middlesex, England; Penguin Books Australia Ltd, Ringwood, Victoria, Australia; Penguin Books Canada Ltd, 2801 John Street, Markham, Ontario, Canada L3R 1B4; Penguin Books (NZ) Ltd, 182–90 Wairau Road, Auckland 10, New Zealand. This selection copyright © 1985 by Granta Publications Ltd. Each work published in *Granta* is copyright of the author.

Cover by Chris Hyde

Granta 14, Winter 1984

ISSN 0017-3231
ISBN 014-00-75674

Published with the assistance of the Eastern Arts Association

CONTENTS

Norman Lewis Jackdaw Cake   7

Raymond Carver Where he was: Memories of my Father   19

Beryl Bainbridge Funny Noises with our Mouths   29

Michael Ignatieff August in my Father's House   37

Doris Lessing Impertinent Daughters   51

Vladimir Rybakov Family Politics   71

Breyten Breytenbach Punishable Innocence   85

Todd McEwen Paramilitarism in Costa del Burger   95

Eddie Limonov Eddie-baby   107

William Boyd Alpes Maritimes   127

Josef Škvorecký Failed Saxophonist   143

Don McCullin A Life in Photographs   171

Reinaldo Arenas A Poet in Cuba   197

Christian McEwen The Business of Mourning   209

Jaroslav Seifert Skating with Lenin   217

Adam Mars-Jones Weaning   231

Notes from Abroad

Bernard Crick On the Orwell Trail   236

Notes on Contributors   256

Literary Meaning
From Phenomenology to Deconstruction
WILLIAM RAY

'One of the finest, most interesting studies in literary theory which I have read for some time. The book offers at once an attractively wide-ranging survey of a whole set of major modern literary theories, and a particular, controversial and challenging case about them. It is packed with insights, a pleasure to read . . .'
Terry Eagleton
240 pages, hardback **£17.50**   (0 631 13457 3)
paperback **£5.95**   (0 631 13458 1)

A View from the Spire
William Golding's Later Novels
DON CROMPTON

This is the first critical study of Golding's later novels, and provides chapter-by-chapter examinations of all his fictions from *The Spire* onwards. It gives special attention to the contrasting problems posed by the three most recent – *Darkness Visible, Rites of Passages* and *The Paper Men.*
208 pages, **£15.00**   (0 631 13826 9)

English Satire and the Satiric Tradition
Edited by CLAUDE RAWSON

Written by some of the most distinguished scholars of the subject, this book represents a major and panoramic reassessment of the satiric tradition in English literature.
304 pages, hardback **£22.50**   (0 631 13271 6)
paperback **£7.50**   (0 631 13272 4)

The Reading of Proust
DAVID ELLISON

An important and original contribution to the understanding of Proust, both in its exploration of the connection between Proust and John Ruskin and in its application of literary theory to detailed readings of Proust's work.
256 pages, **£17.50**   (0 631 13569 3)

Puns
W.D. REDFERN

Puns are traditionally the lowest form of wit. This book asks us to think twice about their place in our lives and our culture. It is at different moments an analysis, a history and an anthology of puns. It collects and dissects them in literature, and finds them too in popular culture, the visual arts, in graffiti, in slips of the tongue, in dreams, cliches and proverbs, and in advertising.
240 pages, **£14.95**   (0 631 13793 9)

Basil Blackwell

ARENA

PROVOCATIVE ...

Two memorable novels from one of the most distinguished and influential writers of our time. In **The Sunlight Dialogues,** John Gardner explores the heart, soul and fantasies of America, silent in its majority and forgotten by its dreams. **October Light** tells of the strange battle of wills between brother and sister; a profound, marvellously touching novel of humour, imagination and compassion.

THE SUNLIGHT DIALOGUES £3.95
OCTOBER LIGHT £2.95

HAUNTING ...

When an artist decides to stay at an almost deserted hotel, he soon becomes haunted by the mystery and sense of tragedy surrounding O-Nami, his strange, almost mad hostess. He wants to paint her portrait, but first he must solve the enigma of her life.
'Soseki doesn't shrink from seeking, and even finding exquisite pearls of beauty' **The Guardian £1.95**

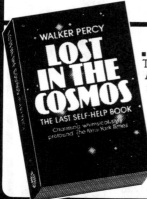

... AND MIND BOGGLING

The ultimate self-help guide from one of America's most respected contemporary novelists and thinkers. Combining philosophy, religion and morals with the wit of The Hitchiker's Guide to the Galaxy, **Lost in the Cosmos** is a provocative, vibrant, sharply funny and dazzlingly clever exercise in popular philosophy which gives no answers but asks the most important questions.
'A true work of innovation' **Library Journal £2.95**

The best in contemporary writing

The publishing of autobiography has been a tradition of JOHN MURRAY since the firm was established in 1768. Among those currently in print, and forthcoming, are:

KENNETH CLARK: **Another Part of the Wood** (£7.95) and **The Other Half** (£7.95) 'Lord Clark's two volumes are among the best written, sharpest and most entertaining memoirs of our time.' Michael Ratcliffe, **The Times**

KENNETH CLARK

PATRICK LEIGH FERMOR: **A Time of Gifts** (£9.50). There will now be three volumes of these memoirs and the second, **Between the Woods and the Water**, will be published in the Autumn 1985

JOHN BETJEMAN: **Summoned by Bells** (£6.95, paperback £4.50) The late Poet Laureate's highly acclaimed verse autobiography

DERVLA MURPHY: **Wheels Within Wheels** (£8.95). 'A very entertaining, as well as a compassionate book.' **The Economist**

JOHN BETJEMAN

FREYA STARK: **Beyond Euphrates** 1928-33: (£12.50); **The Coast of Incense**: 1933-39 (£12.50); **Dust in the Lion's Paw**: 1939-46 (£9.50)

IRIS ORIGO: **Images and Shadows** (£9.50). 'All her work has delighted me, and in this autobiography she is at her best.' Raymond Mortimer, **The Sunday Times**

FREYA STARK

BEATRICE HARRISON: **The Cello and the Nightingales** (June 1985). The memoirs of one of the best-loved British instrumentalists of this century. Foreword by Julian Lloyd-Webber.

JEROME K. JEROME: **My Life and Times** (£9.50) Reissued autobiography of the author of **Three Men in a Boat**

Details of the above, and our other autobiographies, memoirs and letters in print can be obtained from 50 Albemarle Street, London W1X 4BD

JEROME K. JEROME

NORMAN LEWIS

JACKDAW CAKE

When I was first pushed by my mother into the presence of my Aunt Polly, the bandages had only been removed from her face a few days before. They had exposed a patchwork of skin—pink and white—glazed in some places, and matt-surfaced in others, dependent upon the area of thigh or buttock from which it had been stripped to cover her burns. She had difficulty in closing her eyes (sometimes while asleep the lids would snap open). The fire had reached every part of her and she spoke in a harsh whisper that I could hardly understand. It was impossible to judge whether or not I was welcome, because the grey stripe of mouth provided by plastic surgery in its infancy could hold no expression. She bent down stiffly to proffer a cheek and, prodded by my mother, I reached up to select a smooth surface among the puckerings, the ridges and the nests of tiny wrinkles, and touch it with my lips.

In the background the second aunt, Annie, wearing long white gloves, holding a fan like a white feather-duster, and dressed as if for her wedding, waited smilingly. I was soon to learn that the smile was one that nothing could efface. Dodging in and out of a door at the back of the hallway, the third aunt, Li, seemed like a startled animal. She was weeping silently, and with these tears I would soon become familiar.

I was nine years of age, and the adults peopling my world seemed on the whole irrational, but it was an irrationality I had come to accept as the norm. My mother had brought me to this vast house and told me, without discussion, preparation, or warning, that I was to live among these strangers—for whom I was to show respect, even love—for an unspecified period of time. The prospect troubled me, but like an Arab child resigned in his religion, I soon learned to accept this new twist in the direction of my life, and the sounds of incessant laughter and grief soon lost all significance, became commonplace and thus passed without notice.

My mother, bastion of wisdom and fountainhead of truth in my universe, had gone, her flexible maternal authority replaced by the disciplines of my fire-scarred Aunt Polly, an epileptic who had suffered at least one fit per day since the age of fourteen, in the course of which she had fallen once from a window, once into a river, and twice into a fire. Every day, usually in the afternoon, she staged an unconscious drama, when she rushed screaming from room to room, sometimes bloodied by a fall, and once leaving a menstrual splash on the highly polished floor. It was difficult to decide whether she liked or disliked me, because she extended a tyranny in small ways over all who had dealings with her. In my case she issued a stream of whispered edicts relating to such matters as politeness, punctuality and personal cleanliness, and by being scrupulous in their observance I found that we got along together fairly well. I scored marks with her by mastery of the tedious and lengthy collects I was obliged to learn for recitation at Sunday school. When I showed myself as word-perfect in one of these it was easy to believe that she was doing her best to smile, as she probably did also when I accompanied her in my thin and whining treble in one of her harmonium recitals of such favourite hymns as 'Through the Night of Doubt and Sorrow'.

Smiling Aunt Annie, who counted for very little in the household, and who seemed hardly to notice my presence, loved to dress up, and spent an hour or two every day doing this. Sometimes she would come on the scene attired like Queen Mary in a hat like a dragoon's shako, and at other times she would be a female cossack with cartridge pockets and high boots. Later when I went to school, and became very sensitive to the opinions of my schoolfriends, she waylaid me once on my way home, to my consternation, got up as a Spanish dancer in a frilled blouse and skirt, with a high comb stuck into her untidy grey hair.

Li, youngest of the aunts, was poles apart from either sister. She and Polly had not spoken to each other for years, and occupied downstairs rooms at opposite ends of the house, while Annie made her headquarters in the room separating them, and when necessary transmitted curt messages from one to the other.

My grandfather, whom I saw only at weekends, filled every corner of the house with his deep, competitive voice, and a personality aromatic as cigar-smoke. At this time he had been a widower for twenty-five years; a man with the face of his day—a prow of a nose, bulging eyes, and an Assyrian beard—who saw himself as close to God, and sometimes conversed with Him in a loud and familiar voice on business matters. A single magnificent coup had raised him to take his place among the eleven leading citizens of Carmarthen, with a house in Wellfield Road. It was the purchase of a cargo of ruined tea from a ship sunk in Swansea harbour, which he laundered, packaged in bags dangerously imprinted with the Royal crest, and sold off at a profit of several thousand percent to village shops and remote farming communities scattered through the hills.

This had bought him a house full of clocks and mirrors, with teak doors, a wine cellar, and a wide staircase garnished with wooden angels and lamps. After that he was to possess a French modiste as his mistress, the town's first Model T Ford, and a valuable grey parrot, named Prydeyn after a hero of *The Mabinogion*—too old by the time of my arrival to talk, but which could still, as it hung from a curtain rod in the drawing room, produce in its throat a passable imitation of a small, squeaking fart.

My grandfather had started life as plain David Lewis but, swept along on the tide of saline tea, he followed the example of the neighbours in his select street, and got himself a double-barrelled name, becoming David Warren Lewis. He put a crest on his notepaper, and worked steadily at his family tree, pushing the first of our ancestors back further and further into history until they became contemporary with King Howel Dda. For a brief moment the world was at his feet. He had even been invited to London to shake the flabby hand of Edward VII, but on the home front his life fell apart. The three daughters he had kept at home were dotty, a fourth got into trouble and had to be exported to Canada to marry a settler who had advertised for a wife, and the fifth, Lalla, an artist of sorts, who had escaped him to marry a school teacher called Bennett and settled in Cardiff, was spoken of as far from bright.

This was Welsh Wales, full of ugly chapels, of hidden money, psalm-singing and rain. The hills all around were striped and patched with small bleak fields, with sheep—seen from our house as small as lice—cropping the coarse grass, and seas of bracken pouring down the slopes to hurl themselves against the walls of the town. In autumn it rained every day. The water burst through the banks of the reservoir on top of Pen Lan and sent a wave full of fish down Wellfield Road, and then, spilling the fish all the way along Waterloo Terrace, as far as the market.

What impressed me most were the jackdaws, and the snails, on which the jackdaws largely lived. The snails were of every colour, curled and striped like little turbans in blue, pink, green and yellow, and it was hard to walk down the garden path without crushing them underfoot. There were thousands of jackdaws everywhere in the town, and our garden was always full of them. Sensing that my mad aunts presented no danger, they were completely tame. They would tap on the windows to be let into the house and go hopping from room to room in search of scraps.

Weekly the great ceremony took place of the baking of the jackdaw cake. For this, co-operation was forced upon my three aunts, for ingredients had to be decided upon, and bought: eggs, raisins, candied peel and sultanas, required to produce a cake of exceptional richness. Li did the shopping, because Polly was unable to leave the house, and Annie too confused to be able to buy what was necessary, put down her money, and pick up the change.

Each aunt took turns to bake and ice the cake. While they were kept busy doing this they seemed quite changed. Annie wore an ordinary dress and stopped laughing, Li didn't cry any more, and Polly's fits were quieter than on any other day. While the one whose turn it was did the baking, the others stood about in the kitchen and watched, and were for once quite easy to talk to.

On Saturday mornings at ten o'clock the cake was fed to the jackdaws. This had been happening for years, so that by half past nine the garden was full of birds, up to a hundred of them balancing and swinging with a tremendous gleeful outcry on the bushes and the low boughs of the trees. This was the great moment of the week for my aunts, and therefore for me. The cake would be cut into three sections and placed on separate plates on the kitchen table, and then at ten the kitchen windows were flung wide to admit the great black, squawking cataract of birds. For some hours after this weekly event the atmosphere was one of calm and contentment, and then the laughter and the weeping would start again.

Polly did all the cooking, and apart from that sat in the drawing-room, watched over by the parrot Prydeyn, crocheting bed-spreads with the stiff fingers that had not been spared by the fire. Li collected the instructions and the money left for her, and went out shopping, and Annie dressed up as a pirate, harlequin, clown, or whatever came into her head.

My grandfather worked in his tea-merchant's business in King Street, leaving the house early in the morning and returning as late at night as he decently could. On Sunday mornings, like all the rest of the community, he was hounded by his conscience to chapel, but in the afternoon he was accustomed to spend a little time with the Old English Game Fowl he bred, showed and—as the rumour went—had entered in secret cock-fights in his disreputable youth. They were kept in wire pens in the back garden: each cockerel, or 'king' as it was known, separately with its hens. Show judges used to visit the house to test a contestant's ferocity by poking at it through the wire netting with a stick to which a coloured rag had been attached—any bird failing to attack being instantly disqualified.

The comb, wattles, ear-lobes and any loose skin were removed from the head and neck of these birds, and there was frequently a little extra trimming-up to be done. Experience and skill were called for to catch and subdue a king in his prime and sometimes, like a Roman gladiator, my grandfather used a net. Once the bird was tied up and the head imprisoned in a wooden collar, he set to work in a leisurely fashion with a snip here and a snip there, using a specially-designed variety of scissors known as a dubber.

The game cocks often escaped from their pens and strutted about the back garden on the look-out for something to attack. My Aunt Li and I were usually chosen. They had enormously long legs—so long that they appeared to be walking on miniature stilts. My grandfather and my aunt Polly knew how to handle them and carried garden rakes to push them aside, but Li and I went in great fear of them. This they probably sensed, for any king that had managed to break out had the habit of lying in wait well out of sight until either of us came on the scene, when he would rush to the attack, leaping high into the air to strike at our faces with his spurs. In the end my aunt and I formed a defensive alliance, and this brought us closer together.

We based our strategy on cutting down the birds' numbers. Unlike normal chickens the game fowl laid only a few small eggs and had a short breeding season. Polly looked after the brooding hens and chicks, kept separate from the kings, and Li's method was to wait until her sister was out of the way, either having or recovering from a fit, then take several eggs from the clutch under a sitting hen and drop them into boiling water for a few seconds before putting them back. This promised to ease the situation in the coming year but did nothing to help us in our present trouble. My aunt bought a cat of a breed locally supposed to be descended from a pair of wild cats captured in Llandeilo forest about a hundred years ago. She brought it back in a sack one night, kept it in an outhouse without feeding it for three days, then let it loose in the garden. At this time there were two or three game cocks at large, and the scuffle and outcry that followed raised our hopes; but in the morning the kings were still strutting through the flower-beds ready for battle with all comers, and of the cat there was nothing to be seen.

As confidence and sympathy grew between us, my Aunt Li and I took to wandering round the countryside together. Li was a small woman, hardly bigger than me. She would wet me with her tears, and I would listen to her sad ravings and sometimes stroke her hand. One day she must have come to the grand decision to tell me what lay at the root of her sorrow. We climbed a stile and went into a field and, fixing her glistening eyes upon me she said, 'What I am going to tell you now you will remember every single day of your life.' But whatever she revealed must have been so startling that memory rejected it, for not a word of what was said remains in my mind.

The Towy River made and dominated Carmarthen, and it was always with us, whenever we went on our walks, throwing great, shining loops through the fields, doubling back on itself sometimes in a kind of afterthought, to encircle some riverside shack or a patch of sedge in which cows stood knee-deep to graze. In winter the whole valley filled up with floods, and people remembered nervously the prophecy of the enchanter Merlin that the floods would eventually engulf the town where he was buried. For my aunt these offered endless excitement, with drowning sheep and cattle being carried away on the yellow whiplash of the river's current, disappearing beneath the surface one after another as it swept them towards the sea, and the coracle men in their black, prehistoric boats spinning in whirlpools as they prodded at animals with their poles, trying to steer them to safety.

In summer the people of Carmarthen went on trips to the seaside at Llanstephan, at the river's mouth. There was no more beautiful, wilder or stranger place in the British Isles, but the local Welsh no longer saw its beauty, and familiarity and boredom drove all who could afford it further afield to Tenby, which was certainly larger and jollier. The Normans had built a castle in Llanstephan in about 1250, and there was an ancient church, and a few Victorian cottages, but apart from this handful of buildings little in the landscape had changed for thousands of years. Here the Towy finally unwound itself into the sea, its estuary enclosed in a great, silken spread of sand occupying a third of the horizon, to which our century had added not a single detail but the bones of two foundered ships in process of digestion by mud.

For the villagers a shadow hung over this scene. On fine Sundays and holidays throughout the summer, miners and their families would descend upon it. The train brought them from their hellish valleys to Ferryside across the estuary, and from Ferryside they would cross by boat to take joyous possession of the sands. At first warning of this invasion the people of Llanstephan made a bolt for their houses, slamming their doors behind them, drawing their curtains, keeping out of sight until six hours later the turn of the tide released them from their misery.

The miners were despised and hated by the villagers of Llanstephan in those days just as were field labourers in England by their more comfortable fellow-countrymen. To the villagers the miners were no better than foreigners, people whose habits were beyond their understanding—in particular the frantic pleasure they showed, and their noisily offensive good humour, when released in the calm and sober environment of Llanstephan on a Sunday afternoon. When I saw my first miners come ashore in Llanstephan I asked my aunt if they were dwarfs, so reduced in size had these Welshmen—identical in stock to those of Llanstephan—become after three generations of lives spent underground.

I n Carmarthen and its surrounding villages people were obsessed with relationships, and practically everyone I met turned out to be a cousin four, five or even six times removed. Cousins who were old—say over thirty—were respectfully known as Aunties or Uncles, and one of the reasons for our trip to Llanstephan was to see an Auntie Williams who lived in the first of the line of cottages along the sea front. These were like little houses from a child's picture book, with old-fashioned gardens full of rosemary and honeysuckle, tabby cats everywhere, and fantail pigeons on the roofs.

Auntie Williams was a Welsh woman of the kind they still showed on picture postcards wearing black, steeple-crowned hats, and although the old witch's hat had gone she still wore in all weathers the shawl that went with it. She was famous for her early-red-apple tree—perhaps the last of its kind—which bore its ripe, brilliantly red fruit as early as August; and also for her husband, once a handsome man—as proved by the large coloured photograph in her front room, taken in uniform shortly before the Battle of the Somme, in which most of his lower jaw had been shot away. These days he wore a mask over the lower part of his face, and a tube protruding from his right nostril was fixed behind his ear. He was with us for lunch, dressed in a jaunty check jacket. Auntie Williams had boiled a sewin (a Welsh salmon); mixing a scrap of pink fish well-chewed by her into a bowl of gruel she fed her husband through the tube, and gently massaged his throat as it went down. Everybody in Llanstephan admired him for the cheerfulness with which he suffered his disability. He had published a little philosophical book designed to help others to bear such physical handicaps.

The finish of the meal, joined by two more neighbouring aunties, was spoilt by the arrival of the ferry boat, bringing the miners and their families. They came unexpectedly, as the jetty had been put out of action by the villagers in the preceding week; but the villagers had underestimated the miners' determination to enjoy themselves, which caused them to drag the heavy boat with tremendous effort clear of the water and onto the sand.

Until this calamity the three Llanstephan aunties, with their round country faces and polished cheeks, almost hard to tell apart, had been full of smiles, and by his gestures and noises Uncle Williams had seemed brim-full of good humour. Aunt Li, whose vacant expression signified for me that she was not actually unhappy, was teasing a small crab she had found in a pool. Now suddenly, as the mining families climbed down from the boat and advanced towards us, a great change came over our family gathering. The miners' children, shrieking with delight, scampered ahead, and the miners and their wives trudged after them over the wet sand, carrying their boots and shoes, their little parcels of food, and two bulky packages. Watching this advance, the Llanstephan aunties' kindly, homely faces became different, barely recognizable. My Carmarthen relations laughed and wept in their meaningless way—or in the case of Polly were unable to produce a facial expression of any kind—but they had at least spared me the spectacle of anger, which was frighteningly new. The soft sing-song Welsh voices had lost their music and fallen flat as they talked of the wickedness of miners. It was a local theory, supported by the chapels, that poverty was the wage of sin—and the miners looked poor enough. Their women, who often worked alongside their men, were driven into the mines not by hunger, it was thought, but by shamelessness, and discussing this aspect of the mining life the Llanstephan aunties made the loading-up and manoeuvring of coal trucks in near-darkness a thousand feet under the earth seem a carnal indulgence.

Mr Williams went into the house and came back with a placard, which he fixed to a post by his wall. It said 'Remember the Sabbath Day, to keep it Holy', but the miners ignored it. Their children were everywhere, screaming with glee. They threw wet sand at each other, dug up cockles, dammed the little streams flowing on the beach, and even came to stare open-mouthed over the garden walls. When no-one was watching I sneaked away to try to join them, but we did not easily mix. Immersed in their games, they ignored me, and I was too shy to speak.

Presently a miner beckoned to me. He and his wife were setting out their picnic on a cloth spread over the dry sand. The man was short but very strong-looking, with bow legs, and a snake tattooed on each forearm. He asked me my name, and I told him; his wife looked up and smiled and gave me a slice of cake. 'Sit you down,' she said, and I was just going to when Auntie Williams spotted me and let out a screech. 'Come you back by here.'

I went back and Auntie Williams said, 'What she give you, then?' I showed her the cake and she took it away and threw it to the pigeons. Wanting to get away from her I went over to Li, but she was no longer blank-faced as she had been when I left her, and that meant that something had upset her. She had lost her crab, and I thought it might be that. 'Like me to find you another crab, Auntie?' I asked, but she shook her head.

On the beach, sandwiches had been passed out to the children. The man who had spoken to me opened a bottle of beer. He drank from the neck, and passed it to his wife. The couple who had been carrying the two brown paper parcels untied the string and unwrapped them. One of the parcels held the box part of a gramophone, and the other the horn, and these they fixed together. We watched from our chairs under the apple tree while this was going on. No-one spoke but I could feel the astonished horror. The people who had brought the gramophone wound it up and put on a record, and soon a thin, wheezing music reached us between the soft puffs of breeze and the squawking of the herring gulls flopping about overhead.

The people in the cottage next door had come out into the garden to watch what was going on, and one of them shouted a protest. Uncle Williams stood up, picked an apple and threw it in the direction of the couple with the gramophone, but with so little force that the apple hardly cleared our low wall. His example gave great encouragement to the others, though, and the man who had shouted from the garden next door threw a small stone. My feeling was that he never really intended to hit anything, and the stone splashed in a beach puddle, yards from the nearest of the miners, who gave no sign of realizing what was happening and went on eating their sandwiches and drinking their beer, never once looking in our direction. Next a bigger stone thudded on the sand, and there were more shouts from the cottages, and two or three children who had gone off to collect shells gave up and went back to join their parents.

More shouts and more stones followed—all the stones thrown by men whose aim was very bad, or who weren't trying. After a while the miners began to pack up, taking their time about it, and paying no attention at all to the villagers who were insulting them. The gramophone was taken apart and parcelled up as before, and everything they had brought with them packed away; then without looking back they began to move towards the ferry boat, and within half an hour they had managed to push the boat into the water; and that was the last of them.

Uncle Williams took down the placard and put it away, and his wife put on the kettle for tea. Nobody could find anything to say. The weather experts, who could tell by the look of the seaweed, had promised a fine afternoon, but the miners had ruined the day.

Li suddenly got up and said she was going home. 'We got two hours still to wait for the bus, Auntie,' I said. 'Never mind about the bus,' she said. 'I'm leaving now,' and she was off, marching down the path, and I could see by the way she was walking with her head thrown back and slightly to one side, that something had upset her, although there was no way of saying what. I'd seen enough of her by then to know that it wasn't the miners being there that bothered her—in which case it could only be something one of our Llanstephan relations had said or done. But what was it? I couldn't guess. There was no telling the way things took Aunt Li.

I ran to catch her up. It was six and a half miles to Carmarthen, but she was a fast walker, and I expected we'd beat the bus.

RAYMOND CARVER

WHERE HE WAS:
MEMORIES OF MY
FATHER

My dad's name was Clevie Raymond Carver. His family called him Raymond and friends called him CR. I was named Raymond Clevie Carver, Jr. I hated the 'Junior' part. When I was little my dad called me 'Frog', which was okay. But later, like everybody else in the family, he began calling me 'Junior'. He went on calling me this until I was thirteen or fourteen and announced that I wouldn't answer to that name any longer. So he began calling me 'Doc'. From then until his death on 17 June 1967, he called me 'Doc' or else 'Son'.

When he died, my mother telephoned my wife with the news. I was away from my family at the time, between lives, trying to enrol in the School of Library Science at the University of Iowa. When my wife answered the phone, my mother blurted out, 'Raymond's dead!' For a moment, my wife thought my mother was telling her that I was dead. Then my mother made it clear *which* Raymond she was talking about and my wife said, 'Thank God. I thought you meant *my* Raymond.'

My dad walked, hitched rides, and rode in empty box cars when he went from Arkansas to Washington State in 1934, looking for work. I don't know whether or not he was pursuing a dream when he went out to Washington. I doubt it. I don't think he dreamed much. I believe he was simply looking for steady work at decent pay. Steady work was meaningful work. He picked apples for a time and then landed a construction labourer's job on the Grand Coulee Dam. After he'd put aside a little money, he bought a car and drove back to Arkansas to help his folks, my grandparents, pack up for the move west. He said later that they were about to starve down there; and this wasn't meant as a figure of speech. It was during that short while in Arkansas, in a town called Leola, that my mother met my dad on the sidewalk as he came out of a tavern.

'He was drunk,' she said. 'I don't know why I let him talk to me. His eyes were glittery. I wish I'd had a crystal ball.' They'd met once, a year or so before, at a dance. He'd had girl-friends before her, my mother told me. 'Your dad always had a girl-friend, even after we married. He was my first and last. I never had another man. But I didn't miss anything.'

They were married by a Justice of the Peace on the day they left for Washington, this big tall country girl and an ex-farm hand turned construction worker. My mother spent her wedding night with my dad and his folks, all of them camped beside the road in Arkansas.

In Omak, Washington, my dad and mother lived in a little place not much bigger than a cabin. My grandparents lived next door. My dad was still working on the dam and later, with the huge turbines producing electricity and the water backed up for a hundred miles into Canada, he stood in the crowd and heard Franklin D. Roosevelt dedicate the dam. 'He never mentioned those guys who died building that dam,' my dad said. Some of his friends had died there, men from Arkansas, Oklahoma, and Missouri.

He then took a job in a sawmill in Clatskanie, Oregon, a little town alongside the Columbia river. I was born there, and my mother has a picture of my dad standing in front of the gate to the mill, proudly holding me up to face the camera. My bonnet is on crooked and about to come untied. His hat is pushed back on his forehead, and he's wearing a big grin. Was he going in to work, or just finishing his shift? It doesn't matter. In either case, he had a job and a family. These were his salad days.

In 1941 we moved to Yakima, Washington, where my dad went to work as a saw-filer, a skilled trade he'd learned at the mill in Clatskanie. When war broke out, he was given a deferment because his work was considered necessary to the war effort. Finished lumber was in demand by the armed services, and he kept his saws so sharp they could shave the hair off your arm.

After my dad had moved us to Yakima, he moved his folks into the same neighbourhood. By the mid-1940s, the rest of my dad's family—his brother, his sister and her husband, as well as uncles, cousins, nephews and most of their extended family and friends—had come out from Arkansas. All because my dad came out first. The men went to work at Boise Cascade, where my dad worked, and the women packed apples in the canneries. And in just a little while, it seemed—according to my mother—everybody was better off than my dad.

'Your dad couldn't keep money,' my mother said. 'Money burned a hole in his pocket. He was always doing for others.'

The first house I clearly remember living in, at 1515 South 15th Street, in Yakima, had an outdoor toilet. On Halloween night, or just any night, for the hell of it, neighbouring kids, kids in their early teens, would carry our toilet away and leave it next to the road. My dad would have to get somebody to help him bring it home. Or these kids would take the toilet and stand it in somebody else's back yard. Once they actually set it on fire. But ours wasn't the only house that had an outdoor toilet. When I was old enough to know what I was doing, I threw rocks at the other toilets when I'd see someone go inside. This was called bombing the toilets. After a while, though, everyone changed to indoor plumbing until, suddenly, our toilet was the last one in the neighbourhood. I remember the shame I felt when my third-grade teacher, Mr Wise, drove me home from school one day. I asked him to stop at the house just before ours, claiming I lived there.

I had one bad spanking from my dad when I was little. He took off his belt and laid it on me when he caught me walking down a railroad trestle. As he was whipping me, he said, 'This hurts me worse than it does you.' Even at the time, as small and dumb as I was, I knew this wasn't true. It had the sound of something his father might have said to him under the same circumstances.

I can recall what happened one night when my dad came home late to find that my mother had locked all the doors on him. He was drunk, and we could feel the house shudder as he rattled the door. When he'd managed to force open a window, she hit him between the eyes with a colander and knocked him out. We could see him down there on the grass. For years afterwards, I used to pick up this colander—it was as heavy as a rolling pin—and imagine what it would feel like to be hit in the face with something like that.

It was during this period that I remember my dad taking me into the bedroom, sitting me down on the bed, and telling me that I might have to go live with my Aunt LaVon for a while. I couldn't understand what I'd done that meant I'd have to go away from home to live. But this, too—whatever prompted it—must have blown over, more or less anyway, because we stayed together, and I didn't have to go live with her or anyone else.

For a time in the late forties we didn't have a car. We had to walk everywhere we wanted to go, or else take the bus that stopped near where they used to carry our toilet. I don't know why we didn't have a car, some sort of car, but we didn't. Still, it was all right with me that we didn't. I didn't miss it. I mean, we didn't have a car and that's all there was to it. Back then I didn't miss what I didn't have. 'We couldn't afford a car,' my mother said, when I asked her. 'It was your dad. He drank it up.'

If we wanted to fish, my dad and I would walk to some ponds that were only a couple of miles away, or to the Yakima river, only a little farther away than the ponds. With or without a car, we went fishing nearly every weekend. But once in a while my dad wouldn't want to get out of bed. 'He feels bad,' my mother would say. 'No wonder. You better leave him alone.'

I remember her pouring his whisky down the sink. Sometimes she'd pour it all out and sometimes, if she was afraid of getting caught, she'd only pour half of it out and then add water to the rest. I tasted some of his whisky once for myself. It was terrible stuff, and I didn't see how anybody could drink it.

When we finally did get a car, in 1949 or 1950, it was a 1938 Ford. But it threw a rod the first week we had it, and my dad had to have the motor rebuilt.

'We drove the oldest car in town,' my mother said. 'We could have had a Cadillac for all he spent on car repairs.' One time she found someone else's lipstick on the floorboards, along with a lacy handkerchief. 'See this?' she said to me. 'Some floozie left this in the car.'

Once I saw her take a pan of warm water into the bedroom where my dad was sleeping. She took his hand from under the covers and held it in the water. I stood in the doorway and watched. I wanted to know what was going on. This would make him talk in his sleep, she told me. There were things she needed to know, things she was sure he was keeping from her.

Every year or so, when I was little, we would take the North Coast Limited across the Cascade Mountains from Yakima to Seattle and stay in the Vance Hotel and eat, I remember, at a place called The Dinner Bell Café. Once we went to Ivar's Acres of Clams and drank glasses of warm clam broth.

Both my grandparents died in 1955. In 1956, the year I was to graduate from high school, my dad quit his job at the mill in Yakima and took a job in Chester, a little sawmill town in northern California. The reasons given at the time for his taking the job had to do with a higher hourly wage and the vague promise that he might, in a few years' time, succeed to the job of head filer in this new mill. But I think, in the main, that my dad had grown restless and simply wanted to try his luck elsewhere. Things had gotten a little too predictable for him in Yakima. Also, there were the deaths, within six months of each other, of my grandparents.

But just a few days after my graduation, when my mother and I were packed to move to Chester, my dad pencilled a letter to say he'd been sick for a while. He didn't want us to worry, he said, but he'd cut himself on a saw. Maybe he'd got a tiny sliver of steel in his blood. Anyway, something had happened and he'd had to miss work, he said. In the same mail was an unsigned postcard from somebody down there telling my mother that my dad was about to die and that he was drinking 'raw whisky'.

When we arrived in Chester my dad was living in a trailer that belonged to the company. I didn't recognize him immediately. I guess for a moment I didn't want to recognize him. He was skinny and pale and looked bewildered. His pants wouldn't stay up. He didn't look like my dad. My mother began to cry. My dad put his arm around her and patted her shoulder vaguely like he didn't know what this was all about, either. The three of us took up life together in the trailer, and we looked after him as best we could. But my dad was sick, and he couldn't get any better. I worked with him in the mill that summer and part of the fall. We'd get up in the mornings and eat eggs and toast while we listened to the radio, and then go out the door with our lunch pails. We'd pass through the gates together at eight in the morning, and I wouldn't see him again until quitting time. In November I went back to Yakima to be closer to my girl-friend, the girl I'd made up my mind I was going to marry.

He worked at the mill in Chester until the following February, when he collapsed on the job and was taken to hospital. My mother asked me to come down there and help. I caught a bus from Yakima to Chester, intending to drive them back to Yakima. But now, in addition to being physically sick, my dad was in the midst of a nervous breakdown, though none of us knew to call it that at the time. During the entire trip back to Yakima, he didn't speak, not even when asked a direct question. ('How do you feel, Raymond?' 'You okay, Dad?') He'd communicate, if he communicated at all, by moving his head or else turning his palms up as if to say he didn't know or care. The only time he said anything on the trip, and for nearly a month afterwards, was when I was speeding down a gravel road in Oregon and the car muffler came loose. 'You were going too fast,' he said.

Back in Yakima a doctor saw to it that my dad went to a psychiatrist. My mother and dad had to go on relief, as it was called, and the County paid for the psychiatrist. The psychiatrist asked my dad, 'Who is the President?' He'd had a question put to him that he could answer. 'Ike,' my dad said. Nevertheless, they put him on the fifth floor of Valley Memorial Hospital and began giving him electric shock treatments. I was married by then and about to start my own family. My dad was still locked up when my wife went into this same hospital, just one floor down, to have our first baby.

After she had delivered, I went upstairs to give my dad the news. They let me in through a steel door and showed me where I could find him. He was sitting on a couch with a blanket over his lap. *Hey*, I thought. *What in hell is happening to my dad?* I sat down next to him and told him he was a grandfather. He waited a minute and said, 'I feel like a grandfather.' That's all he said. He didn't smile or move. He was in a big room with a lot of other people. Then I hugged him, and he began to cry.

Somehow he got out of there. But now came the years when he couldn't work and just sat around the house trying to figure what next and what he'd done wrong in his life that he'd wound up like this. My mother went from job to crummy job. Much later she referred to that time he was in the hospital, and those years just afterwards, as 'when Raymond was sick.' The word 'sick' was never the same for me again.

In 1964, through the help of a friend, he was lucky enough to be hired at a mill in Klamath, California. He moved down there by himself to see if he could hack it. He lived not far from the mill in a one-room cabin, not much different from the place he and my mother had started living in when they went west. He scrawled letters to my mother, and if I called, she'd read them aloud to me over the phone. In the letters, he said it was touch and go. Every day he went to work

25

he felt like it was the most important day of his life. But every day, he told her, made the next day that much easier. He said for her to tell me he said hello. If he couldn't sleep at night, he said, he thought about me and the good times we used to have. Finally after a couple of months, he regained some of his confidence. He could do the work and didn't think he had to worry that he'd let anybody down ever again. When he was sure, he sent for my mother.

He'd been off work for six years and had lost everything in that time: home, car, furniture and appliances, including the big freezer that had been my mother's pride and joy. He'd lost his good name, too—Raymond Carver was someone who couldn't pay his bills—and his self-respect was gone. He'd even lost his virility. My mother told my wife, 'All during that time Raymond was sick we slept together in the same bed, but we didn't have relations. He wanted to a few times, but nothing happened. I didn't miss it, but I think he wanted to, you know.'

During those years I was trying to raise my own family and earn a living. But, with one thing and another, we found ourselves having to move a lot. I couldn't keep track of what was going on in my dad's life. But I did have a chance one Christmas to tell him I wanted to be a writer. I might as well have told him I wanted to become a plastic surgeon. 'What are you going to write about?' he wanted to know. Then, as if to help me out, he said, 'Write about stuff you know about. Write about some of those fishing trips we took.' I said I would, but I knew I wouldn't. 'Send me what you write,' he said. I said I'd do that, but then I didn't. I wasn't writing anything about fishing, and I didn't think he'd particularly care about, or even necessarily understand, what I was writing in those days. Besides, he wasn't a reader. Not the sort, anyway, I imagined I was writing for.

Then he died. I was a long way off, in Iowa City, with things still to say to him. I didn't have the chance to tell him goodbye, or that I thought he was doing great at his new job. That I was proud of him for making a come-back.

My mother said he came in from work that night and ate a big supper. Then he sat at the table by himself and finished what was left of a bottle of whisky, a bottle she found hidden in the bottom of the garbage under some coffee grounds a day or so later. Then he got up and went to bed, where my mother joined him a little later. But in the night she had to get up and make a bed for herself on the couch. 'He was snoring so loud I couldn't sleep,' she said. The next morning when she looked in on him, he was on his back with his mouth open, his cheeks caved in. *Grey-looking*, she said. She knew he was dead—she didn't need a doctor to tell her that. But she called one, anyway, and then she called my wife.

Among the pictures my mother kept of my dad and herself during those early days in Washington was a photograph of him standing in front of a car, holding a beer and a stringer of fish. In the photograph he is wearing his hat back on his forehead and has this awkward grin on his face. I asked her for it and she gave it to me, along with some others. I put it up on my wall, and each time we moved, I took the picture along and put it up on another wall. I looked at it carefully from time to time, trying to figure out some things about my dad, and maybe myself in the process. But I couldn't. My dad just kept moving farther and farther away from me and back into time. Finally, in the course of another move, I lost the photograph. It was then I tried to recall it, and at the same time make an attempt to say something about my dad, and how I thought that in some important ways we might be alike. I wrote the poem when I was living in an apartment house in an urban area south of San Francisco and at a time when I found myself, like dad, having trouble with alcohol. The poem was a way of trying to connect up with him.

PHOTOGRAPH OF MY FATHER IN HIS TWENTY-SECOND YEAR

October. Here in this dank, unfamiliar kitchen
I study my father's embarrassed young man's face.
Sheepish grin, he holds in one hand a string
of spiny yellow perch, in the other
a bottle of Carlsberg beer.

In jeans and flannel shirt, he leans
against the front fender of a 1934 Ford.
He would like to pose brave and hearty for his posterity,
wear his old hat cocked over his ear.
All his life my father wanted to be bold.

But the eyes give him away, and the hands
that limply offer the string of dead perch
and the bottle of beer. Father, I love you,
yet how can I say thank you, I who can't hold my liquor either
and don't even know the places to fish.

The poem is true in its particulars, except that my dad died in June and not October, as the first word of the poem says. I wanted a word with more than one syllable to it to make it linger a little. But more than that, I wanted a month appropriate to what I felt at the time I wrote the poem—a month of short days and failing light, smoke in the air, things perishing. June was summer nights and days, graduations, my wedding anniversary, the birthday of one of my children. June wasn't a month your father died in.

After the service at the funeral home, after we had moved outside, a woman I didn't know came over to me and said, 'He's happier where he is now.' I stared at this woman until she moved away. I still remember the little knob of a hat she was wearing. Then one of my dad's cousins—I didn't know the man's name—reached out and took my hand. 'We all miss him,' he said, and I knew he wasn't saying it to be polite.

I began to weep for the first time since receiving the news. I hadn't been able to before. I hadn't had the time, for one thing. Now, suddenly, I couldn't stop. I held my wife and wept while she said and did what she could to comfort me there in the middle of that summer afternoon.

I listened to people say consoling things to my mother, and I was glad that my dad's family had turned up, had come to where he was. I thought I'd remember everything that was said and done that day and maybe find a way to tell it sometime. But I didn't. I forgot it all, or nearly. What I do remember is that I heard our name used a lot that afternoon, my dad's name and mine. But I knew they were talking about my dad. *Raymond,* these people kept saying in their beautiful voices out of my childhood. *Raymond.*

BERYL BAINBRIDGE
FUNNY NOISES WITH
OUR MOUTHS

Beryl Bainbridge

My father ended up a commercial traveller; he didn't go from door to door, but that's what he was. Mostly he travelled only as far as Liverpool, twelve miles down the railway line, to a public house called the Caernarvon Castle. He used it as an office and met business contacts there. Sometimes his contacts were in paint, sometimes in scrap metal. For a period he was an agent to a metal-box manufacturer. When he went into town he was dandified—he wore a striped suit and a Homburg hat. His shoes glittered like glass. Indoors, he dressed in Home Guard battledress, with a black beret on his narrow head. When he wasn't cleaning he sat at the table making calculations on the backs of brown envelopes.

Every Friday he stayed at home to see to the house. He got down on his knees to scrub out the kitchen; he was very dedicated and very irritable. He grumbled that it wasn't right for a man to do what he had to do. My mother often said she wished he'd get the hell out and he always said that one of these days he *would* get out of this hell-hole once and for all. Leaping about the kitchen with his scrubbing-brush, he looked like a cross between General Montgomery and Old Mother Riley.

All his great battles had been fought before I was born. When he was fourteen he had gone as a cabin boy on a sailing ship to America. So he said. He'd imported the first matches to Berlin, dealt in diamonds in Holland, lived in Dublin during the Troubles for some dark unspecified purpose. By the time he was thirty he was in a 'good way of doing'. He was in shipping and in cotton and in property. Doors opened to him without appointment. A carnation in his buttonhole, he pranced like Fred Astaire up the steps of his beautiful Cotton Exchange, and when he entered the massive portals of the offices of the White Star Line, men of power nodded in his direction. That's what he said. Life had got at him in the meantime. It was a mystery to us and him where that golden lad before the mast had gone.

After he was dead I always thought of him as down-trodden, defeated, but when I was a child I thought differently. There was a song popular during the war, that my mother used to sing when dusting the furniture—

When that man is dead and gone
We'll go prancing down the street
Kissing everyone we meet
When that man is dead and gone...

It was about Hitler, but I imagined she was referring to my dad.

Once, when my mother sprained her ankle and he'd phoned for the doctor, my father flew into a rage at the state of the sheets on the bed. He'd wrapped a wet bandage about her foot and carried her upstairs like a child, but the sight of the crumpled bedding sent him into a fury. 'Do you want the doctor to think we live in a slum?' he shouted, jerking the sheets from under her swollen foot, making her hop round the room, fetch pillowcases, change the counterpane.

His moods were regular and followed a pattern. Anything could spark off the initial explosion—a political opinion, a lump in a potato, a lost collar-stud. Transformed in seconds from a reserved, rather courteous man into something monstrous—his back grew a hump, his mouth became a gob—he would call my mother a whore and a dirty bitch, spitting out the words like hot fat, stamping up and down on the spot like a Zulu on the warpath. For two or three days after such an outburst he was violent in all his movements. He didn't speak but slammed doors, hurled plates. On the few occasions he did structural harm to the house, Mother told everyone it was delayed war damage. Once he had passed through those days of smouldering containment, he fell into a sullen depression which lasted several weeks and sent him slinking through the house like a dog that had been muzzled. We left his dinner on the landing in a bowl. Recovering, he would emerge sheepishly one night and join us at the table, and if it was summer-time he might be full of fun for weeks at a stretch—listening to the wireless in the dark; taking us for runs in the car; treating us to afternoon tea in Southport. Until, almost at a point when we had forgotten what it was like before the peace treaty had been signed, something or someone would give offence and off he would go again, kicking the hose across the lawn so that the rose bush snapped, or slinging the teapot in its striped cosy clear over the fence into next door's nettles. Then we would run in all directions to avoid the blast.

31

There weren't many places we could go. We lived in a house that should have been large enough for four, but my mother was preserving the rooms for visitors. The lounge and the dining-room were out of bounds and we occupied only two bedrooms out of the four available. It was generally understood that the mattresses in the other rooms were mildewed with the damp and unfit to lie on. My brother slept with my father and I kept my mother warm. I wouldn't have been surprised if I had caught my mother spraying the mattresses in the spare rooms with the watering-can—she'd have gone to any lengths to avoid sleeping with my father. If my brother got up in the night to go to the lav. my father would shout, 'Turn that blasted light off. You're burning electricity.' That was when he was in a sour mood. If he was in a good mood he would call out jovially, 'Many there, son?' and laugh so much that he couldn't go back to sleep. Then he would pad downstairs in his overcoat and make himself a bacon sandwich.

The only room we were allowed to use—it was wisely never referred to as the living-room—was entirely filled with a table and chairs. I had to crawl under the table to get to my chair. My father sat jammed beneath the window-ledge, hunched over because the wireless jutted out. We ate our food as though any moment the Last Trumpet might sound. To this day I have never seen the point of lingering over a meal.

When we were older, my brother and I went out because we had grown too large to stay in. He went to the church, the bowling green and the youth club. I went to the pine woods and the sea. I liked it best when the wind blew strongly. All the time I was walking on the shore I kept looking for interesting objects. There were whole crates of rotten fruit, melons and oranges and grapefruits, swollen up and bursting with salt water; lumps of meat wrapped in stained cotton cloth through which the maggots tunnelled if the weather was warm, and stranded jellyfish, obscene and mindless. Several times I found bad things—half a horse and two small dogs. The dogs were bloated, garlanded in seaweed, snouts encrusted with salt.

When we were out, my mother usually sat upstairs reading a library book; if my father was on the rampage she took herself off to the railway station and read by the fire in the porters' room, pretending she was waiting for a train. My father listened to the wireless or paced the garden in the dark. Years later in a theatre, watching *Death of a Salesman*, I recognized the set, the light in the upstairs window, and Willie Loman—a dead ringer for my father—stumbling about the yard in a dream, muttering of business deals.

The only visitors that ever came to our house were my aunts, Margo and Nellie, and my maternal grandparents, Mr and Mrs Baines. At the height of the blitz, to be out of danger, my grandparents came to stay; but left after two days. My grandfather said he preferred to take his chances with the Luftwaffe. Of my aunts, Nellie was deferred to more than Margo, though Margo was the wage-earner. My mother didn't care for either of them, on the principle that they were related to my father.

Auntie Nellie had a touch of the martyr: she went to church and did the shopping. Whenever my father came in through the front door she made him lie down on the sofa. She said men were frailer than women. Auntie Margo was a dressmaker. She had been apprenticed when she was twelve to a woman who lived next door to Emmanuel Church School: hand-sewing, basting, cutting cloth, learning her trade. When she was thirteen they had given her a silver thimble. She sat at her sewing-machine as though she were playing the organ at the Winter Gardens in Blackpool, pulling out all the stops, head bowed, swaying on her chair, knee jerking up and down as she worked the treadle. When she broke off the thread she turned round, as if she heard applause behind her. For a time during the war she took a job in the munitions factory at Speke, but Auntie Nellie made her give it up. She said Margo was growing coarse. My mother said there were indications of hysteria in her appearance, a kind of giddiness. She wore cocktail dresses and white wedge-heeled shoes. She smoked continuously and her eyes were over-emphatic; they glittered with drama and fatigue. She bought a lot of the material for the dressmaking from shops that had been bombed, and seeing her in a frock of slightly charred cloth, a diamanté clasp at the hip and a scorch mark on the shoulder, she looked like a woman ravaged by fire. She made a fool of herself over a schoolmaster called Seymour, and there was the occasion, never to be forgotten, when the Dutch seaman billeted on them in the first year of the war had given her a length of satin from the East. Secretly, behind Nellie's back, she'd sewn it up into a sarong—she wore it at a meeting of the Women's Guild, a slit up the leg and her suspenders showing beneath the baggy edge of her green silk drawers.

I stayed the night with my aunties once a fortnight. When they got ready for bed they put their flannel nightgowns on over their clothes and then undressed, poking the fire to make a blaze before they removed their corsets. They grunted and twisted on the hearthrug, struggling to undo the numerous hooks that confined them, until panting and triumphant, they tore free the great pink garments and dropped them to the floor, where they lay like cricket pads, still holding the shape of their owners, the little dangling suspenders sparkling in the firelight. Dull then after such exertion, mesmerized by the heat of the fire, the two women stood rubbing their nightdresses to and fro across their stomachs, breathing slow and deep. After a while they sat down on either side of the fender and removed their stockings. Out on to the woollen rug, at last, came their strange yellow feet, toes curled inwards against the warmth.

Mr Baines, my mother's father, was tall and portly. He was a director of Goodlass Walls, the Liverpool paint firm. He'd bettered himself with a vengeance and collected butterfly specimens. Before the war my grandfather had gone on cruises, leaving my grandmother behind; she had failed to rise with him. She was small and bent, and stored a humbug in her cheek. She made a habit of coming over queer whenever she went down town and accepting brandy from sympathetic passsers-by. My mother treated her with contempt and was always telling her to pull herself together. Her dislike of Grandma had to do with a dog called Bill. My mother had been given Bill as a little girl, on the understanding that it wouldn't make a mess of the garden. My grandma didn't like dogs, and she went out and dug up all the daffodils and blamed it on Bill. My grandfather got rid of the animal the next day, though it broke his heart. My father said my mother was talking through her hat—'The old bugger jumped at the chance,' he said. 'He was too mean to pay for its blasted food.' My grandma confided to me that she'd had rickets as an infant and that at ten she'd worked in a boiled-sweet factory in Gateacre. My mother said it was a dirty lie. If we went out to tea in Southport and my mother left a tip under the plate, my grandmother used to pick it up and slide it into her handbag.

L iverpool people have always been articulate, and my family used words as though they were talking to save their lives. Realities might be hidden, like income and insurance and sex, but emotions and judgements flowed from them like blood. If you sat in a corner being seen and not heard, in the space of a few moments you could hear a whole character being assassinated, dissected and chucked in the bin, to be plucked out and redeemed in one small sentence. Thus my mother, in a discussion with Margo concerning Auntie Nellie, would say how lacking in depth Nellie was, too dour, too big for her boots. And Auntie Margo, heaping on coals of fire, would mention incidents of malice and deceitfulness, my mother nodding her head all the while in agreement, until just as Nellie lay unravelled before my eyes, Auntie Margo would say, 'By heck, but you can't fault her sponge cake.'

There were always words in the house, even when we weren't speaking to each other. There was the wireless, balanced on the ledge behind the curtains. The valves never burned out, but it was cracked across the front in three places and had been patched with black adhesive. My mother wanted the wireless thrown out. Once, she nearly succeeded. She was upstairs at the time, shaking the bath-mat out of the window. It was damp and heavy and slipped from her fingers on to the aerial stretched from the outside wall to the top of the fence. The wireless bounced off the ledge and toppled between the chair and table. My father flung himself forward and caught it in his arms. He loved the wireless, not for music but for the voices talking about poetry and politics, which were the same thing for him.

Continually I try to write it down, this sense of family life. For it seems to me that the funny noises we make with our mouths, or the squiggles that we put on paper, are only for ourselves to hear, to prove there's someone there.

**KEEP
YOUR
EYE ON**

CHANNEL FOUR TELEVISION

MICHAEL IGNATIEFF
AUGUST IN MY
FATHER'S HOUSE

Michael Ignatieff

It is after midnight. They are all in bed except me. I have been waiting for the rain to come. A shutter bangs against the kitchen wall and a rivulet of sand trickles from the adobe wall in the long room where I sit. The lamp above my head twirls in the draught. Through the poplars, the forks of light plunge into the flanks of the mountains and for an instant the ribbed gullies stand out like skeletons under a sheet.

Upstairs I can hear my mother and father turn heavily in their sleep. Downstairs our baby calls out from the bottom of a dream. What can his dreams be about? I smooth his blanket. His lips pucker, his eyes quiver beneath their lashes.

I have been married seven years. She is asleep next door, the little roof of a book perched on her chest. The light by the bed is still on. Her shoulders against the sheet are dark apricot. She does not stir as I pass.

At the window, the air is charged and liquid. The giant poplars creak and moan in the darkness. It is the mid-August storm, the one which contains the first intimation of autumn, the one whose promise of deliverance from the heat is almost always withheld. The roof tiles are splashed for an instant, and there is a patter among the trumpet vines. I wait, but it passes. The storm disappears up the valley and the first night sounds return, the cicadas, the owl in the poplars, the rustle of the mulberry leaves, the scrabble of mice in the eaves. I lean back against the wall. The old house holds the heat of the day in its stones like perfume in a discarded shawl. I have come here most summers since I was fifteen.

When I was fifteen, I wanted to be a man of few words, to be small and muscular with fine bones, to play slide guitar like Elmore James. I wanted to be fearless. I am thirty-seven. The page is white and cool to the touch. My hands smell of lemons. I still cling to impossible wishes. There is still time.

The house was once a village wash-house. At one end of the pillared gallery, there is a stone pool—now drained—where women used to wash clothes in the winter. At the bottom of the garden under the lyre-shaped cherry tree, there is the summer pool where the sheets were drubbed and slopped between their knuckles and the slanted stones. That was when the village raised silk worms for the Lyons trade a hundred years ago. When that trade died, the village died and the washing pool was covered over with brambles.

The house became a shepherd's shelter. He was a retarded boy, crazed by his father's beatings, by the miserable winter pastures, by the cracked opacity of his world. One night in the smoke-blackened kitchen, he and his father were silently drinking. When the father got up to lock away the animals, the son rose behind him and smashed his skull into the door-jamb. After they took the boy away and buried the father, the house fell into ruin, marked in village memory by the stain of parricide.

When we came to look at the place that evening twenty-two years ago, my father sent me up the back wall to check the state of the roof tiles. The grass and brambles were waist-high in the doorway. A tractor was rusting in the gallery and a dusty rabbit skin hung from a roof beam. One push, we thought, and the old adobe walls would collapse into dust. But the beam took my weight and there were only a few places where the moonlight was slicing through to the dirt floor below. The tiles were covered with lichen and I could feel their warmth through the soles of my feet. When I jumped down, I could see they had both made up their mind to buy it.

It is my mother's favourite hour. Dinner has been cleared away from the table under the mulberry tree, and she is sitting at the table with a wine glass in her hand watching the light dwindling away behind the purple leaves of the Japanese maple. I sit down beside her. She is easy to be with, less easy to talk to. The light is falling quickly, the heat it bears is ebbing away. After a time she says, 'I never expected anything like this . . . the stone wall that Roger built for us, the lavender hedges, the bees, the house. It's all turned out so well.'

Her voice is mournful, far away.

A Toronto schoolmaster's daughter, squint-eyed and agile, next-to-youngest of four, she rode her bicycle up and down the front steps of her father's school, the tomboy in a family of intellectuals. I have a photograph of her at the age of ten, in boy's skates with her stick planted on the ice of the rink at her father's school. She is staring fiercely into the camera in the manner of the hockey idols of the twenties, men with slick side-partings and names like Butch Bouchard.

It is nearly dark and the lights have come on across the valley. She twirls her wine glass between her fingers and I sit beside her to keep her company, to help the next words come. Then she says, out of nowhere, 'When I was seven, my father said "Who remembers the opening of the Aeneid?" as he stood at the end of the table carving the Sunday joint. "Anyone?" They were all better scholars than me, but I *knew*. "Arma virumque cano . . . ." Everyone cheered—Leo, the cook, Margaret, Charity, George, even Mother. My father slowly put down the knife and fork and just stared at me. I wasn't supposed to be the clever one.'

There is some hurt this story is trying to name, a tomboy's grief at never being taken seriously, never being listened to, which has lasted to this moment next to me in the darkness. But her emotions are a secret river. She has her pride, her gaiety and her elusiveness. She will not put a name to the grievance, and silence falls between us. It is dark and we both feel the chill of evening. She gets up, drains her glass and then says, 'Mother always said, "Never make a fuss." That was the family rule. Goodnight.' I brush her cheek with a kiss. We will not make a fuss.

She was a painter once, and her paintings have become my memory for many of the scenes of my childhood: playing with a crab in a bucket on a rock in Antigonish, Nova Scotia, and watching her painting at the easel a few paces away, her back, her knees and her upraised arm making a triangle of concentration, her brush poised, still and expectant before the canvas, her face rapt with the pleasure of the next stroke.

When I was six she painted my portrait. It was an embarrassment at the time: my friends came to point and laugh because I looked so solemn. But I see now the gift she was handing me across the gulf which divides us from the vision of others: a glimpse of the child I was in my mother's eye, the child I have kept within me. She doesn't paint anymore. For a time, marriage and children allowed her a room of her own. But then it was swallowed up or renounced, I don't know which. She says only, 'Either I do it well, or I do not do it at all.'

She whispers, 'Have you seen my glasses?'
'Your glasses don't matter. You can do the shopping without them.'
'I know they don't matter. But if he finds out . . . .'
'Tell him to . . . .' But now I'm the one who is whispering.

When I find her glasses by the night-table where she put them down before going to sleep, the lenses are fogged and smudged with fingerprints. A schoolgirl's glasses.

She says, 'I know. I know. It runs in the family.'

'What? Forgetting?'

'No.' She gives me a hard stare. 'Dirty glasses. My father's pupils used to say that he washed his in mashed potatoes.'

She owns only one pair. She could hide a second pair in a jar by the stove so she wouldn't be caught out. But she won't defend herself.

I take her into town and buy her a chain so that she can wear them around her neck and not lose them. She submits gaily but in the car on the way back home, she shakes her fist at the windscreen: 'I swore I'd never wear one of these goddamned things.'

When we lived in the suburbs of Ottawa in the fifties, she used to come out and play baseball with the kids in the street on summer evenings. She could hit. In my mind's eye, I see the other boys' mouths opening wide as they follow the flight of the ball from her bat and I see them returning to her face and to her wincing with pleasure as the ball pounds onto the aluminium roof of the Admiral's garage. She puts the bat down with a smile and returns to make supper, leaving us playing in the street under her amused gaze from the kitchen window.

When the Yankees played the Dodgers in the World Series, she wrote the teacher to say I was sick and the two of us sat on her bed and watched Don Larsen pitch his perfect game and Yogi Berra race to the mound throwing his mask and mitt into the air. We saw Sandy Amaros racing across centre field chasing a high fly ball which he took with a leap at the warning track. In life, the ball hits the turf. In memory, its arc returns unendingly to the perfection of the glove.

41

Michael Ignatieff

The *notaire* arrives as dusk falls. We sit down for business under the mulberry tree. When my mother and father bought the house and fields twenty-two years ago, the *notaire* was a rotund Balzacian figure who observed with amused contempt while the peasants from whom we were purchasing the property passed a single pair of wire-rim glasses round the table so that each in turn could pore over the documents of sale. The new *notaire* is a sparrow of a woman, my age, a widow with two young sons and a motorcycle helmet on the back seat of her car.

We pore over deeds of sale and cadastral surveys of the fields: one planted in clover once and now overgrown with mint and high grass. The goat is staked there under the walnut tree and eats a perfect circle for his breakfast. Framed between the poplars in front of the house is the lavender field. Once a year in the first week of August, the farmer comes with a machine which straddles the purple rows and advances with a scrabbling grinding sound, tossing aside bound and fragrant bunches. We watch from the terrace as the field is stripped of its purple and is left a bare spiky green. The butterflies and bees retreat ahead of the mechanical jaws and at the end of the day are found in a desperate, glittering swarm on the last uncut row, fighting for the sweetness of the last plants like refugees crowded into an encircled city.

Then there is the orchard behind the house. It was once full of plums, but the trees were old and wormy and one by one they were dropping their branches, tired old men letting go of their burdens. Father called in the bulldozer, but when it came, we all went indoors and clapped our hands over our ears so that we wouldn't have to listen to the grinding of steel on the bark and the snapping of the tap roots. In a quarter of an hour, the planting of generations had been laid waste. But it had to be done. The field is bare now, but olive saplings are beginning to rise among the weeds.

The deeds of sale are all in order. My mother runs a finger over the old papers and stops at her name: *'née à Buckleberry Bradford, Angleterre, le 2 février 1916, épouse sans profession,'* and at his *'né à Saint Petersbourg, Russie, le 16 décembre, 1913, profession diplomate.'*

'"*Épouse sans profession*" sounds sad, doesn't it?' she says.

They are transferring the title of the property to me and my brother. 'Just once more,' she asks, 'tell me why we have to.'

'Because,' I reply, 'it is cheaper than doing it afterwards.'

Sometimes on the airless August nights, I lie in bed and imagine what it would be like to sell the house, turn it over to strangers and never come back. I find myself thinking of hotel rooms somewhere else: the echo of the empty *armoire,* the neon blinking through the shutters, the crisp anonymity of the towels and sheets. I remember the Hotel Alesia in Paris, eating brie and cherries together on a hot June afternoon; the Hotel San Cassiano in Venice and its vast *letto matrimoniale.* I remember the next morning lying in bed watching her comb her hair at the dressing-table by the open window. A curl of smoke is rising from the ashtray and the swoop of her brush flickers in the facets of the mirrors. Through the window comes the sound of lapping water and the chug of a barge. We have the whole day ahead of us. I think of all the writing I might do in hotel rooms. Words come easily in hotels: the coils spring free from the weight of home.

In my father's house every object is a hook which catches my thoughts as they pass: the barometers which he taps daily and which only he seems to understand; the dark *armoire* they bought from the crooked *antiquaire* in Île sur Sorgue; the Iroquois mask made of straw; the Russian bear on a string; the thermometer marked *gel de raisin, Moscou 1812* at the cold end and *Senegal* at the hot end. My thoughts, cornered by these objects, circle at bay and spiral backwards to the moods of adolescence.

'Old age is not for cowards.' My father looks at me angrily, as if I cannot possibly understand. 'I have no illusions. It is not going to get any better. I know what she goes through. Don't think I don't. You wake up some mornings and you don't know where the hell you are. Just like a child. Everything is in the fog. Some days it lifts. Some days it doesn't.'

He paces slowly at the other end of the long room, at the distance where truth is possible between us. It is late. Everyone else has gone to bed. We are drinking *tisane,* a nightly ritual usually passed in silence.

Michael Ignatieff

There are thirty-four years between us: two wars and a
revolution. There is also his success: what he gave me makes it
difficult for us to understand each other. He gave me safety. My
earliest memory is rain pounding on the roof of the Buick on the
New Jersey Turnpike. I am three, sitting between them on the front
seat, with the chrome dashboard in front of me at eye level and the
black knobs of the radio winking at me. The wipers above my head
are scraping across the bubbling sheet of water pouring down the
windscreen. We are all together side by side, sharing the pleasure of
being trapped by the storm, forced to pull off the road. I am quite
safe. They made the world safe for me from the beginning.

He was never safe. His memory begins at a window in Saint
Petersburg on a February morning in 1917. A sea of flags, ragged
uniforms and hats surges below him, bayonets glinting like slivers of
glass in the early morning sunlight. The tide is surging past their
house; soon it will break through the doors, forcing them to run and
hide. He remembers the flight south in the summer of 1917, corpses
in a hospital train at a siding, a man's body bumping along a dusty
road in Kislovodsk, tied by one leg behind a horse. I see it all as
newsreel. He was there, with the large eyes of a six-year-old.

As he gets older, his memory scours the past looking for
something to hold on to, for something to cling to in the slide of
time. Tonight, pacing at the end of the room while I sit drinking the
tea he has made for both of us, it is Manya who is in his mind, his
nursemaid, the presence at the very beginning of his life, a starched
white uniform, warm hands, the soft liquid syllables of a story at
bedtime heard at the edge of sleep. She followed them south into
exile. She was the centre of his world, and one morning she was no
longer there.

'I woke up and she was gone. Sent away in the night. Perhaps
they couldn't afford her. Perhaps they thought we were too close. I
don't know.'

Across seventy years, his voice still carries the hurt of that
separation, a child's helpless despair. He was her life. She was his
childhood.

I try to think about him historically, to find the son within the
father, the boy within the man. His moods—the dark self-
absorption—have always had the legitimacy of his dispossession.

44

Exile is a set of emotional permissions we are all bound to respect.

He is still pacing at the other end of the room. He says suddenly, 'I don't expect to live long.'

I say: 'It's not up to you, is it?'

He stokes the prospect of his death like a fire in the grate. Ahead of me the prospect beckons and glows, sucking the oxygen from the room. He says he is not afraid of dying, and, in so far as I can, I believe him. But that is not the point. In his voice, there is a child's anger at not being understood, an old man's fear of being abandoned. He does not want a son's pity or his sorrow, yet his voice carries a plea for both. A silence falls between us. I hear myself saying that he is in good health, which is true and entirely beside the point. He says goodnight, stoops briefly as he passes through the archway, and disappears into his room.

On some beach of my early childhood—Montauk Point? Milocer?—he is walking ahead of me, in those white plastic bathing shoes of his, following the line of the water's edge, head down, bending now and again and turning to show me what he has found. We decide together which finds go into the pocket of his bathing suit. We keep a green stone with a white marble vein in it. He takes it to a jeweller to have it set as a ring for her. In some jewellery box back home, it is probably still there.

I don't believe in the natural force of blood ties. There is nothing more common, more natural than for fathers and sons to be strangers to each other. It was only on those silent beach walks together, our voices lost in the surf, our footprints erased by the tide, our treasure accumulated mile by mile, that we found an attachment which we cannot untie.

There was a period in my twenties when that attachment foundered on my embrace of victimhood. It is a natural temptation for sons of powerful fathers. I was elated with destructiveness, righteous for truth. They had sent me away to school when I was eleven, and I wanted to know why. We had ceased to be a family in the flesh, and became one by air mail and transatlantic telephone. Once a year, for a month, in this house, we tried to become a real family again. Such is the story which the victim writes. I wanted to know why. I see his hands covering his face.

Michael Ignatieff

Why did I cling to the grievance? The truth is I loved going away from home, sitting alone in a Super Constellation shuddering and shaking high above Greenland on the way back to school, watching the polar flames from the engines against the empty cobalt sky. I won a first-team tie in football. I listened to Foster Hewitt's play by play of Hockey Night in Canada on the radio under my mattress after lights out in the dorm. I was caned for a pillow-fight, a wild and joyful midnight explosion of feathers, the only true uprising that I have ever taken part in. After such an uprising, the punishment—twelve stripes with a bamboo cane—was an honour.

I read *King Lear* in Gallimore's English class. He frog-marched us through every scene, battering us with his nasal southern Ontario intonations: until I fell in love, for the first time, with the power of words.

I went to my first dances and breathed in that intoxicating scent of hairspray, sweat, powder and the gardenia of girls' corsages, that promise of lush revelations in the dark. I became an adult in a tiny tent on a camping ground north of Toronto. The gravel was excruciating on my knees and elbows. The girl was very determined. She guided my hands in the dark. Afterwards she slapped my face, like a caress.

I did what I wanted. Because I was at school, I didn't have to bring her home; I could keep sex a secret. But I clung to the grievance of banishment.

I clung to another grievance too, but this one as much my making as his. I said to him, You have crushed her. She used to paint. Not any more. She has wishes for you and for me, but none for herself. Not anymore.

He never forgave me for that, for the absolution I had given myself in blaming him. I see his hands covering his face.

'Truth is good, but not all truth is good to say.'

My son is sitting on his grandfather's knee, working over his grandfather's hands with his gums. I notice that his signet ring, a carving in amber of Socrates set in a gold oval—one of the survivors of exile and the pawnshop—is missing from the little finger of his left hand. In its place there is a small university ring which seems to pinch. He notices me looking at it.

'I gave it to your brother. You'll get the watch.'

The tops of his hands are strong and sunburned, but the palms are gullied and clenched with arthritis. He no longer wields the axe.

He is tender and wary with his grandson, this messenger of life and his mortality. He strokes the child's chest absently, as if re-learning a long-forgotten gesture. My son turns in his lap, and with infantile deliberation removes his grandfather's spectacles. They exchange a blue glance across seventy years. 'In the year 2000,' my father says, 'he will be sixteen.'

When I come through the beaded curtain with my breakfast, my mother is whirling the baby around slowly beneath the mulberry tree, cheek to cheek, holding his arm out against hers in the old style and crooning, 'Come to me, my melancholy baby.' My son has a wild look of pleasure on his face.

'You dance well,' I say.

She whirls slowly to a stop and hands him to me: 'No, I lead too much.'

She whispers in the baby's ear, 'Crazy old granny, crazy old granny.' She is not crazy. She is afraid. Her memory is her pride, her refuge. The captions of *New Yorker* cartoons not seen for forty years; lyrics of Noel Coward and Gerty Lawrence songs from the London of the thirties; the name of the little girl with Shirley Temple curls in the desk next to hers at Bishop Strachan School for Girls; the code names of all the French agents she helped to parachute into France during the war: her memory is a crammed shoe-box of treasures from a full life. It is what happened five minutes ago that is slipping away—the pot on the stove, the sprinkler in the garden, what she just said.

The memory which frightens her, which portends the losses still to come, is of the last time she saw her mother. They spent a week together, and as they were leaving, her mother turned to my father and said, 'You're Russian, aren't you? And who is this charming girl?'

Your daughter.

When I was eight, I spent a week-end with my grandmother in the large dark house on Prince Arthur Avenue in Toronto. We ate breakfast together: tea on a silver service, Ryvita biscuits imported from England, with the London *Times* in a feathery edition two

Michael Ignatieff

weeks late. I sat on the end of her bed and we had a conversation, tentative and serious across the gulf of time. I had never seen her hair down before, masses of it—grey, austere and luxuriant against the pillows. There is a kind of majesty in some old women, the deep red glow of a banked fire. I talked on and on, and she followed me with her eyes and a whisper of amusement on her lips.

Then there came a Sunday, not many months later, when I was ushered into the dark mahogany dining room and knew at once from the slope of her shoulders, the terrible diminution of her presence, the slowness with which she turned to meet my eye, that she had no idea who I was. She stared out through the window at the blank wall of the new hotel rising to block her view. She said nothing. Her eyes were still and grey and vacant. I was speechless through lunch with her, and, when I left, I knew I would never see her again. She died several years later in a nursing home north of the city. Her will, that last relinquishing gesture of generosity in a generous life, enabled my father and mother to buy this house.

My mother is cool and lucid about her own prospects. I do not believe these things run in the family, and I tell her so. She nods and then says, 'I'm sure I would make a cheerful old nut. Don't you think so? In any case,' and here she picks up her drink and walks into the kitchen to look to her cooking, 'it's much worse for those you leave behind.'

In the next village, a theatre troupe is staging *Oedipus* on a tiny stage built into the sandstone cliffs at the foot of the village. There is a little boy in front of us in the stands, sitting between his mother and his father. He is about five. Oedipus and Jocasta circle each other slowly against the towering folds of sandstone: the eternal story unfolds in the night air. Oedipus turns his bleeding eyes upon us: 'Remember me, and you will never lose your happiness.'

The little boy rocks backwards and forwards on his seat. He says to himself in a small voice, 'Now I understand everything.'

Then he falls asleep on his mother's lap.

We stay behind afterwards while they dismantle the set. From the top row of the stands, the valley stretches out below us in the amber afterglow of nightfall. The vines and cane wind-breaks are drained of colour. The first lights in the village appear. It was this landscape which made me into a European: man's hand is upon it, the millennia of labour, the patient arts of settlement. The stillness is human: the rim of light at the edge of a shutter, the snake of a headlight, the swish of the irrigation sprinklers drenching the earth in the dark. In Canada the silence among the great trees was menacing. No light for miles. The cold. I had no quarrel with the place. I just wanted to get out.

She is standing beside me looking out into the dark valley. She leans her weight against my shoulder. I met her in a street dance in London eight years ago. Within two weeks I had brought her here, knowing that this was the place which would reveal us to each other.

My favourite photograph of her was taken in the first week we spent in this country. She is on the terrace walking towards me, wearing a white dress and a red Cretan sash. Her right hand is pushing the hair back off her forehead. She is smiling, her gaze directly into mine, shy and fearless. It is the last photograph in which she is still a stranger, approaching but still out of reach, still on the other side of the divide, before we fell in love.

The valley below us is black now. A breeze lifts up from the earth and the olive groves. She points to the sparkling village perched ten miles away on a promontory of ochre: 'It's like an ocean liner.'

I am thinking of the *Andrea Doria*. She went down off Nantucket when I was nine. They sent divers down, and they took photographs. She was lying in shallow water, and the lights of her bridge, by some impossible chance, were still on. Like the livid eyes of some great beast staring at the hunter who has brought her down, the ship's lights streamed through the ocean darkness. As a child I used to dream about those pictures of the great ship glowing on the bottom of the sea. It seems to me now that those dreams were an image of what it would be like to die, sinking in the folds of the ocean, your own eyes blazing in the salty dark.

On the way down the hill from the village, through the vaulted tunnel of the plane trees, white and phosphorescent in the headlights, she sings to me. Verdi as always. Flat as always, her head leaning back, her eyes staring up at the trees rushing by through the sun roof.

'I am *not* flat.'

I am laughing.

She ignores me and sings on in a husky voice, '*Libera me . . . de morte aeterna.*'

From the village road, the house looks low and small, its back hunched against the mistral. By Christmas, when the *notaire* has filed the deed, it will belong to my brother and me. But whatever the deeds say, it will always be my father's house. I cannot sell it any more than I can disavow the man I became within its walls, any more than I can break the silences at the heart of family life.

The lights are out. My parents are both asleep, and our son is in his cot.

She says, 'Let's not go in yet.'

We climb up into the field behind the house where the bee-keeper has his hives, and where you can see the whole of the Luberon mountains stretched out against the night sky. The shale is cool and the dew is coming down. We watch for satellites and for the night flights to Djibouti, Casablanca and Rome. There are many bright cold stars. A dog barks. In the house, our child floats in his fathomless sleep.

'Cassiopeia, Ursus Major, Orion's Belt . . . I must learn the names, I want to teach him the names.'

Out of the dark, as if from far away, she says, 'What do you need to name them for?'

DORIS LESSING

IMPERTINENT

DAUGHTERS

A photograph of my mother shows her as a large, round-faced schoolgirl, full of the confidence I have to associate with her being Victorian. Her hair is tied back with a black bow. She is wearing her school uniform, a full white blouse and a long dark skirt. In a photograph taken forty-five years later, she appears as a lean, severe old thing, bravely looking out from a world of disappointment and frustration. She stands by my father, her hand on the back of his chair. He has to sit: as always, he is ill. It is clear that he is only just holding himself together, but he is in a proper suit, certainly because she has told him he must make the effort. She wears a rather smart tailored dress, made up out of a remnant bought in the sales.

The difference between these photographs is what this memoir has to be about. It seems that it has taken me a lifetime to understand my parents, with astonishments all the way. There is a mysterious process, frightening because there is nothing whatsoever you can do about it, that takes you from fierce adolescence—as if parents and you stood at either side of a battlefield, hands full of weapons—to a place where you can stand where they did, in imagination, any time you want.

Only when I sat down to write this did it occur to me that I could write about my father and hardly mention that dread word 'class', but with my mother it is a different matter. She never freed her judgements from thoughts of class, but then she did not see why she should. Class was then a straitjacket, an imperative, a crippler. Only that time, that place, could have produced her: London, Britain, the British Empire. But the Empire was in its last days: a thought she would have dismissed as treacherous, wrong-headed, soft.

On a mud wall of the old house on the farm in Africa where I was brought up was a large ornately framed portrait of my grandfather McVeagh. He is standing beside his second wife. He was fat-faced and over-fed, with hair slicked down on either side of a parting. He wore a tight smug suit, and a golden chain across his chest. I loathed him, this self-righteous prig, with a violence that stopped me from listening to my mother, whose reminiscences seemed only another attempt to bind me to her. Had she, had my father, not escaped from England? Why, then, was she winding me back into that shroud? I closed my ears, and I am sorry now I did. For instance, who was that elegant, fastidious lady he married? She was Jewish, with a fine curved nose and exquisite hands. Her dress was a miracle of embroidery and little tucks and lace. She came from a different world, by nature if not by class. I think she was a governess. Yet she had chosen to marry him: a thought that didn't enter my head for years; he made two romantic marriages, this philistine bank manager.

Once I had a fit of wanting to know who my forbears were, and before I found what a fussy and tedious business it is and gave it up, I came across birth certificates of McVeaghs from Exeter and Maidstone. They were all called John and Edward and James, and were sergeants in cavalry regiments. In short, my grandfather McVeagh, or his father, had made the jump up into the middle classes, and he was as snobbish as one would expect. Yet his first marriage had been to Emily Flower, the daughter of a contractor for lightering. A marriage for love. There is no picture of Emily Flower. This is because she was such a misfortune. All my childhood I heard of this grandmother thus: 'She was very pretty, but all she cared about was dancing and horses.' It was said with the little cold sniff that probably derived from the servants who brought the children up after wicked Emily died, which was—my mother's tone said it served her right—in childbirth with her third child. That was in 1888, and she was thirty-two. But how was it that the wife of a suburban bank manager was able to dance all the time and be mad about horses? In Blackheath? Blackheath was where my mother said the tall, grim, cold house was; but on Emily's death certificate it says Canning Town.

My mother, Emily Maude, was the first child. Then came Uncle John. Then Muriel, who disgraced herself and the family by marrying back into the working class. Hardly a surprise, judged my mother, for Muriel was always happiest with the servants. In other words she was not happy in the competitive, striving atmosphere of getting on and doing well.

It was a cold home. Her father, so romantic in love, ruled his children as Victorian papas are reputed to have done, with the rod, and without love. There was no affection from the elegant stepmother, who was dutiful and correct and did not understand children. I never once heard my mother speak of her father with warmth. Respect, yes; prescribed admiration, certainly. Never love. As for her stepmother, she might have been a visitor or a distant relation.

Emily was clever at school, much cleverer than her brother John, who was destined for the navy, and who found the exams difficult. He had to be coached and pushed and prodded. She loved examinations, came first in class, adored mathematics, and was expected for a time to become a professional pianist.

The children, as was proper in this Forsytian world, were taken to all public occasions of rejoicing or grief; and my mother spoke of Mafeking night, Queen Victoria's funeral, the coronation of Edward VII, exhibitions, the visits of the Kaiser and of foreign heads of government, as if these milestones were the only possible way to mark the passing of a childhood.

If there was little family life, there was an energetic social life full of friends she kept in touch with for years, even from the farm in Africa. She played tennis and lacrosse and hockey and went on bicycle trips. There were musical evenings. They drew portraits of each other and pictures of appropriate landscapes; wrote humorous and sentimental verses to mark anniversaries. They pressed flowers and collected shells, birds' eggs and stones. They visited the theatre with suppers afterwards at the Trocadero. All this went on in London: she was essentially urban, this woman who would find herself on a farm in the veld.

Modern-minded John William McVeagh, proud of his clever daughter, was thinking of university for her, but was confronted with a rebellious girl who said she wanted to be a nurse. He was horrified, utterly overthrown. Middle-class girls did not become nurses, and he didn't want to hear anything about Florence Nightingale. Any skivvy could be a nurse, and if you become one, do not darken my door! Very well, said Emily Maude, and went off to the old Royal Free Hospital to begin her training. It was hard: conditions were bad, the pay was low, but she did well, and when she brilliantly passed her finals, her father was prepared to forgive her. She had done it all on her own, without him.

Whom, then, did she love, this poor girl brought up without affection? She was fond of her brother John, but this was a far from simple emotion, and of course he was at boarding school most of the time. Her sister Muriel was not her sort. Her many and varied friends? They were good sports, pals . . . . Why did she fight so hard to become a nurse, if not that she needed to care for and to nurture people and to be loved for it? I have only just had this thought: I could have had it before.

Her training completed, she resumed, as far as possible, her social life. She had given up dreams of being a pianist, but continued to play the organ for churches, for instance, in Langham Place. She was part, in a small way, of the musical life of London. 'I could have been a real concert pianist,' she would say, until the end of her days. 'I had my LRAM. The Examiners told me I should go on.' I wonder at her energy. Nurses worked harder then than now. Yet there were musical evenings, and concerts and excursions. Also, holidays—always sea trips, for she loved the sea. She read, too, as did my father. Both knew enough of Wells and Shaw to be affected, and both judged society from a perspective of critical independence. There was a generation of young people, before the First World War, for whom Wells and Shaw played the same tutoring role as Orwell did later.

Then began the War. 1914. She was a sister in the Royal Free Hospital, nursing the wounded soldiers who arrived in train-loads from the trenches. She had an album with verses written by the men she nursed back to life, and she appears as the traditional martinet with a heart of gold.

My father, at that time, was fighting in the trenches. He had two periods there. The first was ended by a timely appendix, otherwise he would have been killed with all his company in the Battle of the Somme. The second, timely again, was when he was wounded—shrapnel in the leg—preventing him from being killed with every other man in the company, at Passchendaele. I do not know exactly how long he was in the trenches, but altogether it was months. He said he was lucky not to have been killed a dozen times over. But the war did him in nevertheless: he lost his leg, and was psychologically damaged. He went into the fighting active and optimistic, and came out with what they then called shell shock. He was in bed for months. My mother nursed him. He was very ill, she said, and what was so worrying was his state of mind. I have a photograph of him in bed in the Royal Free Hospital, a handsome man, but minus a leg and inwardly in torment. Beside him Sister McVeagh sits wearing her full white veil, sewing, her eyes on her handiwork. 'Before she was thought of,' says the caption, meaning me, their first child. The date is September 1917.

She was thirty-three, a year older than her mother had been when she died giving birth to her third child. Sister McVeagh was facing a hard, a very hard, choice. She had been asked if she would accept the matronship of St George's Hospital—an honour, at her age. Usually much older women became matrons and ran great hospitals. But she liked nursing: did she want to become an administrator? Besides, matrons were such martinets! She had suffered under these formidable women, did she want to become one? And here was Captain Tayler, of whom she had become very fond, wanting to marry her. There were no men left, they were all killed. Would she be asked again? She had always thought of herself as—had always been told she was—very plain. Did she want to marry him? Did she want to marry at all, since her real love, the man she ought to have married, was dead?

He had been a young doctor in the hospital with whom, my father confirmed, she had had an understanding. His little picture, torn out of a newspaper that recorded his death by drowning in a ship sunk by the Germans, stood forever on her dressing table. He had a soft, boyish face. The understanding between them, the death, my mother's unhappiness were observed by my father who always spoke of him with pain. 'Your poor mother,' he would say, 'he was a good chap, that young doctor.'

It took her a long time to decide, and she became ill with the strain of it all. As a nurse she should have known what she had to face in a man so damaged. Later she would say, often: 'If we knew when we were young what was going to happen to us, then . . . .'

She really had no idea, then or ever, of the mental world my father lived in. I am not only talking of his depression after the war. Quite simply, he had a dimension that she lacked. For a long time I thought it was the awfulness of the war that had given him his sensitiveness to other people, his broadness of outlook. Their experiences, after all, had not been so different. His upbringing had been as bad as hers—savage, I was going to say, and yes, the word can stand: her impatient ruthlessness, I once thought, was the legacy of her childhood. But he had been much beaten at school and at home, over-disciplined, and harshly misunderstood. He, like her, had escaped as soon as he could. Years later I met people who had known him as a young man—and what the war had done was to confirm his essential nature: he had always been contemplative and philosophical. 'Your father had his own way of seeing things,' cried a former girlfriend, 'and I would often rather not have known what he was thinking.' And another said, not without ambiguity, that she had never been so well understood. He was kind; he was generous; she had not met anyone like him; but there was something detached in him which was hard to take. And this detachment was a part of his deepest characteristic—an understanding of impermanence, change.

I believe that his nature, so different from hers, was why my mother married him. She knew she had limitations—how could she not, brought up constantly against this magnanimity in everything? 'Don't you see, old girl, that's how things *are*?' he would say, amazed at her pettiness, her inability to see: he had been watching Life at it again, working out one of its little games. He was unsurprised, interested: she, always, rebellious.

To put her dilemma squarely: what she respected most in him, what gave her access to a largeness she would never have known without him, was precisely what did both her and him in: these fine ways of thinking, his scope, were always overthrowing her best self, which was a magnificent commonsense. She had married a weak man, then? But his weakness was obviously stronger than her strength, always pulling her further away from what would best suit her. A weak man? Yet he was not weak by nature; it was the war that had distorted him. *Weak!* How else could you describe him? Always refusing to make judgements, take stands; always insisting on what he called the long view—you'd think there was nothing he respected . . . . And yet. Life was not a simple business; she suspected he was nearer to understanding it than she would ever be.

I have an image of them, confronting Life in such different ways. He looks it straight in the face, with a dark, grim, ironical recognition. But she, always being disappointed in ways he could never be, has a defiant, angry little air: she has caught Life out in injustice *again*. 'How can you!' she seems to be saying, exasperated, to Life. 'It's not right to behave like that!' And she gives a brisk, brave little sniff.

They were married. They did not feel up to a proper wedding. For one thing they were Wells and Shaw people, and white weddings were ridiculous (obviously soon to become obsolete!), and for another, his mother disapproved of Sister McVeagh: she was going to rule him with a rod of iron, said this ruler with the rod. My father was elegant, as always, when he still cared about clothes. My mother wore a dress she clearly had given a lot of thought to: only recently, when I was writing the Jane Somers books, did I realize that my mother (who could, I think, be something like Jane Somers if she lived now) very much enjoyed clothes, even though for most of her life she did not have the money to buy them, or the opportunity to wear them.

It was on the wedding night, they joked, that my mother must have got pregnant, though they were armed with the works of Marie Stopes, and had decided not to have a baby yet, if at all. He was still so low in spirits: he simply did not seem able to pull himself out of his ugly state of mind. And she was ill, she did not know why, but it was probably overwork from the war. And there was all that flu about, so many people dying everywhere: everything was so depressing after the war. It was 1919.

They left for Persia. He had to leave England—he couldn't stand it—so why not Persia? My mother, being a woman of her time, was ready to go off and live in the Middle East, even though she knew nothing about it A close friend was a missionary in Japan; her brother John, never at home in the Navy, was about to become a rubber planter in Malaya.

Persia was then divided into spheres of influence, mainly French and British. Britain had finance, and my father was going to manage a bank in Kermanshah. Before the war he had been a clerk in a bank, and to have to go back to it was awful for him; but at least he was getting out of England, where he knew he could never live again. Coming back from the trenches he felt as all the soldiers of that war did: betrayed by the politicians who had lied to them and did not keep promises; betrayed by the civilians who talked patriotic nonsense and had no idea of what the trenches were like; betrayed by the jingoistic newspapers; betrayed by the Armistice which would make another war inevitable. It was stupid to treat the Germans like this, one should take the long view. None of the Tommies felt vindictive. Any Tommy could tell the politicians they were being stupid. A funny thing, wasn't it? he would demand all his life (my mother half agreeing with him, feeling that she should, while her nature rebelled): any ordinary person could see it, the politicians couldn't. Why is it that ordinary people have so much more sense than politicians when it is the politicians' job to be sensible?

This was the first time in her life when my mother would need a lot of clothes, and she took trunks full of them. She also took the necessities for a middle-class nursery as prescribed by one Dr Trudy King and other mentors. The layette for a baby then consisted of dozens of everything. Napkins thick and thin, and napkin liners. Vests long and short, inner and outer. Petticoats of various lengths, of flannel and of lawn, embroidered and tucked and edged with lace. Long and short dresses of pin-tucked and embroidered lawn. Caps. Shawls. Not to mention binders made of thick material which supported the baby's stomach as if it were a wound from which entrails might spill. This layette itself must have been enought to dismay any woman, make her feel helpless, feel at least that an ordeal lay ahead. It all assumed servants of course. Those exquisite dresses alone took hours to iron, not to mention the dressing and undressing of the helpless infant, who was also supposed to be fed every two or three hours day and night, and, if bottle-fed—a recommended practice—the preparations were like those for a surgical operation.

I used to read those lists on the farm in Rhodesia, dazzled by incredulity: I was surrounded by black babies living contented and naked inside a fold of cloth on their mother's backs.

It was 'Maude' and 'Michael' Tayler who arrived in Persia. My mother had always disliked Emily, I suppose because it was the name of her mother, but she liked Maude, because of Tennyson's Maud. She had been trying to shed Emily for years. She would not have Alfred for my father: a common name. And what did he think about it? I can hear him: 'Oh Lord, old thing, who cares? What does it matter? If it makes you happy, then . . . .' He was made Michael because of Peter Pan.

The Westminster Bank allotted Maude and Michael an enormous house, made of stone that was carved and fretted, with great arches along the verandahs and arched windows, and surrounded by wonderful gardens. Servants—gardeners, cooks, people who cleaned the house, shopped—did everything. My mother hardly mentioned the servants, except to say that households were regulated by protocol, and that the mistress of the house knew her place and did what she was told. She thought this amusing: not a hint here of what in Africa became a neurotic preoccupation: the shortcomings of the black servants.

For my father Kermanshah was what he had dreamed of: an ancient town on a high empty brown landscape, the high blue sky, the mountains all around with the snow on them. When I went to Granada for the first time I knew it was like Kermanshah: gardens, the sounds of water running everywhere, the smell of the dust . . . . My father was managing the bank; he was not at anybody's beck and call. He rode everywhere, for he would not allow his wooden leg to make him less active. He liked the spacious house, and the release, at least to an extent, from English respectability.

My mother was having a difficult pregnancy, morning sickness being only one of the complications. She was expecting a son, Peter John. Why did she not even consider the possibility of a daughter? Her passionate identification with a son was, I think, because of her brother John, who was not clever, did not care very much what he did, and yet went as if by right into the Navy. I think she most bitterly envied him, but to feel like this was not being a good sort. She was the one born to be an officer in His Majesty's Navy! She was the clever one, who adored everything about the sea, about ships, was never seasick. She was resourceful and quick-witted. She was decent and good-humoured and able to get on with people. An authoritarian personality, happy in a structured life, she was able to take and to give orders. Of course, the negative aspects of this particular personality were also hers: the inability to put herself into the shoes of people who were different; a contempt for weakness; a lack of understanding of what she described as 'morbid': the ambiguous, the witty, the equivocal—these areas would always be suspect, and she was threatened by them.

I can only guess, hurt for her, at how much she must have felt frustrated as a girl, seeing her slow brother get what ought to have been hers too. And yet she never said anything, except in jolly little jokes, brave jokes. What she felt had to come out indirectly.

The birth was difficult. I was delivered with forceps that left a scarlet birthmark over one side of my face. Above all, I was a girl. When the doctor wanted to know my name, and heard that none had been prepared, he looked down at the cradle and said softly, 'Doris?' This scene: the doctor's weariness after the long night, his soft, tactful, but reproachful query, was vividly enacted by my mother, like many other scenes.

Of course I resented it all bitterly, particularly that she did not even see that it was likely to make me angry. How could she stand there, with her customary determined little smile, her brisk social manner, telling me that I was not wanted in the first place; that to have a girl was a disappointment that nearly did her in altogether, after that long labour; that she had no milk for me and I had to be bottle-fed from the start and I was half-starved for the first year and never stopped screaming because she did not realize that cows' milk in Persia was not as rich as real English milk; that I was an impossibly difficult baby, and then a tiresome child, quite unlike my little brother Harry who was always so good. And so she let the nurse cope with me, and looked after Harry herself.

Better say, and be done with it: my memories of her are all of antagonism, and fighting, and feeling shut out; of pain because the baby born two-and-a-half years after me was so much loved when I was not. She would recognize none of this, nor accept it. The way she saw it was that her childhood had been cold and loveless, and she would make sure that her children were governed by love. Love was always being invoked; and I became an expert in emotional blackmail by the time I was five. She didn't like me—that was the point. It was not her fault: I cannot think of a person less likely than myself to please her. But it would have been impossible for her to admit it: a mother loves her child, a child its mother. And that's that!

My father hated it when he was transferred to Tehran, to a branch of the bank where he was not manager and had to work under someone else, and where he had to live in a house he thought English and stuffy. But my mother loved it. At last, suitable nurseries, instead of those great stone rooms that curtains and rugs could not soften. I remember the tall square day-nursery, the heavy red velvet curtains and the lace ones behind them, the brass fender with the tall dangerous fire, the suffocating plenty of things, things, things. And, of course, my brother, the 'baby' (he was called Baby until he was seven and fought for self-determination) who was the centre of everything. And the scolding, fussy nurse.

In Tehran my mother also loved the social life, which was like the pleasures of her girlhood over again. About 'the Legation set' she would talk wistfully in Africa, while my father, half sighing, regarded her with his familiar expression: incredulity, curiosity, held in check by irony. How could she enjoy those boring jolly evenings with boring jolly people? He loathed musical evenings, with people singing the Indian Love Lyrics and 'The Road to Mandalay' to each other, while my mother played. (She played alone, for her own pleasure, music these people found highbrow.) He hated the dinner parties, receptions, garden parties and picnics; she could not have enough of them. He would tell the story of a certain Englishman in Persia who, urged by his family to let them have a picnic, put his children on donkeys, blindfolded them, and had them led around and around the garden for an hour, when they were unblindfolded, and saw the feast prepared for them in a corner of their own garden. Meanwhile he retired to the library. A fellow spirit! My mother only laughed. 'Don't you dare try it,' she said.

Persia, particularly Tehran, was the best time in my mother's life.

When they had been in Persia for five years, leave was due, after which they intended to come back. He did not much want to: would he really have to work in a bank for the rest of his life? He had had a country childhood, and always wanted to be a farmer.

It was summer, the Red Sea a furnace, and dangerous for children. They decided—which means, my mother decided—to travel back across Russia. Ours was the first family to use that route after the Revolution, through the Caspian to Moscow. 1924, and everything was in chaos. On an oil-tanker in the Caspian, my mother sat up all night to keep the lights on us, for there were swarms of lice. A shadow fell on an arm: mine, which became red and swollen with bites. Typhus abounded. The trains were ancient, also lice-ridden, no food on them. On every station were crowds of starved children, orphans; and the peasant women selling a hard-boiled egg or some bread had to defend themselves against these *besprizorniks*, when my mother got off to buy something, anything at all, to eat. She was still on the platform once when our train left without her. I remember the terror of it: she had vanished. It took her a day and a half to catch up. She had to fight her way on to a goods train, had to 'tell them what to do—*they* didn't know—I had to make them telegraph our train to wait for me.' All in English, of course. At the frontier, informed that we did not have the right visas, she had told the man at Immigration not to be so silly. For years my father collapsed into laughter, remembering the poor ragged half-starved Bolshevik with a rifle 'that wouldn't bring down a pigeon,' confronted by a British matron. 'Oh Lord,' wept my father, 'I can see it now. Don't be silly, she said, and he was raring to shoot the lot of us.' 'Did I get us in or did I not?' demanded my mother, not really understanding why he laughed so much, but knowing she was in the right. 'Oh, you got us in all right!'

In Moscow, in the hotel, the chambermaids begged to bath and dress us, because they had not seen normal well-fed children. My mother spoke of this with calm, proprietary pride: that the Russians were in this terrible disorganized condition was of course only another proof of the virtues of the British and our Empire.

Six months leave, in England. My memories of it are many, all of cold, damp, dreariness, ugliness, a series of snapshots illustrating my loathing for the place. My parents took us to visit relations, such as my mother's stepmother, now a distinguished old lady living on a minute pension. They did not enjoy it. My father wanted only to leave England, even more stuffy than he remembered, and my mother yearned to return to Tehran. They visited the 1924 Empire

Exhibition at Wembley, and the Southern Rhodesia stand had maize cobs eighteen inches long, and the posters, yards high, claimed that anyone could make his fortune in maize-farming within five years.

My father had about £1,000 capital and a pension because he had lost his leg in the War. This was his chance.

What did they imagine they were going to? Certainly they expected a social life not unlike that in Tehran, for my mother had trunks full of clothes from Harrod's. Also curtains and hangings from Liberty's, and visiting cards. Also a governess, Biddy O'Halloran, aged twenty-one. Perhaps they had heard of the lively goings-on in Nairobi? Not that my mother would have approved of those fast ways. She could not approve of Biddy, who had shingled hair and wore lipstick. These modern girls . . . all her life my mother would use phrases like this, without inverted commas.

It must have been painful, giving up Tehran, to go off to be a farmer's wife in yet another new country. She would not really have minded staying in England—that is to say, London. She was still, every fibre of her, a Londoner. Remembering England, she thought of the streets, buses, trams, theatres, parks, of London. She did not mind the conventional in the way my father did. If he had been prepared to go back into the Westminster Bank somewhere in London, she would have given up the pleasures of Tehran with equanimity. And then she would have lived out her life in conformity with her nature, a useful and energetic middle-class woman in, let's say, Wimbledon.

Instead, she set off for the middle of Africa with her crippled husband, who was steadily getting more prickly and solitary, with practically no money, and her two children, one of whom was born to be a trouble and a sorrow to her. Did she know anything about Africa, or about farming? Not a thing! But it didn't seem to matter.

I think she saw Africa as some little interlude, a station on her way, soon to be passed. Nothing had ever happened to my mother to prepare her for what she would find.

It was a slow German boat. My mother loved the gales that sent the other passengers below, leaving her on the bridge with the captain. This, and the deck games and the fancy-dress parties, made up for her husband, who wanted only to sit and watch the sea, and for her daughter, who was being consistently impertinent, and who cut up her evening dresses with scissors when she was forced to go to bed early so as not to interfere with the evening's good times. The boat loafed around the Cape to Beira where they caught the train to Salisbury. Outside Salisbury was a place called Lilfordia that boarded settlers while they were buying farms. (Lilfordia was the farm of 'Boss' Lilford, later Ian Smith's guide and mentor.) My mother left her children with the governess, and went with her husband by Scotch cart to look at farms. The settlers were being offered land at about ten pounds an acre (at today's values), the money advanced by the Land Bank. The land had been cleared of the black people who had been living on it: they were despatched to the Reserves, or told to move to land that hadn't yet been allocated to whites. This was 'opening up the country for white civilization,' a description my mother never could see any reason to criticize.

The farm they bought was in Lomagundi, seventy miles from Salisbury, a modest 1,500 acres, but we were free to run our cattle, and to cut grass and wood on the miles of Government land which remained unallocated all the time we were there. Our farm, then, was at the frontier of 'white civilization' with nothing between us and Portuguese East Africa a couple of hundred miles away.

The land was sparsely settled, the farms huge. The nearest farmhouses to ours were three, four, five miles away. It was virgin bush: a few trees had been cut for mine furnaces. Every kind of animal lived there: sable, eland, kudu, bushbuck, duiker, anteaters, wild cats, wild pigs, snakes. There were flocks of guineafowl, partridges, hawks, eagles, pigeons, doves—birds, birds, birds. Dawns were explosions of song; the nights noisy with owls and nightjars and birds whose names we never knew; all day birds shrilled and cooed and hammered and chattered. But paradise had already been given notice to quit. The leopards and baboons had gone to the hills, the lions had wandered off, the elephants had retreated to the Zambesi Valley, the land was emptying.

But it was still a wilderness that my parents were taking on. The farm itself was approached by a disused mine track, a dirt road. The railway was seven miles away. Not one acre had been cleared for planting. The labourers were people who had been savagely defeated in a war thirty-five years before, and who left their villages and came out to work only because they had to pay the Poll Tax imposed on them precisely to make them work.

Having found their farm, my parents came back to collect the children. Their daughter as usual had been very naughty indeed, much worse than ever before: she had lied, stolen, run away, sulked and screamed. My mother knew it was all the fault of this travelling about: children need an ordered existence. She got us into a covered wagon drawn by twenty or so oxen, while her husband rode alongside it on his horse. The journey took five days. Inside the wagon was everything they possessed.

While the trees were being cleared off the hill where the house was to be built, we lodged at the gold mine just over the ridge.

Settlers always built themselves mud and thatch huts, joined by verandahs, and were expected to last only a year or so, to be replaced after the first good season by brick and tin. Our house was a single elongated hut, divided into four rooms. Its walls were of mud smeared over poles and whitewashed, the roof thatch cut from the grass in the vleis, the floor of stamped mud and dung.

All the floors were covered with black linoleum, and furniture was made from petrol and paraffin boxes stained black and curtained with flour sacks that were dyed and embroidered by my mother. In the front room, which had windows all around it, 'like the prow of a ship' as my mother insisted, were Persian rugs, Liberty curtains, a piano and the heavy display silver of the period.

While my mother supervised the gang of black men building the house, my father watched the teams who cleared the bush for planting.

Then there was the business of Biddy O'Halloran, who turned out so badly. She had definitely expected something like Nairobi, and found herself stuck in this lonely and savage place with suitors of the wrong class. Every unattached male for fifty miles came visiting to propose to her, and she did not have as much time for the children as my mother thought was due. There were quarrels, and she departed back home. Then, about a year after the arrival in Africa, my mother became ill and took to her bed and stayed there. It was her heart! It is clear now that she was in an acute anxiety state, was having a breakdown. Neither her doctor in Salisbury, nor she (a nurse) could see it. The worst for her, of course, was the isolation. What my father revelled in—for he had at last found the life that suited him—was destroying her. Having always been surrounded by people, she now had only the blacks, towards whom she had had from the start all the attitudes typical of the settler: they were primitive, dirty, stupid. She was never able to see that there was anything interesting in them. Her neighbours were lower-middle class and working class, mostly Scottish, who had come out before the War and had got rich on maize. She did not want to seem snobbish, but what did she have in common with them? She had no intention of spending her life talking about gardening and recipes and dress patterns. But that was what her life now was, just like theirs.

She got out of bed, complained of a thousand aches and pains, went back again. She complained continually, and it was unlike her, for it simply wasn't done to make a fuss! She lay in a bed specially made by a neighbour who ran a timber mill, with attachments for books and magazines, and summoned her children to her throughout the day, to comfort her. 'Poor sick mummy,' she insisted, and we responded with fervent but (in my case at least) increasingly resentful embraces.

But this was certainly not all that went on at her bedside. Early childhood is when children learn best, and nothing was going to get in the way of our instruction, according to Montessori. In and out of bed, she read to us, told us stories; she was a marvellous teacher of small children. We were taught geography by means of piles of mud and sand left over from the house building—making continents and countries and mountains that hardened in the sun and that, for oceans and rivers, could be filled with water. She taught us arithmetic with seeds and hens' eggs and baby chicks. She made us understand the solar system through games in which we were planets, the moon, the sun. We were made to notice stars, birds, animals. For a while we were taught by a correspondence course, but its lessons were not nearly as good as hers, and she ordered us books from England, and two periodicals whose impossibly high standards of writing would find no equal today. The *Children's Newspaper* offered news about discoveries, inventions, archaeological finds, beasts and birds, and the *Merry-Go-Round* printed stories and poems by writers like Walter de la Mare and

Eleanor Farjeon. It was my mother who introduced me to the world of literature into which I was about to escape from her.

And then my mother got herself out of bed, and went on living. She had been ill for a year. I wonder if she ever understood that her illness had been a way of denying what she knew she had to face. What courage that must have taken! I know it and I admire it, but I can't put myself in her place. It was the farm, the veld, that she hated, that trapped her. She was planning, scheming, dreaming of escaping from it, from the moment she arrived. But the farm, the veld, Africa is to me, quite simply, the luckiest thing that ever happened.

Writing about my mother is difficult. I keep coming up against barriers, and they are not much different now from what they were then. She paralysed me as a child by the anger and pity I felt. Now only pity is left, but it still makes it hard to write about her. What an awful life she had, my poor mother! But it was certainly no worse than my father's, and that is the point: he was equipped by nature for hard times, and she was not. He may have been a damaged, an increasingly sick man; she was strong and full of vitality. But I am not as sorry for him as I am for her. She never understood what was happening to her.

VLADIMIR RYBAKOV
FAMILY POLITICS

The name Rybakov is a pseudonym; my real name is Szescinski, because my father was Polish. He came from the region around Gdansk. My great-grandfather had been an enterprising peasant who opened a small factory making sewing machines. He prospered, enabling my grandfather to buy a large estate and with it, according to family legend, the title of count. To this day one of my uncles and his family live in Poland; he is a senior officer in the Gdansk police force. Like most of their fellow-countrymen, they confess to having no love for the Russians.

My mother was from Russia, but, like my father, she was not entirely Russian either: she was also part gypsy. Her mother, my grandmother, known in the family as Mémé, was married to a successful architect called Vorobyov. She, in turn, was the owner and headmistress of a private boarding-school for girls, and, at the same time, was a member of the Social Revolutionary Party. The Social Revolutionaries professed a brand of non-Marxist agrarian socialism and were deeply committed to terrorism as a political weapon. It was they, for instance, who assassinated Plehve, the Russian Minister of the Interior, in 1904; the Grand Duke Sergei in 1905; and Stolypin, the Prime Minister, in 1911.

Mémé's brother did not share her political views: he owned forests in Smolensk Province, and when in 1896 or 1897 he caught some peasants cutting down his trees and stealing the timber, he mutilated them by cutting off the fingers of their right hands. It was no doubt those same peasants or their relatives who seized him eight years later during the 1905 revolution, lashed him between two planks, doused him in kerosene and burned him alive. When Mémé learned of her brother's fate, she exclaimed: 'And high time too! At last justice has triumphed. The dog has died a dog's death.' It was not a particularly intimate family.

Around the same time, Mémé left her husband and lived openly with a so-called 'settled' gypsy, who kept a small shop. In those days, at the turn of the century, this was terrible, scandalous behaviour for a middle-class woman. She flaunted the relationship, boldly walking arm-in-arm with him around the main streets of Smolensk, arousing hatred and indignation among respectable folk. She also had a child by him, a daughter, but after a year the gypsy decamped, taking her money with him. It seems that she had been unable to 'civilize' him after all.

Mémé went back to her husband with her baby daughter: my mother. My mother—who had the dark, aquiline, olive-skinned features and dark brown eyes of the gypsy—looked different from everyone else in the family who were typically Russian: that is, ash-blond and snub-nosed.

From early on, my mother had shown a marked artistic talent, and, while still quite young, was sent to Paris to study drawing and painting. This was just before the outbreak of World War I. Thoughout the war and the Russian Revolution, she remained in France, living in a *pension* with other young art students. During the Civil War that followed the Revolution, her mother, who of course was still in Russia, lost almost everything as the Bolsheviks shot, imprisoned or otherwise eliminated most of the Social Revolutionaries. In the early 1920s, Mémé managed to emigrate, and, along with a great many 'White' Russian refugees, turned up in Paris. There she joined my mother. Mémé had succeeded in bringing with her quite a lot of jewellery sewn into her clothes, so she and mother were at least able to make ends meet. When mother graduated from art school, it was decided that she was unlikely to make a living as an artist, and she enrolled as a student at the School of Medicine of the University of Paris. There she met a young Polish medical student: the man who would be my father.

Both my mother and father had considerable artistic talent—it was one of the shared interests that brought them together—and, after they qualified in medicine, got married and set up a practice together, they carried on painting. And they were not just 'Sunday painters': their work was exhibited more than once in Paris during the thirties.

They had two children: my eldest brother Misha, who was born in 1937, and Petya, born four years later. That was about the time that the Soviet Union entered the war. That was always the time my mother became more active in politics.

Mémé had always hoped that her daughter would support the Social Revolutionaries whose party continued to exist in exile. But instead my mother joined the French Communist Party. She was a convinced and fairly extreme communist—an embryonic Stalinist, in fact—although her communism was always tinged with a strong dash of Russian nationalism. It was inevitable that she would join the French Resistance. My father, though, did not. He had always been clay in her hands: she became a communist, he became a communist; she became an artist, he became an artist. And so when the Communist Party issued orders (through her) that he was to adopt a neutral position under the German occupation, he obeyed her. But he didn't collaborate with the Germans, except by selling them the silk scarves he painted and by trading on the black market to keep the family alive.

By the end of the war, mother was quite high up in the Party hierarchy. I know this because my brother Petya told me that Pierre Dex often came to visit us. Until recently Pierre Dex, a poet, was well known as a leading member of the French Communist Party, whose 'eyes were opened' to the true nature of communism by Solzhenitsyn. Dex has written a book about the experience and is now an active contributor to right-wing newspapers. In those days, however, Dex was a Stalinist and first attracted notice as the principal prosecution witness in the trial of Viktor ('I Chose Freedom') Kravchenko. He accused Kravchenko of lying and distorting the truth about the Soviet system.

After the war, the Communist Party ordered my mother to do propaganda work among the former Soviet prisoners-of-war who had remained in France. Her job was to persuade them to return to the Soviet Union, a job she undertook with great zeal.

I was born in 1947 and grew up as a normal Parisian child: I studied at the *Ecole communale*, and, both my parents being doctors, was comfortably well off. In 1947 and 1951 my mother was offered Soviet nationality and officially invited to return to the USSR, and on both occasions she refused, while still remaining a loyal Stalinist: when as a small boy I refused to drink my milk, for example, my mother used to persuade me by saying: 'Drink to Stalin's health'—and I drank it. Later she told me it was the only way she could get me to drink milk.

Mother only finally decided to return to the USSR in 1956, after the Twentieth Party Congress, at which Khrushchev denounced Stalin and all his works. Although she was a Stalinist in France, she knew what would have happened to us if we had gone back to the Soviet Union while Stalin was still alive. But after the

Twentieth Congress she said—and I quote her verbatim—'Now they won't throw us into the Gulag.' And she started to prepare for our departure from France. My father was persuaded fairly quickly, because apart from their shared political allegiance both he and my mother also continued to nourish artistic ambitions, and they somehow imagined that in the USSR they would be granted the recognition as great artists that they had failed to gain in the West. My eldest brother Misha, having joined the French Communist Party in 1954 at the age of sixteen (I was then only seven), did not need to be persuaded. The only anti-communist in the family was my brother Petya: he was fifteen, but already his opposition to communism seemed, to me at least, to be a deeply-rooted part of his character. He was not told that we were leaving France for Russia, because my parents knew he would refuse to go. Just before our departure my mother gave him an injection of a powerful soporific, which put him to sleep for forty-eight hours, and when he woke up we were already in Russia. When he realized what had happened, Petya tried to throw himself off the train, shouting that he refused to live in a communist country and demanding to go back to France. Father tied him up to prevent him from doing anything stupid. He was still tied up when we arrived in Moscow. My parents were confident that Petya would soon accept his new surroundings.

In Moscow, we were told there was no accommodation available for us there, and that we should select some provincial town to live in. We were given a list of about ten towns to choose from. Mother quickly discovered which place offered the most tolerable living conditions—the best housing, the best supplies of food, etc—and she chose a town in the Southern Ukraine, which before World War II had belonged to Romania and before that to Austria: Chernovtsy. The place still had a distinctly 'European' air; it was known as 'Little Vienna'. We were given a flat that was, by Soviet standards, enormous—a room that was little less than twenty feet square.

My father became disillusioned: he missed his tennis court and his horse, and compared to Paris the place was a dull, boring, provincial dump. Although they did indeed enjoy a certain success as artists, and they were communists, they were, of course, communists of the Western European type. Thus when father was

Vladimir Rybakov

asked to paint a picture of prisoners of war, he painted what he had
seen, namely real Soviet POWs. Instead of depicting the version
that he was supposed to—the proud Soviet hero, head held high in
defiance of brutal Nazi captors, etc., etc.—he painted a real POW,
wretched, suffering and crushed. When Party officials told him that
his picture was all wrong, that Soviet POWs never looked like that,
he replied that he had seen them himself and they looked exactly
like that. This was the start of his troubles with officialdom, and
there were no more exhibitions of his work. After a few months he
had become a confirmed anti-communist, and began taking steps to
get permission to return to the West. At first the authorities refused:
he had assumed Soviet nationality, and since Soviet law did not
recognize the concept of dual nationality and immigration was then
impossible for Soviet citizens, there could be no question of
allowing him to go back to France. So father reacted like a
Westerner ignorant of the Soviet system, packed a suitcase and
attempted to leave the country by crossing the frontier at some
remote spot in Central Asia. It was a very rash thing to do. He was
arrested and questioned, and—amazingly enough—released.
Father was then told that, although they couldn't allow him to go to
France, he could apply to return to his place of birth. He was soon
given permission and left for Poland. He remained in Poland for a
while, but then, as emigration from Poland is far easier than from
the USSR, he was able from there to return to France.

All this time my brother Petya remained permanently shut in
his room, not having set a foot outside the flat since our arrival in
Chernovtsy; he declared that he would only leave his room in order
to return to France and freedom. If my memory is correct, Petya
stayed in that room for more than three years. Father sent him
invitations to come to France, but the Soviet authorities would not
accept them. Eventually father went back to Poland and asked for
Petya to be allowed to join him there; this time they let him go. But
in one sense my father was too late; by then Petya had become
mentally ill. He was nineteen. When father saw him and realized
what had happened, he put Petya into a Polish asylum and returned
to Paris.

Meanwhile, my eldest brother Misha had completed his
postgraduate studies and was given a flat in Moscow. He got

76

married, and in time was appointed to the Chair of Romance and Germanic Languages at the University of Vladimir, a city about 150 miles east of Moscow. At the same time he held the job of editor of *Nouvelles de Moscou*, the French-language newspaper published in Moscow by Novosti Press Agency. For years Misha had dutifully worn his communist blinkers, trying not to notice anything to right or left of him, and even when he looked ahead he didn't see what was there but what they wanted him to see. With time, however, he came to admit the reality of what surrounded him, and his communist convictions faded, although by Soviet standards he was prosperous and successful, earning over 1,000 roubles a month. I was gradually changing my views, too. Only mother remained a faithful communist, true to her ideals.

W hen I was about fifteen and still at school, two things happened to me, both equally disastrous. The first was to develop an enthusiasm for the history of the region where I was living. Quite by chance I learned that in 1939 the Soviet Union had *not* liberated the Western Ukraine and Western Byelorussia, as we had been taught, but that in actual fact the Soviet Union, in alliance with Nazi Germany, had attacked Poland. This news amazed and horrified me. The second disaster was the shock I received when I asked my mother whether she knew what had awaited those POWs after the war, when, persuaded by her eloquence, they had returned to the USSR. She answered that she had been quite aware of their impending fate—namely immediate shipment to Siberian labour camps and, in most cases, death. But, she insisted, it was 'necessary': principally because the build-up of world-wide communism was still at the stage where tough methods were inevitable, and we could expect to see plenty more blood, deception and violence for at least another century, perhaps even two centuries. The game was meant to be worth the candle, though, because communism was 'the bright future of mankind'. She said all this with complete seriousness: her ideological faith was unshaken even by the knowledge that the policy of repatriating Soviet ex-POWs was motivated by reasons of crude *Realpolitik*: first, because the Soviet Union needed the ex-POWs to swell its slave labour force; second, because at that time (the late forties) the French

Communist Party was hoping to seize power, and the considerable number of Soviet ex-POWs in France was an embarrassment to the Party. These men did not have good things to say about Soviet-type communism—they *knew* at first hand what it was really like—and they were only too ready to spread this politically damaging information among the French working class, with whom they lived and worked, chiefly as manual labourers.

These two revelations, taken together, made me into a convinced anti-communist. Not yet sixteen, I left home. I was not away for long, because I had no internal passport. But at the age of sixteen I duly received my passport, and I left again. I bummed around the whole vast country, working as a bricklayer, stevedore, welder, fitter, anything . . . . I went to Central Asia, to Kazan and points east, ending up in Verkhoyansk in North-Eastern Siberia, where the winter temperature can fall to minus seventy degrees centigrade. I did not correspond with my mother. At one point I had even forgotten how to speak French. Indeed I had forgotten the existence of France, my birthplace. In the end I enrolled in school again as an extramural student and got my 'Certificate of Maturity', which I needed in order to go to university.

I returned home like the Prodigal Son, mother welcomed me back, and I entered the Faculty of History at Chernovtsy University. Very soon, however, I started to play the fool. I didn't exactly smash any windows, but I drank a lot, horsed around and occasionally got into a fight. My real downfall occurred in my second year, when, again, I started to take a serious interest in history, in particular in Marx's theory of the so-called 'Asiatic Mode of Production'. This theory, I was to discover, was not only not recognized in Soviet universities, but was also taboo. In spite of that, I wrote an essay, showing how Marx himself had pointed out that in addition to his classic five stages of the development of production—primitive accumulation, slave-owning societies, feudal societies, bourgeois societies, socialist societies—there was also a sixth and final category that applied to such Asian countries as China and India, whose historical development did not fit into the 'five stages' that were meant to be more typical of Europe and North America. Marx called this sixth category—characterized by a uniform and repressive subjection of the working population to a vast, centralized bureaucracy (in other words an accurate prediction of the present state of affairs in the Soviet Union!)—'The Asiatic Mode of Production'. I was summoned to the Dean of the Faculty, where I argued that I was only quoting Marx himself. This, it appears, was no defence. In 1968 I was expelled from the university.

I was immediately called up for military service. A month after being expelled, I found myself on a troop train taking me to an army base in the Far East. I was there a year. The methods were harsh—and were meant to be harsh—and they threw the book at us for the slightest misdemeanour. When on one occasion I objected to the way we were treated, I was made to clean out the sewers. This involved wielding a shovel while standing up to my waist in human excrement. As I stood there, I swore to myself that as soon as I managed to get out of this shit, I would find a sub-machine gun and kill as many officers as I could before I was killed myself. But when I got out and had cleaned myself up, I found that I had not suffered any actual harm and was only very hungry. Life, I decided, was in fact worth living; I didn't shoot any officers after all.

I don't think they quite broke me there, but they did bend me a bit.

Even so, although still an anti-communist, I was promoted and became a real, tough Soviet Army sergeant. I would have carried out any order. To some degree, I suppose, I became an automaton: 'Orders are orders': 'You're not paid to think'—and so on.

During that first year in the army I had learned to operate long-distance communications equipment, a top secret sixteen-channel cable-telephone system called a 'Hawk', used as the link between divisions and their corps headquarters and above. But when my training was completed, I was not assigned to the Signal Corps. Somehow or other—presumably from mother—my father discovered the address of my unit and wrote to me from France. For this I was arrested and interrogated for three days and nights, during which I told them nothing, for the good reason that I had nothing to tell. At the end, instead of being posted to a Signals unit, I was transferred to the Artillery as punishment and sent to one of the remotest units stationed near the Chinese frontier—where I served for three years.

At that time the Soviet-Chinese border wasn't really the best place to be. Chinese troops violated the border regularly, even though crossing it was tantamount to certain death. Their officers undoubtedly knew this, because the Chinese soldiers were always drunk. We had standing orders not to take prisoners and to shoot any wounded: no Chinese was to get back alive. Whenever they made an incursion, we would move our guns forward and fire over their heads, in order to lay down what is known as a 'fire curtain' behind them so that the Chinese could not retreat through it. Simultaneously we would open up on them from both flanks with napalm fired from multiple rocket-launchers and burn them up. Then we would be deployed in a long line with the aim of doing precisely what, for instance, the SS did in World War II: advance and kill any remaining wounded. I found this somewhat disturbing. Although we knew that the Chinese objective was to seize large tracts of Soviet Siberia, and that none of their troops was allowed to get away alive, we found that killing wounded men in cold blood is not much fun. When you were advancing and saw a wounded Chinaman in front of you, you tried to move sideways to the right or left so that it would be someone else's job to finish him off. But then your neighbour would notice this, and would refuse to move over. This led to fights between our own men. As a result we would be killing Chinese and punching each other at the same time. Everyone ended the operation with bloody faces.

The first time you took part in this it was an appalling experience. After a salvo from those napalm rockets, the ground would be littered with guts, blood and burned human flesh, which smells horrible; it made you vomit. Then after a while you got hardened to it. I was quite prepared to kill and be killed, just like many of my comrades. You develop an attitude of mindless indifference to human life. During my time, our regiment alone killed 30,000 Chinese. Our casualties were comparatively light. We chiefly lost men during blizzards or heavy rainstorms when, with visibility reduced to almost nothing, the Chinese could cross the frontier, sneak up on our posts, kill the sentries and set fire to our stores. During one of these raids I was concussed, and have partly lost the sight in my right eye and the hearing in my right ear. To this day I still get headaches.

I never saw my mother again, although it must have been around the time that I was stationed on the Soviet-Chinese border that she learned about my poor brother Petya: he had been moved from an ordinary Polish asylum to the psychiatric ward of a prison. Petya, it appears, had tried to spread some sort of anti-communist propaganda among his fellow-inmates. This development seems to have disturbed my mother: clearly she was starting to have serious qualms of conscience about her son. She applied for permission to return to France, believing that if she could get him to the West he might have some chance of being cured. Eventually, she got out. In France, she got a job as a doctor, saved up some money and travelled to Poland where she had to pay to get Petya released. She brought him back to France, and, being a doctor, tried to cure him herself. She failed. Seeing that Petya was a hopeless case, she wrote letters to me and my brother Misha, in which she admitted that she had destroyed not only Petya but the family: she was to blame, and she therefore saw no further point in living. She hanged herself.

I had never wanted to leave the Soviet Union, but my experiences in the army convinced me that I had to get out. On being demobilized, I wrote my father, asking him to invite me and my brother Misha to join him in France. We had to wait three years before being allowed to emigrate, during which time I once more took up the familiar round of manual industrial jobs—welder, lathe-operator and so on. In the end, we got out because of the name of the person who formally requested that we should be allowed to leave: my father had remarried to a rich woman who was an old friend of Mme Pompidou, whose husband was about to make a state visit to the Soviet Union; when he arrived, he handed Brezhnev a list of French citizens who wanted to emigrate. Our names were on it. Although Soviet authorities had steadily declined to grant us exit visas for three years, it was hard to refuse Pompidou.

There was still the problem of the woman I wanted to marry and who I hoped would join me some day in France. She was living in Archangel, where I went to see her ten days before I was due to leave. I had to invent a reason for going there, and said that I was a merchant seaman on leave and that she was pregnant. We were married three days later, but it was an illegal marriage: for obvious reasons, no Soviet citizen who has been given permission to emigrate is allowed to marry before leaving. My marriage, of course, had been entered on the appropriate page in my passport.

To avoid being arrested and tried for breaking the emigration laws, I set fire to my flat. When the table and curtains were well ablaze, I burned my passport almost completely, taking care to destroy the page where my marriage was entered by leaving the passport number intact. After the fire brigade had gallantly put out the fire, I went to the police, showed them my almost totally destroyed passport, and was issued with a new one—as a bachelor again. Meanwhile, my wife travelled down from Archangel to her home town of Nikopol, where on the strength of our perfectly genuine marriage certificate she legally changed her surname to Rybakov, and was duly given a new passport bearing her new name.

Father was waiting for me when I arrived. He introduced me to my stepmother and took me to his new home near Lens, the mining town in northeast France where he had established a lucrative medical practice (a large number of Polish miners worked in the Flanders coalfield, and they naturally wanted to be treated by a Polish doctor). On that first evening I, in typical Soviet fashion, had far too much to drink. It was our first night together, and I spent it shouting at my father: I accused him of being inhuman, of having cruelly abandoned my brother Petya in a Polish asylum, the last straw that had sent my wretched brother hopelessly mad. Father defended himself by throwing all the blame on my mother, insisting that she was the culprit—which was the truth, but only half the truth: they were both equally to blame. But we did not just quarrel; we had a fight. I am strong—stronger than he was—and I punched him a bit too hard and broke two of his ribs. I left his house. I never saw him again.

In that winter of 1973, I found it very hard to find work and adapt to French life. I wasn't eligible for refugee aid; to the French authorities I wasn't a refugee or an émigré—I was just a Frenchman who had been abroad and come home again: '*Tu est français— démerde-toi!*' Having never worked in France, I was not eligible for the dole. I began sleeping under the bridges of Paris with perhaps ten francs in my pocket. I lived for several months among the *clochards*; they fed me, and one of them even gave me a copy of Baudelaire's *Les fleurs du mal*, which for lack of any other reading matter I read over and over again. I couldn't ask my brother for help. As a married man with three children his problems were, if anything, greater than mine, and for complicated reasons I was on bad terms with his wife. I applied for a job on the Renault production line, but was turned down, as their employment policy was to give preference to Arabs from Algeria and Morocco.

One evening I was sitting beside the Seine, staring at the water. I recalled my mother: like her, I could see no further point in living. Here I was in the 'free world', out of work, hungry, huddled on an embankment with water trickling down the back of my neck. Without my warm Moscow overcoat I would probably have died from exposure. I decided that the dirty waters of the Seine could at least offer me oblivion. The thought of suicide, while serious, did not last long. I walked away from the Seine and quickly tried to pull myself together.

But I wasn't able to do that for some time: I next found myself in the police cells. Three young men had tried to mug me; finding I had no money, they attempted to wrench off my watch (which I later had to sell). I reacted in a typically Soviet fashion. In Russia, if three men attack you, there are three possible outcomes: you are killed; you are crippled; you beat them up. On this occasion, I crippled all three very seriously. And then I was arrested. I was desperate: certain that I would get at least three years in prison. But this was France, not the Soviet Union. When my trial came up, I proved that I had acted in self-defence, and was released.

I found work as a welder. By chance, I also came across the Russian-language newspaper *Russkaya mysl* (*La pensée russe*), and wrote a letter to the editor and included a few stories and articles I had written. I had been writing short stories since the age of fifteen, but none of them had been printed. In the Soviet Union, I once showed some to a friend and asked if he thought I could get them published. 'Not only will no one publish them,' he said, 'but each of these stories could earn you five years in a labour camp.' I continued writing, but only for 'the desk drawer', in the expressive Russian phrase.

Russkaya mysl replied by offering me a job. I began as a proof-reader and was later promoted to reporter and then assistant editor. I also resumed my writing and finished a novel I had begun in the Soviet Union, *The Burden*, and started on a second, *The Brand*.

My first novel was published in French in 1978. I sent a copy of it to my father, along with an article about me that had appeared in *Paris-Match*: after our fight he had predicted I would die in some gutter; I wanted him to see that I was not dead in a gutter, but that I had become not only a journalist, but, what's more, a novelist. It was then I learned that he had been dead for two years: he had died suddenly from a heart attack, brought on by the careless use of a needle while treating himself by acupuncture. To this day, I do not know where my mother and father are buried.

My brother Misha now works in Paris as technical translator. Petya is in a mental hospital near Lille. He imagines he is still in the Soviet Union and still longs to escape to France and freedom. He has moments of lucidity, and I have tried to visit him regularly.

Although I was born in France and have lived there for a total of twenty years, I feel instinctively that it is not my homeland. My homeland is Russia. I miss it terribly.

Translated from the Russian by Michael Glenny

BREYTEN
BREYTENBACH
PUNISHABLE
INNOCENCE

Life in the zoological sense consists of such actions as are necessary for existence in nature. But man manages things so that the claims of his life are reduced to a minimum. In the vacuum arising after he has left behind his animal life he devotes himself to a series of non-biological occupations which are not imposed by nature but invented by himself. This invented life—invented as a novel or a play is invented—man calls 'human life', well-being. Human life transcends the reality of nature . . . . Have we heard right? Is human life in its most human dimension a work of fiction? Is man a sort of novelist of himself who conceives the fanciful figure of a personage with its unreal occupations and then, for the sake of converting it into reality does all the things he does—and becomes an engineer?
José Ortega y Gasset, *Toward a Philosophy of History*

M'lord,
I should have liked to have added to the above that this 'invented life', which man calls human existence, is conceived and born in dreams, and that reality does not exist except in opposition to the dream, just as dream is dream only in comparison with reality. They are the ink and the paper for the same piece of writing. And if now this invented life, this created reality, comes alive and truly exists in space and time, then the more orthodox view of reality (daylight, the tedium of work, dying) must therefore be a dream. Do I dream I'm alive or do I live as if I'm a-dream?

The mess in which I now find myself—my reason for turning to you—has outlines at times so vague that I must ask myself if it is a-dream or reality. One thing, however, is as clear as daylight: without any doubt, it did happen. 'Happen' is my private attempt at synthesizing the otherwise irreconcilable opposites of reality and dream: it is in truth the common denominator. For what is 'happen'? Does it depend upon the evidence of witnesses? Just say for argument's sake that I have stubbed my toe somewhere and nobody saw it, and after an hour or more I no longer feel it: did it then still take place? Happening is the heritage of a feeling. In this sense I can assure you that what I intend to describe here truly did happen to me. I furthermore include a duly signed statement from a witness—who will only emerge later in this writing. (That is if I can lay my hand on the statement.)

Almost a year ago exactly—if my calendar doesn't deceive me, it was a Tuesday, the 5th of May— I, together with my wife, Yolande Marie, and my brother, Nicolaas Herman, and my sister, Rebekka Klavdia Maryn (both Breytenbach), came ashore here for what we thought would be a brief holiday. We hired a car locally, and without any fixed plan or predetermined route started visiting the various coastal towns. Since we had been told previously about an impressive, new mountain fortress of a certain sect in a given town, the name of which now escapes me, we decided to visit that as well.

It was a clear windy morning when we arrived. The heart of this little city is not very big: a few streets lined by rows of sad autumn trees and a little further along the suggestion of modern suburbs or outlying districts. The centre of the community—and clearly a place popular with tourists—was a cloistered fort on the hill, safely entrenched behind high walls and encircled by a deep moat. A draw-bridge joined the fort to the main street. Here on this bridge, pedlars and itinerant hawkers and bargain-spitters exhibited their wares and foodstuffs. There was the swell of human voices, the exuberant selling of ice creams and cakes, pennants and other souvenirs.

We each bought a small flag from a man in a cap, and I told him, when he asked, that we intended to visit the fort. A shadow of serious concern darkened his countenance, and he grabbed me urgently by the arm: 'Don't! You will never get out of there again!' I shook off the silly man's hand, laughed and paid him for the pennant, with a hefty tip thrown in. If only I had listened to him then!

It was a pale day, a little as if the turbulent wind had swept away the colours from the sun, emptying its intimacy and leaving just the light. The bottom of the dry moat was strewn with empty paper bags, squashed ice cream cones, orange-peel and other rubbish. Ravens hopped or fluttered awkwardly from one pile to the next. Some boys from the town stood on the bridge shooting at the birds with their air-guns. It was surprising that a wounded raven doesn't bleed much.

With a group of sightseers we walked through the enormous gateway of the fort to the inner courtyard, and immediately we were astonished. One could say that here one was entering another world—except that it probably had much in common with the suburbs and districts that, we suspected, were nearby. But what we saw in the inner courtyard seemed at odds with the ancient stone and moss: it was ultra-modern—glass and neon wherever you looked—and all around you could sense the impersonal efficiency which has become so much the hallmark of Western business civilization. A young man, clad in an anonymous grey suit, had us all kneel down with our faces turned towards a shining loudspeaker, which addressed us courteously but curtly. We were asked to repeat an oath which, if I remember correctly, came from the Bible, or some text which sounded a lot like the Bible. The deference with which the young man treated the disembodied voice was to us a clear indication that it must be that of the abbot, the general, or the commander.

Afterwards we were led to a cloakroom, where we were asked to exchange our town clothes for long, bleached garments. Nobody was opposed to this (were we already convinced that it was too late?), and the general feeling was one of, Well now, in a cloister or an abbey one ought to adapt to the regulations and the dress of the inhabitants, expecially if those regulations are clearly intended to foster humility. We also became aware that we suffered a certain heaviness, an oppressive feeling but also one of resignation. Without speaking, the four of us looked at each other just to make sure that we were all still together. Barefoot, we continued.

It must be admitted that the rest of the building was not as impressive as the entrance. From inside one would never have guessed that, seen from the outside, the castle looked like something from the Middle Ages. The corridors and the halls were dirty and featureless, with the drabness and the greyness that one associates with the neglected schools of the thirties.

The guide and the guards—they, too, were dressed in long gowns—accompanied us from hall to hall. Sometimes we sat down on chairs with the others (also clothed like us) to listen quietly to lectures that were broadcast from the ubiquitous loudspeakers that were placed like altars in every hall. On the way from one hall to the next, we could sometimes glance through an open door into a dormitory where grey and colourless people sat on beds with holy books in their laps.

Towards nightfall a similar dormitory was allocated to us. By every bed there was a small cabinet containing a flannel, a toothbrush and two or three books, all of them written by the voice in the loudspeakers. (That voice, by the way, spoke with the tone, the register and the accent of a practically-minded chairman, or the president of a board of directors—important characteristics which may be of help later for an eventual identification.)

Our watches were in the pockets of our city clothes, and even if we had been brave enough to ask our guards for the time, they probably could not have given us an answer; that is, if they had watches, which was not at all certain. The strange thing was that nobody here opened his mouth. The only audible voice was from the loudspeakers in the many halls. Not that the people were mute—only that you were so overwhelmed, or so exhausted, that you could not emit a sound; or otherwise that you had a guardian angel watching your lips. Even among ourselves we hardly exchanged a murmur.

When I realized what was happening to us, my blood started to boil. I could not comprehend why we were expected to spend the night there. But because at that stage I could not yet find my way back through the innards of the building to the entrance portal, and, as we were all quite exhausted from all the walking and the sitting (not even knowing whether it was dark or not outside—the halls had no windows), we decided to let things ride until the following morning.

If only I had paid more attention at the beginning to the warning of the salesman outside.

Breyten Breytenbach

M'lord, it was as if we were shuffling through a weird dream. *Via dolorosa.* Why do these words now surface in me? You must understand that I am not a believer, that the suffering of Christ is for me no more than a poetic symbol. In reality, through our fear and prejudices and ignorance, we ourselves make our earthly existence a way of suffering for everybody, and one could even say that someone who is allowed to lay down his cross at the age of thirty-three can be considered lucky to be rid of it so soon. Yet the religious speculation forces itself upon me because in that cloister-fort, we felt as if we were living a religious experience: as if the voice were actually that of God, the Father: yes, to sum up, that we had ended up in heaven without knowing it. And yet nobody ever mentioned a word about religion—I can now no longer even remember why I keep on referring to a cloister. Certainly it was never called one in my presence. And why would you be detained in heaven against your own wishes? Or was it really contrary to our wishes?

Ah, but it had nevertheless that special feeling of the sacred— explained perhaps by the continuous obeisances and the respectful way, even if empty and unquestioning, that we lent our ears to the broadcasts of sermons, counsel, exhortations, reprobations and speeches. And finally because we accepted everything. I cannot remember what was written in those books—I can't even remember if anybody ever read them; but after a lecture you usually went back to your dormitory to sit leafing through the books, and that is perhaps why I describe them as holy. Then they were the only objects to which one could apply one's fingers, and in this they assumed an extraordinary value.

The crisis came after several days. I had started feeling that this enforced and tedious rhythm of sleep-walk-listen-kneel-sleep was gradually eroding us, breaking us down. In the course of my thoughts I tried clinging to something I could call 'mind', something I thought of as truth. But I did not know what the truth was, and I did not know whether my mulish mullings were not actually preventing the emergence of truth in me. Or was even that planned, was even that foreseen, was it scheduled to happen in exactly that way? (That too is why I now turn to you. Help me.)

90

On top of all this I realized that I was starting to make compromises. During our daily procession from one hall to the next, we must sometimes have passed near the entrance. That I knew. I discovered that some of the inhabitants occasionally got as far as the entrance itself, yes, and maybe even outside it, had crossed the bridge into town. Were they sent on shopping errands? I started believing that those allowed to leave by the entrance in this way must certainly enjoy the confidence of the guide or the guards, and that therefore also had the approval of the omnipresent loudspeaker. Furthermore I reflected that the warders themselves had to be trustworthy ex-inmates. And that is why I tried to get into the guards' good books.

But I did not know how to go about it. Was I to kneel with more enthusiasm? Should I show a spirit of enterprise? Shake my shoulders with discreet disdain? Was I to nod my head when the voice announced important precepts? (Of which, for the life of me, I now no longer remember even a single phrase; I don't know whether he ever spoke in intelligible sentences or even used a known language.) How could I be sure that this uninterrupted outpouring of words was not taking place on a subconscious level? And if that was the case, how much of this initiation, transformation or indoctrination had taken hold in me and would persist afterwards? What is my truth then? Am I not now perhaps doing exactly what the voice had plotted for me? That is also why I'm asking for your help. Please help me. I'm so impure.

Then, however, my only fear was that, in my attempts to win their trust, I was endangering my own truth, my mind. My 'mine', if you don't mind. Because when you start collaborating with the enemy—imagined or real—you take in far more from them than you are aware of or can control. And even resistance itself can be a form of collaboration.

I am not a *satyagrahi*. Faced by what destroys the insights I succeed in having, I cannot keep my mouth shut. The outburst just had to come—even the most pathetic pimple must sooner or later show its pus. Yolande Marie, Nicolaas Herman and Rebekka Klavdia Maryn were becoming strangers to me. All of us, just like all the other lodgers, had started tying our hair in uniform grey and unimaginative buns. And when one day we were led again to our first lecture after our period of sleep (which was always dreamless), I took hold of the guard by his sleeve and started shouting excitedly. I demanded to know the point of this comedy. I wanted to know when we would be allowed to continue our travels, or at least when we would be free. (But nobody was forcing us to stay here. Why did we not just get up and walk out the door?) I wanted to know who the director was and I wanted to talk to him. I described all the proceedings as despicable, as inhospitable, and as an example of bad taste to boot. I persisted in my complaints, and even claimed I would see to it that the detention of innocent persons be brought to the attention of the right people. Come what may. (Help me.) And above all I was shouting: 'What is the truth, what is the truth, aren't you ashamed of yourself?'

The warder did not budge. His face went a deeper shade of crimson, but showed no other emotion. I noticed that his eyes were bright blue, in striking contrast to the red of his cheeks and forehead. He stared straight ahead without batting an eyelid and brought us to the hall to which we had been walking. There all my spirit left me.

Nevertheless I could have made a much bigger racket; I'm sure I would have been justified in cursing and yelling until the house came down, were it not for my trying to retain a measure of self-control. Because the issues at stake were not only scandalous: no, they were awful. But could I really have carried on shouting more and more loudly? Wasn't I then already too numb? You are now perhaps shaking your head in disapproval: my explosion may seem silly to you; or, worse still, you will now refuse to take my case because in your opinion I went and spoiled it entirely. In your wisdom you may very well have wanted to advise me to persist in kneeling and in leafing through the books. But, My Lord, I too am only human, and I have tried to describe what happened so you may understand how I came to the breaking point. Please try to see my point of view, and help me if you can.

I lost all sense of time and the structure of events. My wife, my brother and my sister disappeared, as it were, from my vision. And perhaps the act of resistance I described just now served to strengthen the loudspeaker's confidence in me. I know only that I found myself in the entrance one day—was it really the first time since our arrival there? Several other inmates were lingering nearby. Perhaps even my wife and my siblings were there: I no longer know; I'm not sure I ever did. Outside the glass doors of the entrance (which were open) a raven flew by in the wind, stunned and stupid, with half an orange in its beak. The black, and then the orange, dripping. Sharp like memory. Sharp like the pain experienced by one chased from the garden of love. I sensed that I had started walking forward. Nobody tried to restrain me. I was in a no man's land: shivering, charged with the power of the voice in the loudspeaker—before which a group of visitors in town clothes was even at that moment kneeling to mouth the oath of allegiance. (Of the damned.) (The saved.)

And then I was outside, with the wind in my bleached garments. I ran fast! Fear was at my heels and I was surprised that my legs were still so strong. Everything was in me and I was in everything. I thought the boys with the air-guns were going to shoot at me; that they, like the hustlers and the pedlars, were put there to foil my attempt at escape. But no. Nobody tried stopping me. The wind whistled over the rocks and the bare outcrops. The sky was the colour of old ice cream. I raced over the bridge into the town, my pale garment around me: bulging, a white raven with rubbish under the feathers, only a tongue of orange fear in the mouth.

Here I live now in an old house next to a mourning autumn tree. How I got here I shall never be able to explain. The facts—if one can speak of facts—have slipped through my fingers. Somebody must have presented me with a suit of clothes, or else I myself found it somewhere, probably in a dustbin. It is too small, and they have forgotten the shoes. I have found that most people in town wear long robes, just like those in the fort, as they move from dustbin to dustbin. To tell the truth: there aren't many people in this town and they all wear the same clothes.

Breyten Breytenbach

It was my intention to approach one of the many lawyers living in the suburbs or the outlying districts, or even in the inner city, to lay my case before them. It is said there is an incredible number of legal experts here. But I understand they are all still young and ambitious and, unfortunately, corrupt. Moreover, rumour has it that they are all, without exception, at the beck and call of the voice of the cloistered fort.

After a short while here an old black woman, with a single garment as her earthly possession and cover, joined me, and now we share our fate in sadness or in peace, or in the sadness of peace, or in the peace of sadness. It was she who really put me on to you. She said you are the only competent one. That your filing system is good. That you will listen. That you will have no truck with ravens or rocks. I think she has also escaped, but a long time before me. This, however, I cannot swear to.

She told me: *The name of the voice is Chuck Huntingdon; he wears glasses and he is fifty-four years old.* Follow it up. Therefore I now turn to you. Help me. I've tried to present my case as clearly as possible, and it is my considered opinion that, with the facts set out here and at your disposal, you could—if the matter interests you—open legal proceedings.

At night I dream of Yolande Marie, and I experience in my bones the deadening of Nicolaas Herman and Rebekka Klavdia Maryn as they become more and more distant. My untutored mind tells me that someone surely ought to be accused firstly of kidnapping and secondly of detaining people against their wishes.

But do those people really want to come out? Did I? Will this letter ever reach you? Do I truly want them out? Am I out? (Excuse me for this obvious question.) Are these *my* naked feet below the short trouser-legs on the bare floor—as the old black lady goes rummaging for orange peel and ice cream cones in the dustbins on the street? Who have I become, or was I always like this, or *am* I at all? How do I dream in my dream about reality? Must I dream you too?

Therefore I address myself to you. Help me please, Mr Huntingdon.

TODD MCEWEN
PARAMILITARISM IN
COSTA DEL BURGER

Todd McEwen

It was to be the Pupae. A word nobody understood. It could easily have been the Romulets or the Hiawathas. I was only seven when they sent me to join up. I say *only* obviously because I'm trying to present mine as a tragic case. Not real tragedy, but, you know, pathetic.

I don't remember getting the idea myself. But that kind of drivel is often dished out by your best friend. In my case, Fard. I liked him though he shared a bedroom with his big waxy ears and his grandmother and her big waxy ears. And a ton of ironing around his house. Not washing. Ironing. That is where mothers transplanted from the midwest fell down. They could wash away in the electric paradise of the Southern California Edison Company. But *ironing*. It was not automatic.

To my surprise the old boy and girl thought it was a terrific idea. I then realized I had made a big mistake. But it was too late. They rushed around like mad getting me the official junk. The handbook smelled like new paint. I thought they could have scented the different chapters: salt air for knot tying, raccoons' bottoms for the camping. But before they got me home with the handbook and lunatic paraphernalia, I started crying all over the place!

I had been looking at illustrations for the tree-climbing badge (the first order of merit). I knew there weren't any trees big enough for even a rickety eyesore like me to climb. The trees. They were zeros. Mere suggestions of bad ideas. Unclimbable. We lived in the middle of nowhere, that is to say in an untangle of brand new homes. An area undistinguished by even the slightest variation of atmosphere. If you got lost, goodbye. You might as well move into another family's house which looked like your own, you would never find yours again.

So I cried. But I had also begun thinking how to get out of it. They were so keen, I couldn't possibly do it.

Around the same time I had been given a bicycle. And I discovered there was political advantage in falling off it. Bam! Waaah! Anything you want. So the way to get out of Pupae was to fall off my bike. Oh I complained here and there, groused during tooth-brushing. Interrupted the bed-time prayer (still said then) with attacks on group activity. But these weren't important. I had my secret weapon. The old girl affirmed: You're Going. That's what you think I smiled in the dark I'm going to fall off my bike.

The afternoon came. It was overcast, always a bad sign in the land of Costa del Burger. I was being plunged into the uniform by the old girl. This hurts and that hurts I said. Casually, half-heartedly. She was resolute: You're Going. Yeah yeah I thought. I felt guilty putting on the cap and kerchief; I liked them in the shop but I really couldn't go through with this. You can't let them get away with it. Next thing they're walking all over you. To re-establish my suzerainty, I would fall off my bike.

Off you go says the old girl. I don't want to go I said. Nonsense, You're Going she said. That's another thing, you can't let them talk to you like that. Bye now she said. Better see me off I said. A bit nervous she wouldn't stay for my crowd pleasing sabre rattling ambulance summoning performance. I got on my machine. She stood admiral-like on her bridge of a porch. Well goodbye she said. Goodbye! I said and came about and then expertly twirled the front wheel so that two seconds later I lay in a dramatic tangle of blue uniform and bathetic, Dada apparatus. If only I had had some ketchup. I looked towards her. Extended my hand. Alms. Imploring. Tragic. Are you all right then? she says. Stupidly, I nodded. She didn't even leave the porch! I had Fallen Off My Bike and she just stood there. I'd get her for this. Ageless drama lost on an ignorant audience. I was a flop. I would close after one performance. I would have to go to Pupae.

I made a last effort. There was no point. I cannot go, I am hurt I said getting up. What Rot, Off You Go, Get Going, You're Going she said. And went inside and shut the door. I stared at its green finality. Life is hell I thought Seven years down the damned tube.

I had a special word, a nonsense word, you might call it a charm or a juju, I said when I was angry. It simultaneously exorcised all bathetic pathetic and bad feelings *and* stirred them up so I could take a shower in them. When I said this terrible word. So I said it.

But. I had to go. Now had to go with appliqués of dirt and bathetic pathetic chain grease on my uniform, for which I would undoubtedly receive Pupae demerits. I had read about the demerits. They were one of the few things I was going to get out of it.

So I got on my bicycle. Bicycle of Pain. I pedalled slowly agonizingly slowly away from the house.

The scenery of our area depressed me. Stupid little trees, new sidewalks, useless storm drains. The tiny thirsting pampas the mad called lawns. The trees will be big someday my father said, so utterly without conviction that I wanted to strike him down. Tiny liquidambars, dusty oleander. You couldn't climb those, it would be arboricide. We lived in a bad model-railway landscape, glued to a plywood board.

As I rode, more fluidly now I was around the bend from the house, but still heroic, heroic, I looked towards the house where the Pupae would gather. It hovered brown and yellow far away in the heat. At the intersection I halted and looked to the right. There at about the same distance was the five and ten. If I veered towards it, if I shirked duty and forwent heroism, I could run free, a dues spending savage, a mad consumer of chewing gum, plastic Army men, rubber balls, wax lips. Life as it should be lived. Anarchy. But this I did not do. The repercussions would rock the globe. It would be the end. No, at that moment I conceived a better plan. Heroically I would go on. On, and pupate. And I heroically would work to destroy them. From within!

I turned towards the hated garage of fascism. I pedalled with renewed energy, fired by purpose. Adventure, thrill drove me on. Past prefabricated rock gardens. Past the partly hedge obscured bald head of ? Past Fard's house and its driveway trailer in which I had on occasion played medic with Fard and his dog. The dog always won.

I arrived and leaned my bicycle against a honeysuckle humming with black bees. I faced the open door of the garage. The maw of heroic destiny. The place already contained a number of pupae, wriggling about, staring at the walls with their only partially evolved eyes, waiting for the inaugural meeting of our nest to begin.

I went into the garage sighing. Where was Fard? The only one I knew there was Julius. I sought out Julius. It was easy. Julius lived constantly in a state of goggling bewilderment. His face was a perennial astonished beacon. If you questioned Julius all you got for a minute was wet workings. Then he would give out with something blisteringly inane. The uniform of Julius was incomplete and untidy. This was like him as well. I saw Julius was holding an ear of Indian corn. This made me sweat. I hadn't thought we were to bring anything save our regulation Pupae uniforms and a willingness to learn certain crafts, songs and ways.

Why have you brought that corn Julius? I said. While I waited Julius operated his mouth and his eyes watered. This is all I could find, he said finally. His eyes continued to run, he was crying, I was mystified. What do you mean it was all you could find? I said. Julius's life must be wretched, all he could find. I could not find a banana, my mother does not have any and she would not buy me one! streamed Julius. I looked at the other pupae. None of them had bananas or Indian corn. Or if they did they had concealed them. I looked back at Julius. His ear of corn. Not much of a snack I said. Julius dashed at me brandishing it. It is not a snack you *crab!* he cried We are supposed to have a banana, it is part of the uniform *stupid!* I got the idea he was going to tear at me but his nails were bitten so short there was little danger. And what he foamed Are those stupid things you are wearing around your necks! The other pupae squirmed uncomfortably and looked sidelong at Julius. I gazed at him. They are bandannas I said *Bandannas,* you're supposed to bring a bandanna, not a banana Julius. No wonder he was in the slow readers. And he had not been able to get a banana so he had brought *an ear of corn.* Seeing it was roughly the same size and shape. But an ear of corn is hardly ever a substitute banana and it is no kind of surrogate bandanna at all. Julius looked wildly around the garage. Conception of his ridiculous error struck him in the full. He shook, he blushed, he turned and deliberately walked into the farthest corner. A real corner sort of fellow, Julius. He stood faced away from us, head bowed, loudly snorkelling.

We were diverted from this Oriental spectacle, this Julius face lost perhaps forever, with the arrival of our Nest Mother.

Our Nest Mother was the real problem. She was as well meaning as any idiot. But her red toenails, her rebounding blonde hair, her impossibly tight (though regulation) blue skirt piped with Pupae gold distressed us immeasurably. Could such a Nest Mother throw a line across a rocky gorge? Instruct in whittling a tiki, give palpable meaning to the mystery and faint erotism of the word *spelunk?*

No.

The Nest Mother could never a climb a tree. But she might scare you up one. Her husband, nominally the Nest Father, was hid in a closet with a bottle of Ruffino. The perfect drone. Another accident of fate dooming our nest was that their kid was in it. Nunzio. This kid was such a stupid bastard, we all hated his guts. He had the powerful malice of all redheads with big teeth. Nunzio was the only pupa with regulation trousers, obtained no doubt through some kind of horrific blatant favouritism. He surveyed us with ministerial contempt, casting especial loathing at the corner dampening Julius. Nunzio stood behind his mother like some kind of pole.

Hello boys said Nest Mama. With difficulty she perched on a high stool. As ya know we will begin with the pledge to the flag. I bucked up a bit. This I knew how to do. But! Where was the flag? The pupae looked around. Nest Mama cleared her throat. Since there ain't much of us, we don't have enough does funds yet ta buy a flag. So in the meantime we will salute this as our flag. Nunzio, bring the flag honey.

So then Nunzio with his molary redhead's grin produced this bathroom fluffy pink rug!

He held it up in front of him. We watched in mute shame, he nailed it to the wall. Nest Mama beamed. Now we will say the pledge she said. Salute, Salute! said Nunzio glaring at us Obey, Obey!

I was very unhappy about this. I longed for home. What were we to say? I Pledge Allegiance To The Rug Of Mr And Mrs Bottla Ruffino? But the others started droning the pledge as it was droned at school so I went along. You were supposed to belt out the pledge like billy-o but we were nonplussed, our rendering was soft. The rug was I noticed stained and had bits of bloody and yellowed toilet tissue caught in its tufts. I felt ill.

In the corner Nunzio poked at Julius. Come out of there stupid, my mother commands it! boomed Nunzio. Julius oh Julius! called Nest Mama C'mon over here dear. Nunzio tugged with increased energy and Julius shot out to the centre of the garage where he stood abject wet and hot on an oil stain. The leaves of the ear of Indian corn hung down, also abject. What's the matter Julius honey? said Nest Mama not caring or really looking at Julius at all. Nothing said Julius. The word came from deep within him. Make him salute! shouted Nunzio advancing on Julius Salute, Salute! Julius covered his eyes with the ear of corn. No no it's all right honey we hafta start the meeting now said Nest Mama. Nunzio stepped back glowering.

Now boys said Nest Mama As ya know the first badge in the handbook is climbin a tree. The pupae rustled. But she said I have spoke with the captains and cause there ain't no trees big enough ta climb here we are excused from this badge. Isn't that nice? Clearly she was relieved. And clearly the pupae were disappointed. Would we get consolation tree badges? Our sleeves ached so to be blazoned. Gomez, a fat kid, had expected to be taken to a forest so he could climb a tree. He was too obese to know there wasn't a forest for a thousand miles. Gomez emitted some very poor-smelling gas. So-o went on Nest Mama quickly As ya know the second badge is Arts an Crafts. An today we are gonna make a Arts an Crafts Project. Collective fed up pupae toothpaste exhalation. A PUPA'S MOUTH IS ALWAYS CLEAN. Nest Mama slid off her slick stool and went over to a table on which were the Materials.

Nest Mama was as vague as one can possibly be while still actually talking about something. We were to cast shields in plaster of Paris, paint them blue, then affix gold-painted letters from alphabet soup. The letters to spell out the Creed of the Pupae. A Pupa Is New, A Pupa Is White, A Pupa Wriggles Bravely. I didn't have the heart for this kind of endless gluey task. The materials would rage out of my control. The macaroni would adhere to my uniform, my legs.

Suddenly I was seized with insight. At this moment I would begin my covert work of evil. Destroy the plaques. Destroy the Creed of the Pupae. Morale will tumble! Ideological sabotage. Bandanna and dagger.

However. I had plotted without considering the stupidity of Nest Mama. While we waited for the gypsum to harden, she *boiled* the alphabet pasta. All the Phoenicians' work for nought. She was a prisoner of package labels, devoid she was of the cool logic of the *Pupae Handbook* (Revised).

And all the little pupae were sad, there were no trees to climb and the very letter of their law was sopping nothingness!

At this juncture I realized there was no point working within a thing like this to destroy it. From that day to this I reject this mode of change. The thing was doing fine on its own. While you are in there fighting changing destroying so you say, the world sees just another jerk drawing a pay cheque and trying like the rest to glue the wet letters of some insane weed on to a shield.

The whirl of silliness filled my throat with phlegm. I wondered how I could get the old boy to extract me from this circus totalitarianismus. Where was Fard?

But Nunzio with the luck of all malicious redheads had somehow got his letters arranged. He paraded his shield about, holding the Nunziotic misspellings of the Creed high above us, running at the terrified Julius with it. But some of the gluten letters slackened and fell away from the blue paint. Letters falling softly falling in the garage as we watched. I Am Finished, I Am Finished! chanted Nunzio martially stamping in his regulation black Pupae shoes for which we all despised him. A revolting mis-whelped Hephaestus. He marched in a circle round Julius, who had got the worst of this: his shield looked like a punched face. It had not hardened when he began to paint it, it was sea blue, not the powerful royal of the Pupae. Nest Mama gave him only the most overcooked letters, and what gold paint he had been allotted had run down his shirt front.

Nunzio stamped around him, it was too much for Julius to bear. He started to hop, to yell, his soft shield flew up in his hand, a great mould spelling uncomfort or death for Nunzio! Julius let it go but Nunzio stooped. We all watched. The shield flew, as if slowly, towards Nest Mama's behind. She's bending over the table, helping Gomez, his fat incapable hands. The flying shield, the Creed cupping itself for a wet impact, a perfect union with Nest Mama's fussy and ignorant ex air hostess butt.

Pow!

We stared, certain that the Creed of the Pupae was not meant to be slapped on a Nest Mother. Nothing about it in the *Handbook* so we waited to see what would happen.

What did: Nest Mama got a queer red face. She turned to her infant protector and sergeant-at-arms. Who did that Nunzio? she asked angrily. Wow. So now we all had to suffer Nunzio's great moment. His eyes became saucers of accusation, his grin unbearably molar. *Julius!* screamed Nunzio *Come here!* But bravely Julius flew at Nunzio who too late saw the ear of Indian corn. As Julius clubbed him with it I was struck by the tone poem of colour, the yellow and purple kernels of corn intersecting Nunzio's pale skin brown freckles and russet hair. Nunzio the helpless, Nunzio the lame, Nunzio the tyrant in whose weakness we all rejoiced.

Quickly though Nest Mama came over. Globules of Julius's creed dropping from her. To save her precious blue plastic Army man of a son from the retarded violent corn wielder. She sent Julius back to his corner. Not realizing that is where Julius wished to be, resting his nose in the meet of the fresh sawn redwood boards. Contemplating the smooth cement floor and furtively fingering the new smelling garden hose.

Nunzio had to be restrained, he was still trying to get at Julius, but Nest Mama held him. Could mean her epaulettes after all, assault. The rest of us stood around. Denim trousers force you to stand *around*, rubbernecks at a scene of death. The morale of our nest had crumbled. Personally I was happy. A few more weeks of this and the pupae would quit *en masse*.

The pupae began to cry. Me too, though mostly to bolster the thrilling sound level. We will now make Arts an Crafts Boxes yelled Nest Mama Ta keep ya Arts An Crafts Materials in. Forgetting we had no materials, just damp lumps. More caterwaul. We would not be stopped. She moved backwards, away, no no, no more, rejecting our ear-shattering gaping aspect. This was not what she wanted, she had tried so hard, had spent so long painting her face and tailoring her skirt. She groped for the doorknob. She escaped into the tiled sanctuary of her modern kitchen.

Immediately she went we stoppered our noise. Deprived of our adult, we lost heart and voice for grief. We started down at our soft projects. Julius looked around at us. Nunzio stared at the door. Looking at it, trying to see his mother through it. He faced us. You made my mother cry! he screamed. I thought he was going to have another go at Julius but instead he heaved his shoulders and went through the door.

We guessed the meeting was over. Saddled our ponies and took to the evening air. Not so different from the afternoon air, o land of cinematic anticyclones.

My ride home. Forgot were the blandishments of the five and ten. Even in the hot amoral desert wind I felt triumphant. The whole neighbourhood seemed dry and stupid enough to snap off and blow away. I thought I should attempt to recapture some physical suggestion of my heroic injury. So the old girl would know I had been hurt and brave. But I could not remember which side I had fallen on! I had to give up. I passed Fard's house, its trailer. Perhaps Fard had been in there with the dog the whole time.

I waited for the old boy to come home. I had my plan. Eventually he did, untying the chin string and removing his Canadian earflap hat. He always dressed for bad weather even though there never was any. He took off his galoshes. He kissed the old girl. He put his head in a pot on the stove to ascertain its contents. Then he sat down significantly and said to me Well how did it go today son? I cleared my throat.

I Fell Off My Bike Dad I said. I detected a crinkling near his left eye. Yes so I heard he said But how was it, *how was your first day at the nest?* The way he hunched forward squirming and blowing brands at me from his bonfire of a pipe he could have been asking How was your first day at the breast! But I was ready for this. He didn't yet know that I knew. Later he would but then he did not. I knew his soft underbelly:

He was of forest fastnesses, miles and miles of tall pines, had actually to snowshoe to a miserable one-room school not even red. I knew he saw my childhood among the trees strangled at birth, the cement, as nothing. Weak, limp, pithless, lacking in Indian possibilities. In short *devoid of woodcraft.*

So I hit him. Right there. I drew in breath and expelled an appalling tale of the abandonment of tree-climbing. I made him see that in all of exciting Technology County there was not a TREE for a BOY to CLIMB, not nowhere, and further insinuated that under this foolish Nest Mother there was no chance for a guy, a Boy, to learn woodcraft and The Things A Boy Must Learn To Be A Boy.

I *trowelled* it on the old guy, all over him, he could hardly move or speak when I was finished. So despondent so filled with grief was he over the polymer shallowness of our sun-baked nonparadise. So filled with compassion for his well-meaning genuine Boy who wanted only to climb a tree and learn to whittle and or whistle. I also spared no detail of the ridiculous shield trouble.

After staring far into the past of America for a deal of time he got up. Heavy of heart he tramped into the kitchen. This boy he said to the old girl This boy is no longer a Pupa. Do you hear? It's a ruse she said You should make him go, he Fell Off His Bike. For a moment the old boy looked at me, they both knew I was a scheming bicycle tumbler. But he turned back to her. No he said He must not go. He stared out the door at the brown grass. No trees he said bleakly. Then, lowly; *I will take him in hand.* The old girl's eyes widened at this and so did mine. what did he mean, pretty ominous, probably take me out in the family tank to some insect kingdom like Holy Jim Canyon and cast me into the flood.

But that was to come. I was the age when the future *is the future,* not that steam calliope horror nearly upon you whenever you look out the window.

Contemporary Writers

Patrick White
J Colmer
96 pages
Paperback
0 416 36790 9

Malcolm Lowry
R Binns
96 pages
Paperback
0 416 37750 6

Iris Murdoch
R Todd
112 pages
Paperback
0 416 35420 3

Harold Pinter
G Alamansi and
S Henderson
112 pages
0 416 31710 3

Joe Orton
C Bigsby
80 pages
0 416 31690 5

Saul Bellow
M Bradbury
112 pages
0 416 31650 6

Richard Brautigan
M Chenetier
96 pages
0 416 32960 8

John Fowles
P Conradi
112 pages
0 416 32250 6

Donald Barthelme
M Couturier
and R Durand
80 pages
0 416 31870 3

Alain Robbe-Grillet
J Fletcher
92 pages
0 416 34420 8

Kurt Vonnegut
J Klinkowitz
96 pages
0 416 33480 6

Philip Roth
H Lee
96 pages
0 416 32980 2

Seamus Heaney
B Morrison
96 pages
0 416 31900 9

Philip Larkin
A Motion
96 pages
0 416 32270 0

Graham Greene
J Spurling
80 pages
0 416 31850 9

Thomas Pynchon
T Tanner
96 pages
0 416 31670 0

All paperback £2.25 each

METHUEN
11 NEW FETTER LANE, LONDON EC4P 4EE

EDDIE LIMONOV
EDDIE-BABY

It was at the age of eleven that Eddie-baby's life changed abruptly. That was the day after his fight with Yurka. Yurka was a year older than Eddie-baby, and had the pink, healthy cheeks and the strong healthy torso of a boy born in the Siberian town of Krasnoyarsk. In Eddie-baby's opinion, Yurka was an absolute fool. Eddie, however—eleven years old and still inexperienced—did not yet realize that a fool can be as strong as a young bullock. Strong and dangerous.

The fuss was about nothing. Eddie-baby had drawn an absolutely inoffensive caricature of Yurka, which showed him asleep during a lesson. This healthy boy, in fact, was always inclined to doze off in the hot classroom. When Eddie-baby and another artist, Vitka Proutorov, pinned up the wall-newspaper, Yurka elbowed his way through to Eddie and said that he wanted to 'have a knock' with him. 'Let's have a knock, Savekha,' he said. 'Savekha' was a derivative of Savenko, Eddie's surname. Among the pupils of No. 8 Middle School it was fashionable to call each other by a name that ended in 'kha'. Sitenko was called Sitekha; Karpenko, Karpekha; and so on.

Yurka the Siberian beat up Eddie-baby until he was unconscious. And he abruptly changed Eddie's life, just as the appearance of the Archangel Gabriel changed the life of Mahomet and made him a prophet, and the falling apple made Newton Newton.

When Eddie-baby came to his senses, he was lying on the floor in the classroom; around him stood several of his classmates with frightened faces, while a little further away Yurka was sitting calmly at one of the desks.

'Well, did you get it?' said Yurka, when he saw that Eddie-baby had opened his eyes.

'I got it,' Eddie-baby agreed. Whatever else he may have lacked, he had a firm grasp of objective reality. Together with his sympathizers he made his way to the toilet, where with water they cleaned off the chalk and dust that had stuck to his trousers and his black velveteen jacket. Five-kopek pieces, amiably proffered by his classmates, were applied to Eddie-baby's bruises, his whole physiognomy being adorned with bruises and scratches. The incident was closed.

Going home after school that day, Eddie-baby analysed his life, all eleven years of it, examining it from various points of view. Only at home was he slightly distracted from this process by his mother's frightened cries and by the business of parrying her questions: 'Who?' 'Where?' 'When?'

All that Eddie-baby said was that he had been in a fight. He did not say who had beaten him, rightly considering this to be his own affair. In Eddie-baby's opinion, questions such as 'Where?' and 'When?' were pointless.

That day he did not touch his French kings or his Roman emperors, did not look at any of his notes nor surround himself with books. He lay on the divan, his face turned to its upholstered back, and thought. He heard his father come home, and even stood up obediently so that his father might inspect his bruised and scratched physiognomy, but almost at once lay down again in the same position, nose to the wall. When his father and mother began to bore him a great deal droning away behind his back, he pulled one of the divan cushions from under his head and covered his head with it. His father used to do this whenever he lay down for a nap after Sunday lunch. Eddie-baby, however, was not sleeping; he was thinking.

To this day Eddie-baby clearly remembers the next morning down to the slightest detail—the bright spring sunshine, and how he walked along the path behind the house, his usual route, in order to come out on First Transverse Street, which should have led him straight to school. On that day, however, Eddie-baby stopped for a short while behind the house, under Vladka and Lenka Shepelsky's windows, put his haversack on the ground, untied and took off his Pioneer's kerchief and stuffed it into his pocket. This gesture was unconnected with any renunciation of the Pioneer organization; by taking off his kerchief Eddie-baby was rather symbolizing the start of his new life. Eddie-baby had decided to abandon his books, to enter the real world, and in the real world to become the strongest and the boldest.

He decided to become a different person and became one that same day. Usually taciturn and self-absorbed, on that day Eddie bombarded the teachers with witticisms and cheeky, caustic remarks, for which the French mistress, shaken, sent him out of the classroom. He spent the rest of the lesson hanging about in the corridor, along with a tough second-year boy called Prikhodko, catching flies basking in the first spring sunshine as they sat on the window-ledge. Then, together with Prikhodko, he committed his first sexual crime: they invaded the female toilet on the fourth floor, where several girls from class 5A were hiding to escape from a PE class, and there they 'squeezed' them. Eddie-baby had seen other schoolboys do this before, but he himself had never felt any desire to commit an act of 'squeezing'.

In the raid on the girls' toilet, he imitated Prikhodko and flung himself on his victim, a plump girl called Nastya (Eddie-baby did not know her surname) from behind, and seized what might have been approximately called her breasts. The girl tried to wriggle free, but she could not shout very much because then she would have been heard in the classrooms, and punishment awaited those who skipped classes; she scratched, and squealed quietly. Stimulated by the resistance and, once again following the example of Prikhodko, who at that moment was pressing the truly full-breasted Olya Olyanich up against a wash-basin (she was already fourteen) and had his hands under her skirt, the new Eddie-baby also put both hands under Nastya's school-uniform skirt and gripped her in the place where girls have their 'cunt'. Eddie-baby had learned the word 'cunt' in his second year at junior school and knew where the cunt was located.

In his second junior year his classmates Tolya Zakharov and Kolya, nicknamed 'Backstreet Scrounger' (his other nickname was less complicated and more humiliating—it was 'Pisser'; the kids used to say that he still pissed himself, that is to say wet his bed), had tried to rape Lara Gavrilova. They had tried to rape her during long break on a heap of overcoats. In those days the school had not yet installed coat-hooks and a changing room, and the coats simply lay in a pile on the back benches. Today's Eddie-baby, aged fifteen, recalls this incident and can't understand how two eight-year-old boys could have 'tried to rape' an eight-year-old girl. 'What with?' smirks today's Eddie. What sort of a penis could an eight-year-old boy have, even if he were as much of a tearaway as Tolya Zakharov and Kolya the Pisser? Tolya and Kolya were expelled from school, but two weeks later they were taken back again.

Eddie-baby seized Nastya by her 'cunt' under her skirt. It was very warm where Nastya's cunt was. Eddie-baby grasped this warm spot and squeezed. At the moment when Eddie squeezed her cunt, Nastya started to howl. Eddie-baby had the impression that Nastya was not only warm there but wet too. No doubt she just finished pissing, guessed Eddie-baby.

The girls' cries, although they were not loud, brought in the cleaning woman Vasilievna, wife of Vasya the school porter (they lived in a small house in the school yard), who began walloping the boys with a wet cloth, shouting that they were 'mad dogs' and ought to be in prison. 'Clear off!' shouted Prikhodko. Letting go of the girls and shielding themselves with their hands from Vasilievna's cloth, he and Eddie-baby tore out into the corridor and raced away.

After that incident in the girls' toilet, Eddie-baby earned the unconcealed amazement and patronizing approval of Prikhodko. It was then, too, that Eddie-baby began to be friends with Chuma the Plague—Vovka Chumakov—and in March ran away with him to Brazil.

Their escape to Brazil became widely known throughout No. 8 Middle School owing to pure chance. When they ran away to Brazil, Eddie-baby and Chuma the Plague hid their satchels under some pieces of rusty iron in the cellar of the house where Chuma lived, because why should anyone need a satchel in Brazil? God knows why they didn't throw their satchels away altogether instead of carefully hiding them; they were not proposing to come back to Kharkov from Brazil.

At all events, the satchels were found by some electricians who had gone down to the cellar to repair the wiring, and were triumphantly brought by them to the school and handed over to Rakhilya, the boys' form mistress. By then a search was already under way.

When recalling his escape to Brazil, today's Eddie-baby smiles condescendingly. One's first naive experiments. Why they had to go to Brazil on foot and by compass, he now has no idea. At the time, he and Chuma had set off to the south. Naturally they soon got lost, and instead of Brazil they reached the municipal rubbish-tip, ten kilometres out of town, where tramps and cripples robbed them and

111

seized their entire capital—135 roubles and ninety kopeks—which they had saved up for their escape to Brazil, leaving them with nothing but a couple of geography text-books; Eddie-baby had brought these in order to keep up his own and Chuma's determination to reach Brazil by looking at the photographs and drawings of tropical animals and birds and the torrid landscapes of Amazonia. One of these books was called *A Journey through South America*.

It was the end of March and still very cold, although the snow had all gone during a thaw in February. Without money—thus Chuma (son of a laundress and the more practical of the two) reasoned to the still obstinately romantic Eddie-baby as they sat round a campfire burning in an old steel barrel—they would never reach Brazil. They couldn't even reach the Crimea, where Eddie-baby proposed to wait till the really warm weather began, and then move by compass westwards to Odessa, where they would sneak aboard a ship going to Brazil. 'Let's go home!' said Chuma.

Eddie-baby didn't want to go home; he was ashamed of returning. Eddie-baby was much more obstinate than Chuma. Without a compass, Chuma the Plague set off in the direction of a bus-stop, while Eddie-baby stayed and spent the night, stripped down to his singlet, beside the steam-raising boiler in the boiler-room of a large block of flats. Mice or rats were rustling in the corners and Eddie-baby never closed his eyes. Next morning he was caught by the sales-girls when he tried to steal a loaf in a bakery shop, and was handed over to the police.

Today's Eddie-baby is standing in front of his house, No. 22 Transverse Street, but he very much doesn't want to go home or to Aunt Marusya. For this reason, having stared for a while at Aunt Marusya's lighted windows on the first floor, he decides to pay a visit to the benches under the lime trees; maybe some of the boys will be there, and perhaps they can all have a drink and a chat. Therefore, zipping up his yellow jacket to the throat, thrusting his hands into his pockets, Eddie-baby sets off boldly for the Saltovsky Road, choosing to go by the asphalted path that leads past Karpenko's house. Near Karpenko's house there is a large, stinking public lavatory. If all he wanted was a 'leak', he would have stood against any wall—manners are unpretentious in Saltovka—but unfortunately he wants to do a 'big job' as Eddie's parents say, or to 'dump a load' as Karpenko says, or to 'shit' as the rudest inhabitants of Saltovka put it. Eddie-baby is indeed shy of uttering aloud this latter definition of a daily physiological process because it is so rude.

The lavatory is a stone hut with two entrances, male and female; it is practically the only public lavatory on this, 'their', side of the Saltovsky Road. Eddie-baby can't bear going in there, but since he is now spending the greater part of his time on the streets (his father and mother recall with nostalgic longing, as for some Paradise Lost, the era when he could not be forced out of doors), he is obliged to utilize this convenience.

Pushing open the wooden door, Eddie-baby sees with horror that the entire floor of the lavatory is awash with a mixture of half water, half urine, and that some anonymous folk-genius has laid a temporary causeway across the liquid, made of bricks brought from outside, leading to the wooden eminence in which three holes are cut. Trying not to breathe the noxious air, Eddie-baby balances his way along the bricks over the turbid midden, and, after lowering his trousers, sits down on one of the holes. Since he is nevertheless obliged to breathe now and again, Eddie-baby is made involuntarily aware that the stench is compounded not only of urine and excrement, but also of vomit. The opposite end of the wooden eminence is covered in a thick layer of vomit. The vomit is an artificial red in colour: obviously the victim who left the contents of his stomach here had been celebrating the forty-first anniversary of the Great October Socialist Revolution by drinking exclusively Cahors or Strong Red. Specialists or professionals—and Eddie-baby is a professional—consider that fifty per cent of Soviet Strong Red wine actually consists of dye and that it corrodes the stomach of any idiot incautious enough to drink it.

Eddie-baby tears off from a rusty nail on the lavatory wall a scrap of newspaper, which some kind soul—and such there will always be—has left there, and wipes himself, recalling with a chuckle the theory propounded by Slavka the Gypsy that the printers' ink on newspaper is harmful to the arsehole, and that from constant wiping of it with newsprint one can get cancer of the rectum.

113

Today the lavatory is so repellent that Eddie-baby hurries to get out of it as quickly as possible, but he makes an unpardonable mistake. Standing up to throw the paper in the hole, he unintentionally looks down and notices that the level of shit under the dais is unusually high, that no more than ten or fifteen centimetres separates the shit from the seat and that here and there pinkish-white worms are squirming around in it!

'Fuck this!' exclaims Eddie in horror, and hurries over the bricks away and out of the disgusting cloaca, cursing himself for having looked down. After putting fifty metres between himself and the revolting, lighted building, he sighs with relief.

On the benches under the lime trees, to his delight Eddie-baby unexpectedly finds not only Cat and Lyova, but Sanya Krasny too, who somehow oughtn't to be there.

Standing between Cat, Lyova and Sanya are a half-litre of Stolichnaya vodka and a white bowl full of cucumbers and slices of roast meat. The bowl has obviously been brought by Cat and Lyova, whose house—No. 5—is nearby. Sanya's house is closer to Eddie's.

'Ed!' the three lads shout with delight.

Eddie-baby does not call out in reply but goes up to them, smiling and silent. He knows that if he responds with 'Yes!' or 'What?', all three heroes will shout back in unison: 'Go suck a cock for lunch!' and roar with laughter. Eddie-baby is never offended by this; it is a traditional, jocular greeting, but remembering it, he refrains from replying.

To be fair, it should be said that the same relationship exists between Cat, Lyova and Sanya. If Sanya calls out 'Cat!' and if Cat forgets himself and replies 'What?', then he will get the invariable response: 'Fuck you in the mouth!' and a roar of laughter. It is a friendly if coarse joke, nothing more.

'Sit down, Ed,' says Sanya. 'Lyova, pour the boy a drink.'

Lyova pours out Eddie-baby half a glass of vodka. Eddie drinks the cold, biting liquid. Having downed his vodka, Eddie-baby pauses, then says nonchalantly to Sanya: 'Didn't you go to Rezany's party, Sanya?'

Only after he has spoken this sentence does Eddie-baby allow himself to stretch out his hand for a piece of meat and a cucumber. Never to be in a hurry is a sign of the utmost cool when drinking.

It turns out that although it is only half-past nine, Sanya has already managed to have a furious row with Dora, his hairdresser girl-friend, has told her to go to hell, slapped her face and left Tolya Rezany's party slamming the door (Tolya is also a butcher, with whom Sanya and Dora generally celebrate holidays); now Sanya is sitting on the bench under the lime trees. Where else should a young man from Saltovka go, where else to take his grief and troubles, and who is there to console him if not his cheerful friends and a good glass of vodka?

'Fucking slag!' says Sanya, referring to his abandoned hairdresser, as he chews a cucumber after his vodka. 'Tries to make out she's a virgin. Abanya told me a month ago that Zhorka Bazhok, a guy from Zhuravliov, was fucking her. I didn't believe him, but now I see Abanya was right!'

'You ought to dump her altogether, Sanya,' says Lyova. 'Mean to say you can't find yourself another cunt? You only have to whistle and a dozen of them'll come running.'

'Ask Svetka,' says Eddie-baby in support of Lyova, meaning Sanya's sister Svetka. 'She's got a whole heap of girl-friends, she'll pick one out for you.'

'Why the fuck should I ask anyone?' Sanya objects, slightly offended. 'I only have to walk into a dance and every cunt in the place is looking at me, waiting for me to invite them out and fuck them. As for my sister Svetka'—here Sanya turns to Eddie—'she's still wetting her bed, and her friends are more your age, Eddie. As far as I'm concerned, they're just kids.'

Eddie-baby says nothing. He is ashamed that he's still a kid.

Crunching their cucumbers, the group falls into a melancholy silence. Now and again they can hear a drunken song, snatches of music or a burst of laughter coming from the neighbouring houses.

'Well, how about getting another bottle?' Cat breaks the silence, speaking to Sanya.

'OK, why not . . . ,' Sanya agrees and fumbles in his pocket for money. 'No. 7 Grocery is open till midnight tonight.'

'I've got some cash.' Cat stops Sanya. Cat's a decent lad and earns good money in his factory. As a butcher, of course, Sanya earns far more, on top of which he always has plenty of meat, but he also spends his money fast. Cat wants to do the honours now, which is his right, so Sanya doesn't object and takes his hand out of the pocket of his Sunday-best Hungarian overcoat.

Cat gets up from the bench, pulls on his jacket (he and Lyova came out without overcoats), says: 'OK, I'll be back in a minute', and sets off.

'If they've got any Zhiguli beer, buy a couple of bottles,' Lyova calls after him as he goes.

'OK, Fatty,' Cat replies without turning round.

After taking only a few paces, however, Cat stops and stares hard in the direction of the tram-stop.

'Hey, boys, it's a pig,' he announces, 'running this way!'

'Fuck him, let him run,' says Sanya calmly. 'We don't owe him anything. There's no more vodka left. He's wasting his time running.'

Heavy boots thumping, greatcoat unbuttoned, a policeman comes running towards the benches. Eddie baby knows him, as do the others. Stepan the pig, a man of around fifty, cannot of course be a good man, but Stepan Dubnyak is not a complete shit, though he's a crafty one. If he ever gives any of the lads fifteen days in the cells for being drunk and disorderly, he always brings them a bottle in his pocket, although drinking in the cells is naturally not allowed. Several times Stepan has managed not to arrest boys when he should have arrested them, and so on. Stepan wants to live at peace with the local tearaways.

Now that Sanya has stopped working at the Horse Market and moved to the new food-store on Materialist Street, the same one that Eddie-baby and Vovka the Boxer once robbed, Stepan's wife goes to Sanya to buy meat. He puts aside some nice pieces for her. Or he says they're nice. Sanya likes to make fun of his customers. One day for a bet, in Eddie-baby's presence, he pulled out the thick red lining from someone's galoshes, hacked it up with a cleaver on his wooden butcher's block, smeared it in blood and there and then sold it—all of it—as a makeweight to someone's order of meat.

'What's the matter, Stepan?' Sanya asks in a phoney-sympathetic voice. 'Are the dogs after you?'

'Help me out, lads, please!' Stepan blurts out, panting. 'Some black-arsed buggers in the 12th Construction Battalion have mutinied. They were smoking hash and now they're moving this way up Materialist Street towards the Stakhanov Club. They're beating up everyone in their way, they've already raped one girl . . . and they're coming this way! They beat up my mate Nikolai, he's unconscious, I had to leave him in the club . . . .'

Judging by Stepan's face, the matter is serious. He has a terrified look, and he's not easy to frighten.

'How many of them are there?' Cat asks. 'Is it the whole battalion?'

'There were about twenty,' says Stepan, breathing heavily. 'Now there are about ten or a dozen of them. All Uzbeks. But the ringleader is a sergeant—he's Russian. Obviously their relatives brought them this hash from Uzbekistan for the holiday. They're completely insane, foaming at the mouth . . . .'

'Why the fuck should we stick our necks out,' growls Lyova, 'just to help the pigs? I've done time, thanks to you pigs, so you can count me out.'

'Are they armed?' Sanya asks Stepan, disregarding Lyova's grumbling.

'No, thank God. They've taken off their belts and are swinging the buckles as weapons. They're beating up everybody, doesn't matter if it's women or children. Help me, lads, I'll never forget it if you do! There's no one at the station except the duty officers, and by the time they've called up some help from the other stations, God knows how many people these black-arsed bastards will have injured!'

'Well?' asks Sanya, speaking principally to Cat. 'Shall we help the forces of Party and government in the struggle against the black-arsed hooligans?'

Eddie-baby, glancing at Sanya, realizes that he needs a target on which to vent the fury he feels for Dora the hairdresser.

'Party—hell! Government—hell! They're bashing up your own girl-friends. They've just gang-banged a girl in the park!' shouts Stepan.

'If they caught my slag she'd love it!' laughs Sanya.

'Come on,' Cat agrees, 'let's go.' He doesn't ask Lyova, knowing that he'll come with them anyway.

They all run after Stepan, across the tram-tracks and into the darkness beyond. Stepan is followed by the hefty twenty-two-year-old Sanya; the powerful Cat, heavy as the bar-bells that he lifts; Lyova; and Eddie-baby, though nobody asked him to come and he is slightly afraid.

At the poorly-lit Stakhanov Club (closed because it is a holiday), a couple of frightened old caretakers inform Stepan that the drugged, mutinous soldiers did not head for the Stakhanov Club as Stepan had expected, but have for some reason run on towards a practically deserted and uninhabited region in the direction of the Saburov dacha. The area is bounded on one side by the fence surrounding the Hammer and Sickle factory that extends for several kilometres; along the other side is the fence of the Piston factory, while between and parallel to them runs the tram-line along which the trams carry people to and from Saltovka.

It is quite possible, thinks Eddie-baby, that the soldiers have simply lost their way, because there is absolutely nothing for this horde, drug-crazed by some Asian narcotic, to do there. However, beyond these two kilometres of wasteland, covered as it is with several years' growth of weeds and marshy in places, there are more residential suburbs and after them there is the town. Perhaps the soldiers want to go to the town?

'Where are your fucking vigilante squads today?' Sanya shouts to Stepan. Elbows working like pistons, they are running in the direction pointed out to them by the club caretakers, as they attempt to catch up with the band of savage nomads.

'They're fucking useless!' shouts Stepan in despair. 'None of them wants to go on patrol on a public holiday.'

For some time, breathing noisily, they all pound away in silence past the fences that flank the open space. The numbered sections of steel fencing flash past: two, three, five, seven . . . twenty and more, Eddie-baby counts to himself.

At the point where one fence meets the other and the narrow asphalt path suddenly turns towards the tram-tracks in order to cross them, the little group is met by a terrifying howling sound and several flying stones. It is not even a howl, but more of a concerted roar, something like a distorted 'Hurra-a-a-a-h!' coming from throats invisible in the darkness.

'Oh fuck!' Stepan curses angrily but impotently as he ducks away from the cobble-stones, heavy as cannon-balls. Stepan's voice quivers, as if he is crying. 'We'll never smoke them out from here! Just our luck that those fucking workmen haven't finished repaving the road.'

The black-arsed buggers have taken cover behind a ready-made barricade of cobble-stones, a metre and a half high, left behind by road workers, who are now probably out drinking somewhere, not even suspecting what is happening at their abandoned workplace. Stepan, Sanya, Cat and Lyova, followed by Eddie-baby, beat a forced retreat out of range of the heavy cobble-stones and hold a conference.

'We must arrest them before the police cars arrive,' says Stepan.

'Not fucking likely,' Sanya objects. 'The most important thing is to get that sergeant, and then all the rest will run away'.

'Get him, get them!' The policeman sneers at Sanya, imitating him. 'How? There are four of us, and at least ten of them.'

'Five of us,' Eddie-baby puts in grimly and firmly, pushing his way into the circle, but no one pays him any attention.

'Why don't you shoot, you cunt?' Sanya asks Stepan. 'What the fuck d'you think they give you a TT automatic for? So you can catch villains with your bare hands?'

'I can't!' says Stepan firmly. 'If I kill someone and he's unarmed, and a soldier into the bargain, I'll be put on trial. I can't shoot.'

'You prick!' Sanya says bitterly. 'Just shoot and they'll shit themselves. We're all witnesses that you were firing in self-defence. If you're afraid of killing one of them, aim at their legs . . . .'

'I can't!' Stepan cuts him off. 'I can't.'

'Well, give me the gun then,' says Sanya, 'and I'll get that sergeant.'

'I can't entrust a police automatic to you!' Stepan is losing his temper. 'Are you joking?'

'You prick! Oh, you prick!' Sanya curses him.

Their argument is interrupted by an outburst of roaring and a hail of stones. This time the situation is far more serious. The maddened soldiery have run out from behind the barricade and are advancing on them. Eddie-baby catches sight of them for the first time. Only a few of them are in greatcoats, despite the cold. Lacking belts to tighten them, their uniform tunics are hanging around them like peasant shirts, collars open, baring their white undershirts that emphasize their dusky oriental features. Wrapped around his right hand, each one of them has a wide, army-issue belt with its heavy cast-bronze buckle. Anyone getting one of these buckles on the temples or the top of the head usually falls unconscious. Fighting with belt-buckles is a normal army pastime. The soldiers are now running straight at them, swinging their belts in the air.

Sanya, Cat and Lyova, the latter limping, pick up the cobble-stones thrown by the soldiers and hurl them back. Eddie-baby follows their example, without much success. As in a slow-motion film, Eddie-baby sees the swarthy, infuriated faces getting dangerously larger.

A hitherto inaudible tramcar rolls up and comes to an enforced halt, furiously ringing all its bells; it can go no further—some of the soldiers are running across the tram-lines, and several large cobble-stones are lying right on the tracks.

The soldiers are now fewer in number than the young men and the policeman, who are hiding behind bare tree-trunks at about ten metres distance. Stepan's trembling fingers are poised over his holster.

'Shoot, you prick, or they'll smash us all—shoot!' shouts Sanya.

Cat seizes Stepan by the arm and tries to take the revolver from him. Stepan wrenches his arm free. He holds the revolver at arm's length. It is shaking in his hand. Stepan is terrified.

'Shoot!' shouts Sanya.

'Shoot, you cunt!' Lyova shouts in fury.

'Shoot at their legs!' yells Cat.

'Shoot!' shouts Eddie-baby.

Accompanied by the unceasing carillon of tram-bells, the police sergeant finally presses the trigger several times in succession. 'Bang! Bang! Bang! Bang!' Four shots resound in the night air and four times the invisible bullets strike sparks from the cobbled roadway under and between the feet of the band of soldiers, bringing it to a sudden stop.

Clustered behind Stepan, the lads see the soldiers running back into the darkness to seek cover behind the barricade. In a shower of sparks a second tramcar, also ringing its bell, stops behind the first one. The doors are closed, the passengers press up against the windows.

Stepan fires a few more rounds and changes the magazine.

Not all the soldiers have taken cover behind the barricade. One large figure stops, as though having second thoughts, then utters a desperate roar: 'A-a-a-h!' and again sets out towards Stepan and the lads.

'The ringleader!' says Stepan hoarsely. 'The sergeant!' and staggers back.

'He's the one we want,' says Sanya. 'Distract his attention, Stepan, annoy him, while Cat and I sneak round along the fence and then grab him from behind. He's in such a state, he won't notice what we're doing.'

Cat and Sanya drop on to all fours and make for the fence, keeping close to the ground.

The sergeant is no longer running but advancing ponderously towards the retreating Stepan, Lyova and Eddie-baby.

'Shoot, you bastard!' shouts the sergeant. 'Shoot, you rotten fucker! Go on, shoot at a Russian soldier, sodding police bastard!'

'Give up, you stupid prick, or it'll be the worse for you!' Lyova shouts to the sergeant. All three, including Eddie-baby, retreat before the advancing hulk of the sergeant, waiting for the moment when Sanya and Cat will jump him from behind.

Suddenly the tramcar driver switches on his headlights and the whole scene is flooded in yellow light. The sergeant ceases to be a massive, dark figure and can at last be properly seen. He stands there, his uniform tunic pulled open with both hands to bare his chest; despite the cold, drops of sweat can even be seen on his forehead. Unlike the soldiers, whose heads are shaved bare, his red hair is clipped in a crew-cut. He comes nearer and nearer. Nervously Stepan waves his TT pistol, holding it out as before at arm's length.

'You prick! You can't do it!' Lyova shouts at the police sergeant.

What can't he do? wonders Eddie-baby. At that moment, glancing at Stepan, almost bent double as he points his TT forward, Eddie-baby realizes that Stepan is not very good at shooting. I wonder if Stepan was at the front in the war? Eddie thinks.

'Shoot me in the chest, you pig! Shoot a Russian soldier!' The sergeant keeps shouting in a senseless, animal-like roar. Suddenly he bends down and picks up a cobble-stone at his feet and raises it over his head.

'I'll kill you!' he shouts in a wild voice and lunges forward, only to crash to the ground, together with the stone, under the weight of Cat and Sanya, who have flung themselves on him from behind.

This time silently, the soldiers dash out from behind their fortification in a bid to rescue their leader and superior officer, but Stepan fires at their legs again, this time more coolly, once more striking beautiful yellow sparks off the roadway.

Almost at that very moment the scene is enlivened by the sudden arrival of three police cars. Policemen jump out of them and attempt, under Stepan's leadership, to catch the soldiers. Simultaneously both tram drivers open the doors of their cars and a crowd of slightly drunken men, dressed in their holiday-best, leap out and try to discover what's going on.

Eddie-baby hears his name: 'Ed!' It is Sanya calling him. He has obviously been calling for some time, as he sounds angry.

'Ed, you mother-fucker! Come here.'

Eddie-baby runs towards the voice.

Sanya and Cat are holding down the giant, defeated Russian sergeant. The giant is croaking and trying to move. In spite of Sanya's hundred kilograms and Cat's trained muscles, they are clearly not finding it easy to keep the sergeant immobile.

'Ed, where the fuck have you been?' Sanya says in a slightly more friendly tone. 'Pull the belt out of this bugger's trousers!'

Eddie-baby cautiously pushes the sergeant's tunic upwards and unbuckles the belt on his trousers.

'Don't touch me you little bastard, or I'll kill you!' the sergeant croaks through his bloodstained mouth.

'Shut up!' Sanya addresses the sergeant almost affectionately and punches him in the face from above as though with a hammer. Sanya's punch weighs several pounds and his hand is hard. Sanya constantly toughens it by hitting the edge against a hard surface, so that he can easily smash a plank of wood with it. The sergeant falls silent.

'We'll just go and take a look around, and you, Ed, stand guard on this criminal,' says Cat sarcastically. He is clearly amused at playing the role of a guardian of law and order. Seeing the nervous glance that Eddie-baby is giving the sergeant, he adds: 'Don't be afraid of him. If anything happens, kick him in the throat or the face with the steel tip of your boot.'

'And don't feel sorry for him,' adds Sanya. 'If he gets loose he won't have any pity on you.'

Several policemen, along with Sanya, Cat, Lyova and Stepan return to the scene of action, where they lift the sergeant from the ground and stand him on his feet. Only now does Eddie-baby appreciate how unusually tough the sergeant is. Sanya and Cat grip him by his arms, still tied behind his back, and lead him towards one of the police cars.

But Stepan has other plans. He stops the lads, and, taking Sanya aside from the other policemen, says to him in a half-whisper: 'Listen, Sanya, don't be a fool! The sergeant is yours and mine. These boys have just come to collect all the credit when we did all the work'—he says, nodding towards the other policeman. 'What we must do is take the sergeant to the station ourselves and hand him over directly to Major Aleshinsky.'

Stepan stops for a moment, then, changing his business-like tone to one more confidential, he goes on: 'Major Aleshinsky has got his knife into you, Sanya. But when we turn up with *this* package of goods'— Stepan nods at the sergeant—'he'll change his mind. Perhaps even arrange some official reward: "For collaboration with the police force in the maintenance of law and order." Well?'

'OK, let's go to the station,' Sanya agrees, though not very willingly.

The pigs don't object, so Stepan quickly forms a little procession. Stepan and Cat take the lead, each holding an arm of the arrested Uzbek soldier. His tunic is torn at the shoulder and soaked in blood. He looks frightened: obviously the effect of the drug has started to wear off, and now he realizes that something not very pleasant has happened. Behind the Uzbek come Sanya and Lyova. The inquisitive Eddie-baby—first running ahead a bit, then dropping back—brings up the rear.

The assembly is accompanied by a dozen or so extraneous civilians, largely made up of drunken passengers from the two tramcars, eager for sensation.

Eddie-baby notices from the behaviour of his older comrades that they really want to be off somewhere else as quickly as possible: further developments are of little interest to them, despite the exotic temptation of appearing in front of the chief officer of No. 15 Precinct not as tearaways or criminals but as conscientious auxiliaries of the police in the struggle against crime.

Cat is the first to duck out. Eddie-baby sees him hand over the arm of the Uzbek soldier to a keen little man in a white cap and a shabby raglan raincoat. The little man grasps the arm with ferocious willingness. Free and glad of it, Cat drops back a little and for a time walks alongside Sanya and Lyova, whispering something to Lyova, obviously telling him to detach himself from the procession. Indeed, a short while ago Lyova had loudly announced that he needed a leak, and now he hands over his post as escort to yet another onlooker who is eager to take part in the event: a Georgian of criminal aspect delightedly seizes hold of the sergeant's rock-like biceps.

Eddie-baby's observations are interrupted by Sanya, who says to him, quietly so that neither the giant sergeant nor the Georgian will hear him: 'Ed, take this animal to the police station—but whatever you do, *don't* go inside, got it? I'm going to . . . take a leak too.' Sanya gives Eddie a meaningful look, winks, and disappears into the crowd.

Eddie-baby doesn't understand why his friends should want to forgo the triumph that they have all earned. Why were the lads refusing to go to the police station and for the first time present themselves to the dreaded Major as heroes instead of criminals and culprits? Stupid! thinks Eddie-baby. Stupid. The next time one of them is booked, the Major might have to let him off. After all, the police are always lenient if one of their regular vigilantes gets mixed up in any trouble . . . .

Later, however, when they reach the 15th Precinct station-house—built, like almost all the houses in Saltovka, out of white brick—Eddie-baby feels certain inexplicable pangs of conscience. He stays outside, pretending to dawdle and allows the Georgian the honour of squeezing through the door with his prisoner, the granite-like sergeant. All the onlookers, too, crowd into the entrance lobby of the station. Eddie stands by the doorway for a minute or so, then calmly goes away. Sensible Eddie.

Translated from the Russian by Michael Glenny

One Writer's Beginnings
EUDORA WELTY

Eudora Welty has been called by the *Times Literary Supplement* 'one of the most entertaining, evocative – and underrated– of American writers.' In *One Writer's Beginnings* she recreates the world of her small-town Southern childhood, revealing how her family and surroundings shaped both her personality and her writing.

'Haunting…a gentle, reflective book, full of insights into the nature of memory.'
Daily Telegraph

'a book of great sensitivity – as controlled and yet aspiring as a lyric poem.'
New Statesman

'Vivid…her gifts for listening and seeing …have never deserted her, as this luminous book testifies.' *Observer.*

'makes for entrancing reading – an evocation of a parochial southern life in the 1920s in delicate prose that now and then comes up with a phrase of power and vividness that unforgettably conjures up for the reader a time and a place.'
Sunday Telegraph
£8.50   Hardback   136pp with 17 halftones   0-674-63925-1

Letters of Henry James
Volume IV, 1895-1916
Edited by LEON EDEL

This volume, the conclusion of Leon Edel's masterful edition, covers the letters written by Henry James in his last twenty years.

'With this fourth volume, Leon Edel completes his edition of the letters. It is wonderful to have them.'
The Sunday Times

'(the letters) have a breadth of vivacity and originality and critical intelligence which no other writer in English of that period can for a moment be thought to equal.' *Books and Bookmen*

'marvellous letters they are – written at the height of James's career, rich in his views on the art of fiction and of course beautifully composed, but also expressive of a "new" James who has shucked off his emotional reticence and opened himself to the life of passion.' *Publishers Weekly*
The Belknap Press of Harvard University Press
£26.40 Hardback 864pp illus. 0-674-38783-X
Volume III, 1883-1895, also available
£27.00 0-674-38782-1

HARVARD
UNIVERSITY PRESS   126 Buckingham Palace Road   London SW1W 9SD

WILLIAM BOYD
ALPES MARITIMES

Anneliese, Ulricke and I go into Steve's sitting-room. Steve is sitting at a table writing a letter. 'Hi,' he says, looking up. 'Won't be a second.' He scribbles his name and seals the letter in an envelope. The three of us watch him. He stands up and turns to face us. His long hair, brushed straight back from his forehead, falls to his shoulders. Perhaps it's something to do with the dimness of the room but, against the pale ghost of his swimming trunks, his cock seems oddly pigmented—almost brown. 'Make yourselves at home,' he says. 'I'll just go put some clothes on.'

I have a girl now—Ulricke—and so everything should be all right. And it is, I suppose, except that I want Anneliese, her twin sister. I look closely at Anneliese to see her reaction to Steve's nakedness (Steve wants Anneliese too). She and Ulricke smile at each other. They both press their lips together with a hand, their eyes thin with delighted amusement at Steve's eccentricity. Automatically I smile too, but in fact I am covered in a hot pelt of irritation as I recall Steve's long-stride saunter from the room, the way his cock slapped on his thighs....

Bent comes in. He is Steve's flat-mate, a ruddy Swede, bespectacled, with a square bulging face and unfortunate frizzy hair.

'Does he always do that?' Anneliese asks.

'I'm afraid so,' Bent says, ruefully. 'He comes in—he takes off his clothes.'

The girls surrender themselves to their laughter. I ask for a soft drink.

It wasn't easy to meet Ulricke. She and Anneliese were doing a more advanced course than me at the *Centre* and so our classes seldom coincided. I remember being struck by rare glimpses of this rather strong-looking fashionable girl. I think it was Anneliese that I saw first, but I can't be sure. But the fact is that the one I met was Ulricke. How was I meant to know they were twins? By the time I discovered that those glimpses were not of one and the same person it was too late.

One lunchtime I was walking up to the university restaurant by the *Faculté de Droit* (the *restauru* by the *fac* as the French have it) when I heard my name called.

It was Henni, a Finnish girl I knew, with Anneliese. At least I thought it was Anneliese but it turned out to be Ulricke. Until you know them both it's very hard to spot the difference.

We had lunch together. Then Ulricke and I went for coffee to a bar called Le Pub Latin. We spoke French, I with some difficulty.There was no mention of a twin sister, that first day, no Anneliese. I talked about my father; I lied modestly about my age, with more élan about my ambitions. Soon Ulricke interrupted to tell me that she spoke very good English. After that it was much easier.

Ulricke: tall, broad-shouldered, with a round, good-complexioned face—though her cheeks and nose tend to develop a shine as the day wears on—thick straight peanut-coloured hair parted in the middle.... She and Anneliese are not-quite-identical twins. To be candid, Anneliese is prettier, though by compensation Ulricke has the sweeter temperament, as they say. Recently, Anneliese has streaked her hair blonde which, as well as distinguishing her from her sister (too late, too late) adds, in my opinion, dramatically to her attractiveness. In Bremen, where they live (father a police inspector), they were both prize-winning gymnasts as youngsters. Ulricke told me that they ceased entering competitions 'after our bosoms grew', but the strenuous training has left them with the legacy of sturdy well-developed frames. They are thin-hipped and broad-shouldered, with abnormally powerful deltoid muscles which give their figures a tapered manly look. When naked, Ulricke's round soft breasts seem almost like an afterthought—like a Michelangelo female nude. When she removes her T-shirt one expects to see the flat, tiny-nippled slab breasts of a champion swimmer. As for Anneliese, I imagine she's the same. Although one night I felt her breasts—beneath the yellow lambswool sweater that she often wears—I have yet to see her naked.

Steve returns, in pale jeans, sandals and a cheesecloth smock-shirt he brought back from his last trip to Morocco. He pours wine for everyone. Steve is an American, somewhat older than the rest of us—late twenties, possibly even thirty. He is very clean, almost obsessive with his cleanliness, always showering, always attending to the edges of his body—the callouses on his toes, his teeth, his cuticles. He has a moustache, a neat blond General Custer affair which curls up at the ends. It's a similarity—to General Custer—which is amplified by his wavy shoulder-length brown hair. He has spent several years travelling the Mediterranean—Rhodes, Turkey, Ibiza, Hammamet. It's quite likely that he sells drugs to support himself. He's not rich, but he's not poor either. None of us knows where he gets his money. On his return from his last Moroccan trip he had also purchased a mid-calf, butter-coloured Afghan coat which I covet. I've known him vaguely since I arrived in Nice, but lately, because of his interest in Anneliese, I tend to see him rather more often than I would wish. Whenever I get the chance I criticise Steve for Anneliese's benefit, but subtly, as if my reservations are merely the result of a disinterested study of human nature. Just before we arrived at the flat I managed to get Anneliese to accept that there was something unappealingly sinister about Steve. Now, when he's out of earshot, we exchange remarks about his nudism. I don't believe the girls find it as offensive as I do.

'I think it's the height of selfishness,' I say. 'I didn't ask to see his penis.'

The girls and Bent laugh.

'I think he's strange,' Anneliese says, with a curious expression on her face. I can't tell if she finds this alluring or not.

Ulricke and I continued to see each other. Soon I learned about the existence of Anneliese, duly met her and realised my mistake. But by then I was 'associated' with Ulricke. To switch attention to Anneliese would have hurt and offended her sister, and with Ulricke hurt and offended, Anneliese would be bound to take her side. I found myself trapped; both irked and tantalised. I came to see Anneliese almost as often as I saw Ulricke. She appeared to like me—to my deep chagrin we became 'friends'.

I forced myself to concentrate on Ulricke—to whom I was genuinely attracted—but she was only the shadow on the cave wall, so to speak. Of course I was discreet and tactful: Ulricke—and Anneliese at first—knew nothing of my real desires. But as the bonds between the three of us developed I came to think of other solutions. I realised I could never 'possess' Anneliese in the way I did her twin; I could never colonise or settle my real affections in her person with her approval.... And so I resolved to make her instead a sphere of influence—unilaterally, and without permission, to extend my stewardship and protection over her. If I couldn't have her, then no one else should.

'When ought we to go to Cherry's, do you think?' Bent asks in his precise grammar. We discuss the matter. Cherry is an American girl of iridescent, unreal—and therefore perfectly inert—beauty. She lives in a villa high above the coast at Villefranche which she shares with some other girl students from a college in Ann Arbor, Michigan. They stick closely and rather chastely together, these American girls, as their guileless amiability landed them in trouble when they first arrived in Nice. The Tunisian boys at the *Centre* would ask them back to their rooms for a cup of coffee, and the girls, being friendly, intrigued to meet foreigners and welcoming the opportunity to practise their execrable French, happily accepted. And then when the Tunisian boys tried to fuck them they were outraged. The baffled Tunisians couldn't understand the tears, the slaps, the threats. Surely, they reasoned, if a girl agrees to have a cup of coffee in your room there is only one thing on her mind? As a result, the girls moved out of Nice to their high villa in Villefranche where—apart from their classes at the *Centre*—they spent most of their time and their French deteriorated beyond redemption. Soon they could only associate with anglophones and all yearned to return to the USA. They were strange gloomy exiles, these girls, like passengers permanently in transit. The present moment—always the most important—held nothing for them. Their tenses were either past or future; their moods nostalgia or anticipation. And now one of their number—Cherry—was breaking out, her experiences in Nice having confirmed her in her desire to be a wife. She was returning to marry her bemused beau, and tonight was her farewell party.

We decide to go along, to make our way to Villefranche. Mild Bent has a car—a VW—but he says he has to detour to pick up his girl-friend. Ulricke announces that she and I will hitchhike. Steve and Anneliese can go with Bent, she says. I want to protest, but say nothing.

William Boyd

Ulricke and Anneliese live in a large converted villa, pre-war, up by the *Fac de Lettres* at Magnan. They rent a large room in a ground floor flat which belongs to a Uruguayan poet (he teaches Spanish literature at the University) called César.

One night—not long after our first meetings—I'm walking Ulricke home. It's quite late. I promise myself that if we get to the villa after midnight I'll ask if I can stay, as it's a long walk back to my room in the rue Dante down in the city. Dependable Ulricke invites me in for a cup of coffee. At the back of the flat the windows are at ground level and overlook a garden. Ulricke and Anneliese use them as doors to avoid passing through the communal hall. We clamber through the window and into the room. It is big, bare and clean. There are two beds, a bright divan and some wooden chairs which have recently been painted a shiny new red. A few cute drawings have been pinned on the wall and there is a single houseplant, flourishing almost indecently from all the attention it receives—the leaves always dark green and glossy, the earth in the pot moist and levelled. The rest of the flat is composed of César's bedroom, his study, a kitchen and bathroom.

We drink our coffee, we talk—idly, amicably. Anneliese is late, out at the cinema with friends. I look at my watch: it is after midnight. I make my request and Ulricke offers me the divan. There is a moment, after we have stripped off the coverlet and tucked in an extra blanket, when we both stand quite close to each other. I lean in her direction, a hand weakly touches her shoulder, we kiss. We sit down on the bed. It is all pleasantly uncomplicated and straightforward.

When Anneliese returns she seems pleased to see me. After more coffee and conversation, the girls change discreetly into their pyjamas in the bathroom. While they're gone I undress to my underpants and socks and slide into bed. The girls come back, the lights go out and we exchange cheery *bonsoirs*.

On the hard small divan I lie awake in the dark, Ulricke and Anneliese sleeping in their beds a few feet away. I feel warm, content, secure—like the member of a close and happy family, as if Ulricke and Anneliese are my sisters and beyond the door in the quiet house lie our tender parents....

In the morning I meet César. He is thin and febrile, with tousled dry hair. He speaks fast but badly flawed English. We talk about

London, where he lived for two years before coming to Nice. Ulricke tells me that as a poet he is really quite famous in Uruguay. Also she tells me that he had an affair with Anneliese when the girls first moved in—but now they're just friends. Unfortunately this forces a change in my attitude towards César: I like him, but resentment will always distance us now. Whenever he and Anneliese talk I find myself searching for vestiges of their former intimacy—but there seems nothing there any more.

We all possess, like it or not, the people we know, and are possessed by them in turn. We all forge and own an image of others in our minds that is inviolable and private. We make those private images public at our peril. Revelation is an audacious move to be long pondered. Unfortunately, this impulse occurs when we are least able to control it, when we're distracted by love—or hate....

But we can possess others without their ever being truly aware of it. For example, I possess Steve and Anneliese in ways they would never imagine.

I often wonder what Anneliese thinks about while Ulricke and I are fucking across the room from her. Is she irritated? Curious? Happy? The intimacy of our domestic set-up causes me some embarrassment at first, but the girls seem quite unperturbed. I affect a similar insouciance. But although we live in such proximity we maintain a bizarrely prim decorum. We don't wander around naked. Ulricke and I undress while Anneliese is in the bathroom or else with the lights out. I have yet to see Anneliese naked. And she's always with us too—Ulricke and I have never spent a night alone. Since her affair with César she has had no boy-friend. My vague embarrassment swiftly departs and I begin to enjoy Anneliese's presence during the night—like some mute and unbelievably lax chaperone. One day, to my regret, she tells me how happy she is that Ulricke 'has' me; how pleased she is that we are together. The twin sisters are typically close: Anneliese is the more self-composed and assured and she feels protective towards Ulricke, who's more vulnerable and easily hurt. I reassure her of my sincerity and try not to let the strain show on my face.

William Boyd

With some dismay I watch Steve—an exotic figure in his Afghan coat and flowing hair—join Anneliese in the back of Bent's VW. Ulricke and I wave them on their way, then we walk down the road from the apartment block towards the Promenade des Anglais. Although it is after nine o'clock the night air is not unpleasantly cool. For the first time the spring chill has left the air—a presage of the bright summer to come. We walk down rue de la Buffa and cut over to the rue de France. The whores in the boutique doorways seem pleased at the clemency of the weather. They call across the street to each other in clear voices; some of them even wear hot pants.

It's not that warm. Ulricke wears a white PVC raincoat and a scarf. I put my arm around her shoulders and hear the crackle of the plastic material. The glow from the streetlamps sets highlights in the shine on her nose and cheeks.... I worry about Steve and Anneliese in the back of Bent's car.

I begin to spend more and more nights at Ulricke's. Mme D'Amico, my landlady, makes no comment on my prolonged absences. I visit my small room in her flat regularly to change my clothes but I find myself increasingly loath to spend nights alone there. Its fusty smell, its dismal view of the interior courtyard, the dull conversations with my fellow lodger, remind me of how impoverished my existence was—in every respect—before I met Ulricke and Anneliese. I had felt quite proud and pleased with myself during my first weeks in Nice, but now the change in my circumstances casts a baleful gleam of hindsight over my early history in this curious town. I am happy to have exchanged lonely independence for the hugger-mugger intimacy of the villa. Indeed, for a week or so life there becomes even more cramped. The twins are joined by a girl-friend from Bremen, called Clara—twenty-two, sharp-faced, candid—in disgrace with her parents and spending a month or two visiting friends while waiting for tempers back home to cool. I ask her what she has done. She says she had an affair with her father's business partner and oldest friend. This was discovered, and the ramifications of the scandal spread to the boardroom: suits are being filed, resignations demanded, take-over bids plotted. Clara seems quite calm about it all, her only regret being that her lover's daughter—who hitherto had been her constant

134

companion since childhood—now refuses to see or speak to her. Whole lives are irreparably askew.

Clara occupies the divan. She sleeps naked and is less concerned with privacy than the other girls—several times I have caught glimpses of her small white breasts. I find I relish the dormitory-like aspect of our living arrangements even more. At night I lie docilely beside Ulricke listening to the three girls talking in German. I can't understand a word—they could be talking about me, for all I know. Clara smokes French cigarettes and their pleasant sour smell lingers in the air after the lights are switched out. Ulricke and I wait for a diplomatic five minutes or so before making love. That fragrance of Gauloises or Gîtanes is forever associated with those tense palpitating moments of darkness: Ulricke's warm strong body, the carnal anticipation, the sounds of Clara and Anneliese settling themselves in their beds, their fake yawns.

O n the Promenade des Anglais the shiny cars sweep by. Ulricke and I stick out our thumbs, goosing the air. We always get lifts immediately and have freely hitched, usually with Anneliese, the length of the Cote d' Azur, from San Raphael to Menton, at all hours of the day or night. One warmish evening, near Aix-en-Provence, the three of us decided spontaneously to sleep out in a wood. We huddled up in blankets and woke at dawn to find ourselves quite soaked with dew.

A car stops. The driver—a man—is going to Monte Carlo. We ask him to take the *haute corniche.* Cherry's villa is perched so high above the town that the walk up from the coast road is exhausting. Ulricke sits in the front—the sex of the driver determines our position. To our surprise we have found that very often single women will stop for the three of us. They are much more generous than the men as a rule: in our travels the women frequently buy us drinks and meals, and once we were given 100 francs. Something about the three of us prompts this largesse. There is, I feel, something charmed about us as a trio, Ulricke, Anneliese and me. This is why—quite apart from his rebarbative personal habits—I so resent Steve. He is an interloper, an intruder: his presence, his interest in Anneliese, threatens me, us. The trio becomes a banal foursome, or—even worse—two couples.

135

F rom the small terrace at Cherry's villa there is a perfect view of Villefranche and its bay, edged by the bright beads of the harbour lights and headlamps of cars on the coast road. The dim noise of traffic, the sonic rip of some lout's motorbike, drift upward to the villa, competing with the thump and chords of music from inside. *Crosby, Stills, Nash and Young – Live, The Yes Album, Hunky Dory*... curious how these LPs pin and fix humdrum moments of our lives—precise as almanacs. An *ars brevis* for the quotidian.

The exquisite Cherry patrols her guests, enveloped in a fug of genial envy from her girl-friends. It's not her impending marriage that prompts this emotion so much as the prospect of the 'real' Coca Cola, 'real' milk and 'real' meat she will be able to consume a few days hence. The girls from Ann Arbor reminisce indefatigably about American meals they have known. To them France, Nice, is a period of abstention, a penance for which they will be rewarded in calories and carbohydrates when they return home.

I stroll back inside to check on Steve and Anneliese. My mistake was to have allowed them to travel together in Bent's car. It conferred an implicit acknowledgement of their 'coupledom' on them without Steve having to do anything about it. Indeed he seems oddly passive with regard to Anneliese, as if content to bide his time. Perhaps he is a little frightened of her? Perhaps it's his immense vanity: time itself will impress upon her the logic and inevitability of their union...? Now I see him sitting as close to Anneliese as possible, as if adjacency alone is sufficient to possess her.

Ulricke talks to Bent's girl-friend, Gudrun, another Scandinavian. We are a polyglot crew at the *Centre*—almost every European country represented. Tonight you can hear six distinct languages.... I pour myself a glass of wine from an unlabelled bottle. There is plenty to drink. I had brought a bottle of Martini Rosso as my farewell present to Cherry but left it in my coat pocket when I saw the quantity of wine on offer.

T he wine is cold and rough. Decanted no doubt from some huge barrel in the local *cave*. It is cheap and not very potent. We were drinking this wine the night of my audacity.

César had a party for some of his students on the Spanish Lit. Course. After strenuous consumption most people had managed to get very drunk. César sang Uruguayan folk songs—perhaps they were his own poems—to his own inept accompaniment on the guitar. I saw Anneliese collect some empty bottles and leave the room. Moments later I followed. The kitchen was empty. Then from the hall I saw the bathroom door ajar. I pushed it open. Anneliese was reapplying her lipstick.

'I won't be long,' she said.

I went up behind her and put my arms round her. The gesture was friendly, fraternal. She leant back, pursing, pouting and repursing her lips to spread the orange lipstick. We talked at our reflections.

'Good party,' I said.

'César may be a poet but he cannot sing.'

We laughed, I squeezed. It was all good fun. Then I covered her breasts with my hands. I looked at our reflection: our faces side by side, my hands claws on her chest.

'Anneliese...' I began, revealing everything in one word, watching her expression register, interpret, change.

'Hey, tipsy boy,' she laughed, clever girl, reaching round to slap my side. 'I'm not Ulricke.'

We broke apart, I heeled a little, drunkenly. We grinned, friends again. But the moment lay between us, like a secret. Now she knew.

The party is breaking up. People drift away. I look at Steve, he seems to have his arm round Anneliese. Ulricke joins me.

'What's happening?' I ask Steve.

'Cliff's taking us down to the town. He says they may be at the café tonight.'

I confirm this with Cliff who, improbably, is French. He's a dull, inoffensive person who—we have discovered to our surprise—runs drug errands for the many tax-exiled rock musicians who while away their time on the Côte d'Azur. Every now and then these stars and their retinue emerge from the fastnesses of their wired-off villas and patronize a café on the harbour front at Villefranche. People sit around and gawp at the personalities and speculate about the hangers-on—the eerie thugs, the haggard, pale women, the brawling kids.

A dozen of us set off. We stroll down the sloping road as it meanders in a sequence of hairpins down the steep face of the hills to the bright town spangling below. Steve, I notice, is holding hands with Anneliese. I hate the look on his face: king leer. I feel a sudden unbearable anger. What *right* has he got to do this, to sidle into our lives, to take possession of Anneliese's hand in that way?

The four of us and Cliff have dropped back from the others. Cliff, in fractured English, is telling us of his last visit to the rock star's villa. I'm barely listening—something to do with a man and a chicken.... I look back. Anneliese and Steve have stopped. He removes his Afghan coat and places it cape-like round Anneliese's shoulders. He gives a mock-chivalric bow and Anneliese curtsies. These gestures, I recognise with alarm, are the early foundations of a couple's private language—actions, words and shared memories whose meaning and significance only they can interpret and which exclude the world at large. But at the same time they tell me that nothing intimate—no kiss, no caress—has yet passed between them. I have only moments left to me.

The other members of our party have left the road and entered a narrow gap between houses that is the entrance to a thin defile of steps—some hundred yards long—that cuts down the hill directly to the town below. The steps are steep and dark with many an illogical angle and turn. From below I hear the clatter of descending feet and excited cries. Cliff goes first, Ulricke follows. I crouch to tie a shoelace. Anneliese passes. I jump up and with the slightest of tussles insinuate myself between her and Steve.

In the dark cleft of the steps there is just room for two people to pass. I put my hands on the rough iron handrails and slow my pace. Anneliese skips down behind Ulricke. Steve bumps at my back. Soon I can barely make out Anneliese's blonde hair.

'Can I get by, please?'

I ignore Steve, although he's treading on my heels. Below me Anneliese turns a bend out of sight.

'Come *on*, for God's sake.'

'Bit tricky in the dark.'

Roughly, Steve attempts to wrest my arm from the handrail. He swears. I stop dead, lock my elbows and brace myself against his shoving.

'You English fuck!' He punches me quite hard in the back. I run down the steps to a narrow landing where they make a turn. I face Steve. He is lean and slightly taller than me, but I'm not interested in physical prowess, only delay. Further down the flights of steps the sound of footfalls grows ever fainter. I hold the bridge. Steve is panting.

'What do you think you're doing?' he says. 'Who do you think you are? Her father? You don't own these girls you know.'

He takes a swing at me. I duck my head and his knuckles jar painfully on my skull. Steve lets out a yip of pain. Through photomatic violet light I lunge at him as he massages blood into his numbed fist. With surprising ease I manage to throw him heavily to the ground. At once I turn and spring down the steps. I take them five at a time, my fingertips brushing the handrails like outriggers.

Ulricke and Anneliese are waiting at the bottom. The others have gone on to the harbour front. I seize their hands.

'Quickly,' I say. 'This way!'

Astonished, the girls run with me, laughing and questioning. We run down back streets. Eventually we stop.

'What happened?' Anneliese asks.

'Steve attacked me,' I say. 'Suddenly—tried to hit me. I don't know why.'

Our feet crunch on the pebbles as we walk along Villefranche's *plage publique.* I pass the Martini bottle to Ulricke, who stops to take a swig. We have discussed Steve and his neuroses for a pleasant hour. At the end of the bay's curve a small green hut is set on the edge of the coast road. It juts out over the beach where it is supported by thick wooden piles. We settle down here, sheltered by the overhang, spreading Steve's Afghan coat on the pebbles. We huddle up for warmth, pass the bottle to and fro and decide to watch the dawn rise over Ventimiglia.

The three of us stretch out, me in the middle, on Steve's convenient coat. Soon Ulricke falls asleep. Anneliese and I talk on quietly. I pass her the Martini. Carefully she brings it to her mouth. I notice how, like many women, she drinks awkwardly from the bottle. She fits her lips round the opening and tilts head and bottle simultaneously. When you drink like this some of the fluid in your

139

mouth, as you lower your head after your gulp, runs back into the bottle.

'Ow. I think I'm drunk,' she says, handing it back.

I press my lips to the bottle's warm snout, try to taste her lipstick, raise the bottle, try to hold that first mouthful in my throat, swilling it round my teeth and tongue....

Ulricke gives a little snore, hunches herself into my left side, pressing my right side against Anneliese. Despite what you may think I want nothing more from Anneliese than what I possess now. I look out over the Mediterranean, hear the plash and rattle of the tiny sluggish waves on the pebbles, sense an ephemeral lunar greyness—a lightening—in the air.

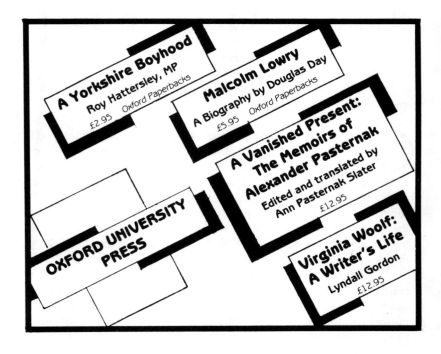

KEITH WATERHOUSE Thinks

The vindictive private fantasies of a choleric commuter are hilariously detailed in this new novel from our finest comic writer. £8.95

"A masterpiece of High Farce, the funniest and most effective book I have read for years"
Auberon Waugh, Daily Mail

KEM NUNN Tapping the Source

An obsessive quest for his runaway sister draws Ike Tucker to California's sleazy beach world where his search swiftly becomes one for his own manhood and identity. £8.95

"Kem Nunn is the bright son of a very good family... Hammett and Chandler, Raoul Whitfield, Paul Cain, James Cain, Horace McCoy and, yes, Ross Macdonald. What Kem Nunn has done is... (to) surpass them all."
Carolyn See, Los Angeles Times Book Review

SARA MAITLAND Virgin Territory

This powerful, provocative second novel confirms the winner of the Somerset Maugham Award as one of the most talented and original writers to emerge from the British Women's movement. £8.95

"A feminist theological novel... extravagant, didactic, densely infiltrated by myth, metaphor and history."
Victoria Glendinning, Sunday Times

JULIAN RATHBONE Nasty, Very

Black political satire coupled with a chilling observation of human behaviour motivated by greed and ambition make Julian Rathbone's 16th novel his most successful yet. £8.95

"A savage parody of the Britain that is no longer great, his novel deserves attention"
Elizabeth Berridge, Daily Telegraph

ROSELLEN BROWN Civil Wars

A broad, passionate new novel from the highly-acclaimed author of THE AUTOBIOGRAPHY OF MY MOTHER and TENDER MERCIES. £9.95

"The graceful energy of Brown's prose is such that the impulse to read fast, to get ahead with the action... conflicts with the simultaneous desire to ponder each rewarding sentence."
Marion Glastonbury, New Statesman

MICHAEL JOSEPH

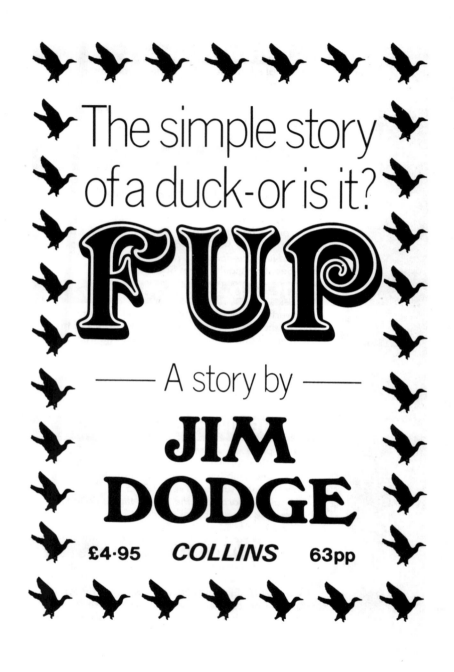

The simple story
of a duck-or is it?

FUP

— A story by —

JIM
DODGE

£4·95   COLLINS   63pp

JOSEF ŠKVORECKÝ
FAILED
SAXOPHONIST

Josef Škvorecký

I was born in 1924 in Náchod, a small town on the north-eastern border of Bohemia, the westernmost part of Czechoslovakia.

Náchod was a town of cotton mills. All the mills had exhaust pipes which channelled the debris from the machines into peculiar little towers on the factory roofs, where the dust was then puffed out into the air. The smog was so heavy that if, towards evening, you climbed the mountains surrounding the valley, the town lay in what looked like thick soup. But in those days nobody knew there was such a thing as smog. It was a constant puzzle for the local doctors why, in spite of the healthy mountain climate, so many people suffered from respiratory trouble.

I was one of them. After a brief career as right back in a soccer mini-league, I fell ill with pneumonia. This was before the days of antibiotics and one could easily die. I very much did not want to die and promised, therefore, to say ten Our Fathers and ten Hail Marys daily, if I survived. As the days, made hazy by fever, dragged on, I kept raising the number until I ended up with a burden of about a hundred Our Fathers and Hail Marys per day. In the year that followed my recovery I tried to live up to my promise. For hours I knelt beside my bed, night after night, and in the morning I looked like a child suffering from a bad hangover. The intense religiosity exhausted me so much that in another year I had another bout of pneumonia. This time I was wiser. I vowed only that, if I recovered, I would—at the age of eighteen—enter a monastery. When that deadline was approaching, I postponed the day until I was twenty-one. A girl—well, two girls, in fact—were unwittingly involved in that decision. With my twenty-first birthday closing in on me, I shifted the date once again: to twenty-five. Eventually, it was the Communists who saved me for secular life. When they took over the country, one of their first acts of class justice was to close down all monasteries.

Religion played an important part in the groping around of my childhood. Before our first communion, in grade three of primary school, we searched our souls, then counted our sins, and compared notes. With fourteen sins to be unburdened in the confessional, I was apparently the greatest sinner in my form. Berta Grym, the richest boy in the class, committed only four, and was, therefore, a model of saintly purity. Moreover, among my sins was

144

one called 'Doubts about the Articles of Faith'. When I mumbled this phrase into the big ear of Father Meloun, he looked up at me through the grille of the confessional and asked in a tone of astonishment: 'Which one?' 'That the world was created in seven days,' I stammered. I had read a book about dinosaurs, and somehow it stimulated my imagination more than Moses. 'That's not an article of faith,' said Father Meloun comfortingly. Instead of relief I felt confusion. Why does the Bible contain misinformation?

Another aspect of religious groping: my parents used to send me to a summer camp called 'Onkel Otto und Tante Blanka Ferienpensionat', in order to perfect my German. Since German was mandatory at the camp, everybody tried to speak Czech. Ninety per cent of the inmates were Jewish. Ninety per cent of them perished a few years later. When I spent my first summer with Onkel Otto, I already knew a little about Jewish religion. I had been taking German lessons from the cantor of the local synagogue, but I met him only twice a week, whereas now I was in daily touch with Jews, and learned a lot about their traditions and rituals. The one that fascinated me most was the circumcision of their penises, and I realized that I had never given a thought to the implications of Jesus being a Jewish male. Circumcision had been just a word for me, with no image attached to it. Now the word was made flesh; at night it was projected, by means of an electric torch, on to the wall in the boys' dormitory, its length and thickness ascertained by a tape-measure.

A group of orthodox youngsters did not compete in the penis-Olympics. They indulged, instead, in long prayer ceremonies, their *cicitls* affixed to their foreheads. They also held various fasts. There was one Quido Hirsch, a Fatso, who was fasting practically all the time. The reason was not theology, but doctor's orders; however I did not know that. Quido gave his fastings various Hebrew-sounding names, and I was envious. In order to beat him at his own game, I invented a three-day Catholic liquids fast and almost died of thirst. But it was Quido who was dead, a short three years later....

Alex Karpeles, my closest friend, was one of the few who did not perish in Auschwitz: his family left the country in time. After the war Alex returned—briefly—in a British uniform. He then went back to Palestine, and if he survived all the ensuing wars, he may still be alive. He was responsible for my literary début.

Josef Škvorecký

I became a writer in the classic Freudian way. Owing to my two bouts of pneumonia I developed into a sickly, overprotected child, accompanied to and from school every day by an anxious mother, and forced to wear shameful knitted headgear that looked like a Spiderman's mask and was to prevent my catching cold. Bereaved of adventurous activities, I began to dream about them. One day I put a dream on paper. It happened after I had read—in a Czech translation—the first two parts of an unfinished trilogy by the Canadian novelist, James Oliver Curwood. Many years later, when I came to Canada, I was surprised that nobody there knew this master. He had written many romantic novels featuring red-coated mounties and beautiful Indian girls: the *Rose Marie* stuff. Frustrated because the happy ending was missing, I completed the saga as *The Mysterious Cave,* and, for the first time in my life, experienced the bliss of creation. My second novel, inspired by yet another Canadian, Ernest Thompson Seton and describing a war between the French and the British in America, was called *Men of Iron Hearts* (under the spell of feminine beauty the hearts melted). It was this novel which Alex Karpeles mimeographed in a magazine he edited for the Club of Young Zionists at the Prague English Grammar School. After the Commie coup in Czechoslovakia, I wisely refrained from mentioning my début.

As I grew into puberty, there followed a series of novel fragments no longer inspired by Canadian literature. All featured a young Czech actor who makes it big in Hollywood, and vows eternal friendship to one Freddie Bartholomew.

I am devoutly heterosexual, but apparently most young people go through a phase of Platonic homosexuality and I was enchanted by this Hollywood boy-star after seeing him in a tearjerker based on *Little Lord Fauntleroy.* The next summer, the local cinema announced another opus starring Freddie: *Captains Courageous.* Without explanation I staunchly refused to spend my vacations in Switzerland where, at a *pension* near Geneva, I was to learn French. I was afraid I would miss that saccharinized distortion of Kipling. Well, I did not, neither did I see Switzerland until some thirty-five years later, by which time the dimple-cheeked Freddie had long since faded into dim memory.

146

For some time after that ingloriously-spent summer, I continued to write the fragments, but after *Thoroughbreds Don't Cry* the Czech hero's counterpart became a girl by the name of Judy Garland. She remained the staple female character of a third set of fragments, in which the Czech actor turned into a nightclub tenor-sax player.

For like a revelation, that strange way of making music entered my life. It was the only revelation I have ever experienced. I am not a mystic. My religious life has been all in the head. I have been indifferent to marching men, waving flags, to slogans, to little girls kissed by statesmen, to arms raised in Roman or proletarian fashion. But—

In the general store of old Mr Maršík, shortly before the outbreak of the war, I spotted a few records with American labels. I brought one home, put it on my wind-up gramophone, and heard the swinging saxophones. Kepler's heavenly spheres must have made music like that. It was a true epiphany, a marijuana of the soul.

My initiation into jazz later proved to have been the beginning of my decisive step into literature as well. I talked my father into buying me a tenor sax, and tried my luck with several local swing bands. But I did not have much more luck as a jazzman than I had as Judy Garland's lover. A sentence from Faulkner's *The Unvanquished* has always struck me as fitting my case extremely well: '*Those who can, do; those who cannot, and suffer long enough because they cannot, write about it.*' I could not, I suffered, and eventually I wrote *The Cowards,* the novel that unmade, and later made me. The celluloid girl of my dreams was replaced by flesh-and-blood beauties from Náchod, and the locale of my fictional fragments shifted from California to my home town, which became the Kostelec of my books. The melancholy superstar of the nightclubs on Sunset Boulevard assumed humbler proportions and turned into a cynic by the name of Danny Smiřický.

The choice of that name was not accidental, and curiously enough, I owe it to the politics of the Great Aryan.

Although my Father had no interest in his ancestry, the Nazis had: like everyone else, we were required to prove our Aryan origin. The proof, partly obfuscated, was provided by my Father's brother, who was a Catholic priest and liked to research old parish registers. Three surprising things came to light. First, the legend of my mother's French background was confirmed, though not much to her liking. On her father's side she was indeed descended from a Frenchman. But this man's only connection with aristocracy was his profession: he was a butler who accompanied his master into the Count's temporary exile in a West Bohemian château, succumbed to the charms of a Chod girl from a nearby village, and defected from the nobleman's service. If this was something of a disappointment to my mother, my venerable uncle's second discovery was, in the light of the new law, embarrassing. It appeared that the maiden name of one of my Father's grandmothers was Silbernagel. The chances of a Silbernagel being Aryan are slim, but fortunately, in the wedding entry of the parish register, the lady was listed as 'of Catholic faith'. Of course, the Nazis didn't care about a Jew's religious beliefs, and the pathetic efforts of some Jews in Náchod to save themselves by asking the ever-ready Father Meloun to baptize them proved absolutely futile. But according to the Nuremberg Laws, if a grandparent's race could not be established beyond reasonable doubt, but he (or she) was listed as Catholic or Protestant, he (she) was to be regarded as Aryan. My uncle, having slightly tampered with the evidence, cunningly proved that this was Granny Silbernagel's case, and we were safe.

My uncle's third discovery was a pleasant surprise for my aristocratophile of a mother. The Škvoreckýs were apparently an extremely old family, first mentioned in the fourteenth century as yeomen who owned a castellet east of Prague, in the village of Škvorec. An ancestor, Martin Škvorecký, a turncoat who switched from Protestantism to Catholicism after the defeat of the Czech Protestants in the battle of the White Mountain in 1620, was even of some importance to historiography. He had managed the estates of Count Czernín, one of the biggest landholders in Bohemia, and his weekly reports on the state of the Count's farms survived and serve as a priceless source for the study of the economy of the Thirty Years' War. Martin ended his life miserably, though. His seventeen-year-old second wife, at that age already the mother of two sons, ran away with Swedish soldiers, and the old husband went mad. The 'Swedish' soliders were, most probably, Protestant Czechs who fought in the Swedish army in the hope of reconquering their land. When they saw their case was hopeless, they took Czech girls with them to Sweden, irrespective of their marital status, to become their wives, the mothers of their children, and the cooks who would nourish the fading memories of the old fatherland with dumplings, pork and sauerkraut.

The Škvoreckýs were a sort of sideline to the powerful Smiřický family, one of the most prominent aristocratic houses in Bohemia. Hence Danny Smiřický.

He, however, was not born until after the war. During the first four years of that *Götterdämmerung*, I attended the local *real-gymnasium*, a very traditional institution, with mandatory Latin and mathematics as the two main subjects at matriculation. In the course of those four years, Czech grammar schools were quickly Germanized, first by increasing the number of German classes from three to seven per week, then by decreeing that the ideologically important subjects, such as history and geography, be taught in German. It was the Nazis who introduced the term 'ideology' into our vocabulary, and can anyone wonder why I have mistrusted the word ever since? Something called *Die deutsche Ideologie* became part of our German instruction, and was reluctantly taught by a pretty Sudetengerman, Eva Althammer, who racially forgot herself to the extent of marrying a Czech with the hopelessly non-Teutonic name of Švorčík. She did it, however, before the war: such a *mésalliance* would not have been permitted after the establishment of the *Protektorat Bömen und Mähren*. The German *Ideologie* consisted mostly of memorizing biographies of the leading Nazis. More fun was provided by 'Race Theory', taught, as part of history, by a gentle old spinster whose German was so poor that—although in Czech she was an excellent lecturer—she had to instruct us by reading slowly and with many mispronunciations from mimeographed sheets. The theory was quite something. We learned that the Germans, far from being a 'pure' race, were in fact a '*Rassenmischung der besten Germanischen und Nordischen Elemente*': a top-quality race cocktail. The 'pure' race were the Jews. No admixture of noble blood there, only a parasitic instinct, greediness, and thick lips drooling at the sight of Aryan girls.

Aryan girls were objects of interest also to the *Rassenforscher*, the racial researchers from the Institute of Racial Origins, housed in the former Philosophical Faculty of Charles University in Prague, which had been closed by the Nazis in 1939. Some time in 1943, all fifteen-year-old Czech girls in Prague were summoned to the Institute, where the scientists photographed them in the nude, and took measurements of their skulls, hips and bosom. About a year later, during a visit to Prague, I bought a set of nude photographs from a waiter. To my surprise, among the shy-looking lovelies I recognized my niece. The race researchers apparently were not above more practical applications of their theories.

We had fun, too, in those grim times: we had our swing bands, and the town was full of lovely mountain-climbing girls. When my novel *The Swell Season* appeared in Canada, some critics doubted its authenticity. Why, they wondered—he describes life under the Nazis as almost devoid of hardships and rather full of merriment. In fact, like life anywhere. One critic found the occasional intrusions of the Nazi threat into the idyll of Kostelec 'rather unexpected'.

This bewilderment comes, I suppose, from seeing too many trashy films about Nazism, and from forgetting about the irrepressible ability of youth to enjoy life under almost any circumstances. My late friend, J.R. Pick, wrote a humorous novel about the Theresienstadt ghetto which functioned as a gate to the hells of Auschwitz, Maidanek, Treblinka. It is called *The Society for the Prevention of Cruelty to Animals,* and features a group of Jewish youngsters who catch and eat the pets of the SS guards to protect the beasts from exposure to their Nazi masters. Gallows humour, to be sure, but humour nevertheless. Most of the models for Pick's characters perished in the gas chambers. He himself survived, but lost one lung. He died, at the age of fifty-seven, of heart failure.

Of course, the horrors of Auschwitz did exist. But when you were sixteen, seventeen, not Jewish and therefore not in any immediate danger, you did not think about the horrors all the time. Besides, the knowledge of them was vague. The Nazis kept their secrets well. Also: the Nazi presence in Bohemia was less conspicuously bloody than in some other occupied lands. Bohemia—unlike Poland, for instance—was a heavily-industrialized country, famous for its armament factories, and the Nazis needed to maintain production of the Škoda three-purpose guns, the *Panzerjäger* armoured attack vehicles, and other fruits of Czech weapon design. The boss of Bohemia, SS Obergruppenführer Reinhard Heydrich, posed as a convinced socialist and a protector of the working class. That's why the terror in the Protectorate was not as indiscriminate as elsewhere—except, of course, during the weeks after the Czech and Slovak paratroopers from England had killed Heydrich, the workers' friend.

People were, at first, jubilant. Then the executions started. About 5,000 of them, announced on red posters day after day. The villages of Lidice and Ležáky were erased from the face of the earth; all males over fifteen years of age were shot, all women transported to the Ravensbrück concentration camp, all small children sent for adoption by childless German families.

During the Heydrich terror, life in Náchod did not differ much from that of the Warsaw ghetto. But at other times it went on as normally as possible during a war, in a town far removed from the battlefields. Now and then the Gestapo took someone, usually an intellectual or a former professional soldier. Some returned after a few months—my father among them—some after the war. Some did not return. But death was not as indiscriminate as in Poland or the Balkans. Besides, totalitarian regimes are not only bloody, but pompous, and pomposity is always ridiculous. Consequently, every bloody dictatorship has its comic aspects. Do you remember the *Paradeschritt* of the SS? Their absurd goose-stepping to lyraphone music? When people saw it for the first time in occupied Prague they burst out laughing and whistled the Laurel and Hardy theme tune. Some, of course, were arrested right away, and some never came back.

In 1943 I matriculated and my coming of age coincided with the announcement of the *Totaleinsatz,* according to which all able-bodied Czech men and women were drafted into the armaments industry. In dictatorships always read 'all' as 'except the more equal'. Greater equality may be acquired in different ways: sometimes by knowing where to pull strings, and sometimes by having enough pre-war French cognac to bribe an influential Nazi or quisling. My father, unfortunately, was a teetotaller, and whenever he tried to pull any strings—catastrophe. I was drafted and was to be sent to Bremen, then one of the prime targets for carpet-bombing raids. However, there is a Czech saying, 'If the Devil is unable to do a job, he substitutes a woman.' As I walked, utterly dejected, away from the draft board in the district capital of Hradec Králové, with an order to

Josef Škvorecký

report for transport in three days, I ran into the jolly wife of my
godfather. She was a model of neither marital fidelity nor Czech
propriety, and that afternoon she was compromising herself with a
man in a German army officer's uniform: at least he was not SS. 'Why
so gloomy, young man?' she teasingly asked me and, with a savage
look at her consort, I told her why. 'Thank God it's not a broken
heart!' she laughed. 'This can be fixed. Go home.'

And she fixed it. I never asked her how, but she did. I never saw
her afterwards, but instead of being sent to Bremen I was dispatched
to the Metallbauwerke Zimmerman und Schilling, a Messerschmitt
subsidiary in Náchod. I don't even know what became of that 'auntie'
of mine: after the war my godfather lived alone.

So in the summer of 1943 I became a *Hilfsarbeiter*—an auxiliary
worker. Quite a shock for a pampered middle-class youngster whose
only physical exertion until then had been pressing the keys on his
tenor saxophone. But it started a new chapter of my education which,
some years later, culminating in my army service, made me into what
I am: a writer who, as some of my readers kindly say, has been able to
portray, with equal verisimilitude, an assortment of Czechs of both
sexes and all walks of life.

It was a unique experience. The fourteen-hour shifts we tried to
spend mostly in the latrines: partly to escape the boredom of mass
production, partly to avoid working for the Nazis. The company that
assembled in that smelly and smoky space was an amalgam of all
classes, more than you would find in a jail: textile workers, students,
bank clerks, tailors, gardeners, businessmen, barbers, lawyers,
waiters—all turned welders, locksmiths, drill-operators and
Hilfsarbeiter. The discussions were profound, lively and on many
subjects; sometimes the shit-house resembled a philosophy seminar.

There was also a pathetic working-class girl, toiling on a drill,
who helped me to get rid of the young man's burden. She almost
became the end of me. Since she made me feel like a man, I tried to
behave like a man, which in those days meant like a war hero. She was
a very patriotic girl, prepared, I am sure, to die for her country
without much ado. I wasn't. But I realized that only after I had
figured out and executed a rather clever act of sabotage aimed at
reducing radically the fire-power of the Messerschmitt fighter plane.
Luckily, the sabotage was discovered by the Czech foreman, who did

not inform the Gestapo but tried to cover things up. He explained to me quite unequivocally that my stupidity could indeed turn into an act of heroism, sanctified by death on the gallows. I did not become a Dostoevsky only because I do not possess Dostoevsky's talent. But my mortal fear, I guess, was equally strong. I survived. The girl did not. She wasn't hanged, though. She died of the classic illness of her class: tuberculosis. And soon I was to witness another TB death.

That was in the sweet, sunny summer of 1945. I was helping out at a hospital where a young survivor of Auschwitz was dying. She looked to me like a living skeleton: she was beyond help. She survived the horror only to die amid the jubilant lilac blossoms of that spring, amid universal rejoicing of newly-won freedom. I almost despaired. Lying in my comfortable bed at night, I felt that nobody had the right to enjoy life while there, behind the antiseptic partitions, that quintessence of hopeless sadness lingered on, expiring slowly, day by day, until she faded out into nothingness.

That sweet, sad summer of 1945, I enrolled at the Medical School of Charles University. It seemed to me, young and idealistic, that only selfless service to those who suffer desperately could justify my own survival. Very few young men, I believe, ever decided to study medicine who were worse equipped for that strenuous vocation than I. My service to my fellow beings—if service it was—was to be of an entirely different kind.

Náchod was the setting of probably the last fighting of the war in Europe. On 10 May, the SS rearguard of Marshal Schörner's army group made a last stand on the outskirts of the town, to inflict casualties on the advancing spearhead of the Russian Army under Marshal Malinowski. The army was Russian in name only. The officers looked Russian: but the drafted men were soldiers from the Asian republics of the USSR.

The fighting was soon over. The surviving SS were savagely butchered by the Czechs and, after the Soviet spearhead, thousands upon thousands of horse-driven buggies rolled into town, followed by vast numbers of captured horses. I had never seen so many in my life. The meat-ration tickets, which even during the war entitled one to a double portion if the meat chosen was horse, shot up in value like shares on a stock exchange. Half a kilo of horsemeat for a ten-gram coupon. Then two kilos. Then five. Then fifteen. In the first few days after the war my native town must have devoured the equivalent of a century of four-legged participants in the Kentucky Derby.

But there was not only the memory of the dying Jewish girl in the hospital: there were other shadows, too, among the bright lights of that spring and summer. A few months earlier, when the war was still on, I came across a leaflet which had been issued by a local Communist cell. In this, the comrades were exhorted to be ready for the liquidation of 'bourgeois resistance groups' as soon as the war was over. I was a member of one such group, and this was my initiation into Marxist-Leninist dialectics. This was the first time I'd read anything which used the word 'bourgeois' as a synonym for 'bad, wrong, despicable'. Since then, this usage has been mindlessly adopted by far too many people in the West. In my opinion—and I have an incurable tendency to base my opinions on experience and solid reading, not on hearsay and ideology—the bourgeois are no worse than any other class. In fact, I have a suspicion that they, the middle class, neither too rich to become decadent, nor too poor to become enfeebled, are the backbone of society. I know many—far too many—bourgeois who, with coolness, courage, self-sacrifice and honesty, faced deadly situations during the Hitler regime and then again during the Stalin years. I also met quite a few perfumed red-nailed girls, exuding sweet bourgeoise charm, who survived courageously the degrading conditions of Communist camps. I do not subscribe to the view that 'bourgeois' is synonymous with 'bad, wrong, despicable'.

Soon I received another lesson in dialectics. I became the editor of a local youth weekly published by the just-founded Union of Czech Youth. Covertly, this was a Commie organization from the very beginning, but overtly, in 1945, it was still non-partisan. For the first issue I wrote a lead article entitled 'Goodbye, Mr Churchill', an enthusiastic tribute to the great war leader who had just lost—inexplicably to me—the first post-war elections. For the second number I contributed a 'critical' analysis of the work of a young local painter who specialized in expressionistic portraits of girls, including my two great and, out of necessity, Platonic loves, Irena and Marie. In my article I defined Art as Love, inspired by the gentle colours of

Marie's portrait which was, indeed, a product of love. Before the third issue was out, I was summoned to the Union's headquarters in Prague where some grim-looking functionaries told me that Churchill was a War-Monger and a Reactionary, and that Art was not Love but Class Struggle. Unfortunately for them—fortunately for me—I had read that Churchill was a war-monger before, in the display window of the Náchod Hitler Jugend Club. In my mind, I was forming an equation between Communism and National Socialism that I have never been able to erase. Probably because reality is inerasable.

It was also the end of my career as the Youth Union's editor.

At the Medical School I lasted exactly one term. To memorize the Latin names of all the bones in the human body proved an insurmountable task. I switched over to philosophy, where you can talk yourself out of any problem and successfully pass any exam without knowing anything; at least not by heart. Instead of attending lectures—all I needed for the *colloquia* was to borrow notes from diligent colleagues—I threw myself into the life of the big city. I also started writing seriously and made a few literary discoveries. My mentors were a shopgirl who called herself Maggie, and Ernest Hemingway.

Although nominally I was also studying phonetics with the celebrated Professor Trnka, one of the founders of the Prague Linguistic Circle, it was Maggie, grandiosely loquacious, who made me aware that the language as it is actually spoken differs considerably, often radically, from what appears on the printed page—or used to in those days. The gap is, or was, much greater in Czech than it is in post-Mark Twain American English. Maggie was a natural-born *raconteuse,* unable to recount anything except as a dramatic scene, and incapable of expressing a thought without compressing it into the most bare, monosyllabic essentials. Like Archimedes, I jumped out naked from the restricting corset of classical Czech usage, and produced a novel called *The Nylon Age.* On paper it looks like phonetic transcriptions; scarcely a compulsively readable text. With thousands of apostrophes, the book tells the story of a love affair between a university student and a shopgirl.

Josef Škvorecký

And then I read *A Farewell to Arms.*

In my many fragmentary Hollywood novels, I had been pretty good—as is every young adept of fiction—at describing nature and creating mood, preferably of the gloomy-sentimental variety. My evocations of Los Angeles must have been second only to Chandler's. But when it came to dialogue—well, it was wooden characters lecturing each other. From the pages of Hemingway, I realized that people in a novel can talk about nothing particularly important and yet not be boring at all. Their dialogue can be amusing, captivating, full of nuances, and, when you come to think about it, quite profound. So Hemingway taught me to write dialogue, and Maggie acquainted me with the scenic method and the use of the vernacular. Her lesson proved the more fateful one, for it eventually led to charges of my imitating the decadent naturalists like Louis-Ferdinand Céline, and of irreverence for the mother-tongue.

I was also writing poetry. It was poetry, not prose, that propelled my eventual entry into the Prague literary scene, underground variety. In 1945 I penned a long Whitmanesque poem entitled *Don't Despair!*—its title taken from a line by the surrealist poet Jindřich Heisler. It was in all respects very derivative. I submitted it to the jury of a poetry competition in 1946. Instead of a prize I received a letter from František Halas who expressed a wish to see me.

To my mind, Halas was hardly a lesser poet than, let's say, William Carlos Williams or W.H. Auden. But he performed his rhymed miracles in an unknown tongue. Internationally, Halas is a nobody. But to Czech poetry, and to me.... In a trembling voice I made an appointment with the poet's secretary, and a few days later I entered his office on shaky legs. As is the common lot of poets, Halas had to make a living as a bureaucrat. He began by telling me that he had not recommended my poem for a prize because—here I interrupted him: 'Oh, I never intended to have it published!' A transparent lie, of course. Halas looked at me with mocking eyes, then said: 'C'mon! The defloration must come one day!' This sentence from his gentle lips silenced me, and he proceeded to explain that he feared, should the poem come out, I would be slaughtered by the critics on both the Right and the Left.

Perhaps he was only trying to make the loss of the prize more palatable to me. Anyway, I didn't understand him, then. Why, in my poem I was just trying to present the world as I saw it—to express my feelings as they were! In my inexperience I had no idea that simple realism is the last thing ideologically-minded critics want. Their concept of the writer's subject—of the world and of human life in it—was a combination of idealization and diabolization. Reality was not their friend. It never is. It never fits their vision.

That was my third major literary lesson: through no fault or credit of mine, I was apparently walking some strange sort of tightrope which neither the political Right nor the political Left approved. Halas spoke from personal experience. He was one of those kind but fallible Catholics who, moved by genuine social feelings in the years of the Great Depression, had joined the Communist Party. In the sweet, tragic summer of 1945 he travelled, for the first and last time in his life, to the Soviet Union. He returned a broken, desperate man. Three years later he died, only a few months after the Commie *coup d'état* of 1948. Before his death he wrote a testament which was circulated underground in the fifties, and, after many years, published abroad. It is a compassionate confession of the big mistake he made, and a bitter critique of the absurd dream of justice called Communism.

He also left his notebooks to his friend and factotum, the literary and art critic Jindřich Chalupecký. In one of them, he had jotted down a few remarks about me and my poem. So I received another letter, this time from Chalupecký, inviting me to attend a meeting at the apartment of the poet and artist Jiří Kolář.

Thus I became a member of one of the very few underground groups in the early fifties. That was the time of the hangings and of the Soviet-operated Czech uranium camps. You qualified for hanging either by openly acting against the new dictators—for instance, by continuing with the banned Socialist Party, as Milada Horáková did, the only woman ever hanged by her own people for political 'crimes'—or by being Jewish and high-up in the Communist Party hierarchy and therefore conspicuous to the evil eyes of Stalin and his Czech sycophants. As for the uranium mines, simple bad luck sufficed. Two or three times I was lucky; others were arrested.

One of the most remarkable members of the Chalupecký-Kolář circle was the surrealist painter Mikuláš Medek, who once actually painted the evil eyes of Stalin. Surrealism was, of course, strictly taboo. To paint like Magritte or Toyen, or to indulge in *Entartete Kunst* (eviscerated art) as Comrade Goebbels had called it could be punishable, and so poor Medek had to do his real work in secret, while making a living as a hack on the socialist market. There he was not a success. His first commission was a poster advertising a bedbug-killing powder. Medek produced a beautifully realistic human torso, surrealistically bitten all over by bedbugs (*before*), and the same torso shining with a mysterious inner light (*after*). He almost got himself arrested because one of the wise men of the Approving Committee found the bitten torso slanderous, and useful to enemy propagandists for its depiction of housing conditions in socialist Czechoslovakia.

The times were lunatic. We would meet at Jiří Kolář's apartment, read aloud unpublished and, under the circumstances, unpublishable stories, talk about literature and about art, and indulge in similar subversive activities. Kolář presided over the group; he is now well-known for his collages, rollages, muchlages, etc., and lives in exile in Paris. Bohumil Hrabal read the first version of the story which later became world famous as the Oscar-winning film, *Closely Observed Trains*; the first draft was definitely *Entartete Kunst*. Hrabal still resides in Bohemia, is in close contact with trouble-makers, and is protected solely by the love of the hundreds of thousands of his readers. Věra Linhartová, the experimental fiction writer and art historian, was also in the group and now lives in exile in Paris. So does Jan Vladislav, the poet and translator, among many other things, of Shakespeare's Sonnets. Jan Rychlík, the modernist composer, jazz theoretician and percussionist, died early. Jan Hanč, the existentialist athlete and poet, followed him to the grave a few years later. Then there was Zdeněk Urbánek, the Shakespearian translator, who has become a Charter 77 signatory; Jiřina Hauková, a poet and close friend of Dylan Thomas; her husband, Jindřich Chalupecký.... We were a stubborn lot, and we survived—moreover, it was through this group that I first became interested in my future wife, Zdena. The interest thus proved fatal. However, the fatality was of the best sort.

I wrote several books during those dark and colourful years. *The Cowards* in 1948 and 1949, right after the *putsch. The Tank Corps,* after my discharge from the army in 1954. *The Stories of a Tenor Saxophonist* in 1955 and 1956. And with P.L. Dorůžka, a jazz historian, musicologist and friend, and Ludvík 'Louis' Šváb, a psychiatrist by profession but the guitarist of the Prague Dixieland Band by vocation, I put together a musical show called *Really the Blues,* the very first jazz revue to be produced after the Commie takeover. All these efforts spelled trouble; some brought me within reach of the prison gates. But I was lucky. Or, maybe, I had a guardian angel.

None of these works of my young maturity came out until much later. *The Tank Corps* had to wait for its première until 1969, when Gallimard published it in French as *L'escadron blindé.* A chapter from it was printed in a Czech magazine—with disastrous results. In a fit of rage, the political commander of the army issued orders forbidding any Czech magazine to print any kind of satire on any aspect of army life. The novel was printed in Alexander Dubček's tenure of office, but then the Russians came and the entire printing was destroyed before publication. It was first brought out in Czech in 1972—eighteen years after I had written it—by my wife's firm, Sixty-Eight Publishers, in Toronto, Canada.

When the tanks arrived in Prague, in August 1968, one of their first objectives was to occupy the building of the Writers' Union, which also housed the offices of the Union's publishing house. After about three weeks, the Red Army withdrew, and the editors moved back in. They found nothing missing except some felt pens and the original of one of the illustrations for *The Tank Corps.* It was the frontispiece, showing a group of army officers' faces in magnificently cheeky caricature. But then one of the editors found the drawing. It was stuck among some old proofs and the man who had put it there had obviously got scared of what he had done to it. Under the most repulsive-looking officer's head there was an inscription: *This is the head of that fucking pig, General Gretchko.* The general was the commanding officer of the invading Soviet forces. Apparently, the Good Soldier Švejk has his siblings even in the World's Best-Disciplined Army.

Josef Škvorecký

Speaking of Švejk: many people say that *The Tank Corps* is a kind of *Good Soldier Švejk* in a Communist army. The name of Švejk is known to most Western readers, but I wonder how many have actually read the novel? Few, I suspect, know who Švejk is and what he stands for.

He is, to put it briefly, one of the major embodiments of passive resistance: the essence of one of the few ways open to the powerless who intend to survive the dangers of living under the powerful. Whenever Švejk is called upon to do something that a loyal citizen of an authoritarian state is supposed to do, he does it not just obediently, as most subjects would, but with exemplary enthusiasm. Whenever he is given an order, he carries it out to the letter, eagerly. He ostentatiously displays an unshaking and unshakeable belief in every authority and every piece of wisdom emanating from that authority's mouth. He is an energetic shouter of officially-approved slogans. In short: by behaving always as a model citizen, an exemplary soldier, a super-obedient orderly, he exposes the impossibility of such behaviour. The good soldier is too good to be true. He, to define his philosophical meaning—for he has a very deep one—shows the absurdity of ideological orthodoxy. Lieutenant Lukáš, for instance, whose orderly Švejk is, instructs him to see to every need of his mistress while he is away on duty. Guess what the needs of that lady are? And Švejk's obedience is unquestioning....

The irony is that, by the time I wrote *The Tank Corps,* I had not read *Švejk* either. I was certainly aware of its existence; I knew some of its episodes from oral renditions by enthusiastic connoisseurs—in Czechoslovakia, one cannot escape some knowledge of the book. But I had never perused the work. This seems to corroborate a hypothesis I have that *The Tank Corps* is not a literary satire, but plain realism. I did not intend to write a satire; I was endeavouring to recapture experience. I was not inspired by a world-famous book, but by a world-wide phenomenon: the army and its inherent absurdities. The basic absurdity is similar to *Švejk*'s: the discrepancy between ideological concepts and the reality they are meant to describe. But I wasn't even aware of that principle when I was writing the book. It's *post factum* knowledge, or rather analysis, revealed to me by a clever critic in Sweden.

T he major disaster of my literary career was the publication of *The Cowards.* I had written the novel between 1948 and 1949 and did not offer it to a publisher for ten years. In it, I made a conscious effort to produce a work of 'magic realism'. What I had in mind, however, was not the type of magic performed by some South American novelists, such as Gabriel García Márquez, who uses gag-like surreal exaggeration to stress the craziness of the world he describes, or simply distorts historical facts to serve his ideological purposes. The term 'magic realism' had been coined before the war by a Czech poet, Josef Hora, who meant by it an infusion of poetry into epic prose. However, the only permissible kind of realism in the early fifties, as I well knew, was socialist realism, a type of socialist Western, and I was not very good at that genre.

Curiously enough, my first *published* work *was* a Western. I only ghost-wrote it, with a friend, who soon afterwards died of a brain tumour. We did it for a professional hack who was trying to cure himself of alcoholism in the spa of Běloves, on the outskirts of Náchod. This derelict fell in love with my beautiful sister Anna, and since he spent all his time either drinking the curative waters or playing tennis with Sis, he had none left to fulfil his obligation of one Western per month for a penny-dreadful weekly called *Rodokaps* (*Pocketnovels*). When he learned from my sister about my literary aspirations, he offered me a deal: he would provide me with a synopsis, I would put some flesh on its bones, he would then paint it over and we would split the profits fifty-fifty. The opus, called *The Smoking Guns of Rio Presto,* had an archetypal plot. It featured a Rancher and his beautiful Daughter and a band of Thieves who were stealing his cattle. The incompetent local Sheriff was helpless. Then a Stranger appeared, first against the rising sun on the Horizon, later in the local Saloon. He saw the Daughter and offered help. He shot up the Thieves and saved the Rancher from penury. However, the Daughter then revealed to the Stranger that she was engaged to a Young Rancher, the owner of the neighbouring B Ranch. The Stranger left, first the Saloon, then the county. He was last seen against the setting sun on the Horizon.

This, of course, is also the formula of the socialist realist novel of the Stalinist era. It invariably features a factory (or collective-farm) Manager, and the beautiful local Schoolteacher (or Doctor). A gang of hard-drinking Workers, infiltrated by CIA Agents, is stealing material from the factory or farm. The incompetent local Chairman of the town council is helpless. A Secretary appears, first at the Railway Station, then in the Party Secretariat. He turns out to have been sent from Prague (or Moscow, or Warsaw, or Sofia). He sees the Schoolteacher (or Doctor), and offers help. He uncovers the Agents, reforms the Working-class alcoholics, and thus ensures the fulfillment of the Production Quotas. However, the Schoolteacher (or Doctor) then reveals to the Secretary that she is engaged to the Young Shockworker in the factory (or on the farm). The Secretary leaves first the Secretariat, then the county. He is last seen at the Railway Station.

As you see, only the rising and setting suns are missing. Both genres are based on the same archetypal story. And as there are, contrary to documented reality, no Negro cowboys in the Western, there are no incompetent Secretaries in the Eastern. Both types are pure fantasies.

As I said, I knew that the only magic permissible to realism in those days was the twisting of reality to suit ideological purposes. Therefore the first book I offered for publication in 1956, after Stalin had safely died, was another novel I naively considered safe, called *The End of the Nylon Age*—a spin-off from my unpublished tribute to Maggie, the shopgirl. It was quickly seized by the censors and banned before publication as 'pornography', owing to my use of the word 'bosom' to describe a woman's (certainly not bare) breasts. When I suggested to the censor that I could replace 'bosom' by 'tits', as the working people call them, she threw me out of her office.

It therefore surprised me when the censor raised no objection to *The Cowards*, which I had offered for publication thinking that I had nothing to lose, after the disaster with my 'pornography'. I had no idea that my novel was being used as an example of the consequences of liberalization: it was redolent of decadent naturalism and reactionary individualism. I was a non-Party man, had never previously been published, and the story, which presented an important historical event not from the 'objective' (that is, Marxist) point of view, but through the eyes of a tenor-sax-blowing bourgeois youngster, was ideally suited to became the target of righteous fury.

Which it duly became. For two weeks, day after day, reviews appeared in all the national papers and journals, and then the hunt continued in local weeklies. The director of the Union's publishing house was fired, and so was the editor-in-chief, together with six other editors. A journalist who managed to sneak in a favourable review was dismissed as well. I lost my job on the staff of the *World Literature* magazine. Then the President himself condemned the novel at a Party Congress and my mother-in-law, a simple woman of the people, offered to look after my valuables and bank books. My wife transported my manuscripts to my father in Náchod, who got a friend in a mountain village twenty miles away to hide them. It looked as though I would get a belated opportunity to become a uranium miner.

But Stalin had been dead for six years, so I missed my chance and, although I was banned, I became a literary celebrity: scandals have always been the best publicity gimmicks. When policemen were dispatched to bookshops to seize unsold copies, they found that they had all gone. Of course, they had been carefully hidden by the enterprising shop managers, and when the immediate danger was over, were sold at many times the original price.

On New Year's Eve 1959, a few weeks before the critical bombardment began, we had received several hundred Christmas cards. One year later only a few dozen came. Nothing extraordinary. Those were the times that tried friends' souls.

One day, when my fortunes were at their lowest, the doorbell rang. Instead of the two people we expected, two unexpected ones stood in the doorway: the most famous Czech film star at the time, Jana Brejchová, and her totally unknown husband Miloš Forman. I had known Miloš in the war: he was a little boy then, staying in Náchod with his uncle, a grocer and my mountain-climbing buddy. Miloš's parents had been sent to a concentration camp from which they never returned, and so he spent most of the war 'visiting' with various uncles. He was pitied by all, but he was too young for me to take any interest in him, and, besides, he pursued his own childish pursuits, not girls like me.

Now, not so many years later, he reappeared in my life with a request: he'd like to write a script from a story of mine, 'Eine Kleine

Josef Škvorecký

Jazzmusik', and make it into his first feature film (he had just
graduated from the Film Academy). The story had appeared in the
first *Yearbook of Jazz* which, partly because of it, was immediately
banned, but Miloš got hold of a copy saved by the printers. I was
moved by this demonstration of fearless loyalty, and reminded of the
war and of the little grocery shop where Miloš used to steal
sauerkraut from a big barrel. Why should I say no?

We set to work. In those days, each script had to be approved by
a dramaturgical body of about seventy members, who considered it
their duty to suggest editorial changes. We entitled our script *The
Band Has Won,* and the story was about a students' swing band that
outwits the Nazis. It was subtitled 'A Musical Comedy'. After a year's
comments and suggestions from the seventy sages, the script, still
bearing the same title, no longer had a swing band in it, and was a
tragedy about a working-class anti-Nazi saboteur in an armaments
factory. However, about this time, the political climate changed, and,
at the end of that year, one of the seventy wizards pointed out that,
although the screenplay was called *The Band Has Won*, there was no
band in it; and although it promised to be a musical comedy, it was a
tear-jerker without any music whatsoever. We set to work again, and
after less than a year, the band was back, the tragedy was out and the
script bore the unmistakable touches of Forman and the dialogue of
The Cowards. By then the political climate had turned almost
pleasant, and one night our work was approved. In an elated mood
we walked across Wenceslas Square, Miloš fantasizing about casting
his sister-in-law in the leading role and I nodding silently in amazed
disbelief.

My feeling proved to be right. That night, my friend the
President listened to the ten o'clock news. An enterprising newscaster
smuggled in an item about a new director's first film, based on a story
by Škvorecký. In the President's mind, only one story was associated
with my name. Next morning, he issued orders to the effect that to
film Škvorecký would be considered serious political provocation.
Miloš tried to get an appointment with the President and explain the
matter to him, but he only got to one of his secretaries who told him
confidentially: 'Comrade, we know the boss made a mistake. But who
do you expect will have the guts to tell him so?'

Six years later, in the summer of 1968, we wrote a synopsis of *The Cowards* which was to be filmed in the summer of 1969. But by then the Russians had come, Miloš had left for Hollywood, and I for Canada.

Eventually, the Party decided to permit an edition of *The Cowards*, and I was officially launched on a literary career. The novel went through several editions and sold well over 100,000 copies in hard cover, in a country of ten million readers. I was a success, and everybody eagerly awaited my next book. To say that the second book is always a problem is a platitude.

I wonder if any artist is ever absolutely sure that what he or she is doing is good? What I often find in writers' confessions is that with every new book the author is faced with a new problem and that all his or her previous experience, though useful, does not guarantee success. I certainly found myself in this dilemma after the *succès de scandale* of *The Cowards*. And at the time some of my colleagues were discussing, in all seriousness, their 'art'. But can I be sure that what *I* am doing is art?

The sixties in Prague were a glorious time, except for one thing: they were also a time of unparalleled literary snobbery. Franz Kafka, previously seen as the prototype of decadence, was suddenly rehabilitated. The Marxist scholars now argued that alienation, the mode of Kafka's existence, was not the monopoly of the Jews or of Capitalism. In fact, profound feelings of alienation were wide-spread in a country where political prisoners were mining uranium used for the manufacture of Soviet atomic weapons, and where children were led to proclaim their disbelief in Santa Claus, and their faith in Granpa Frost, Santa's Soviet substitute.

So far so good. However, the reluctant acceptance of Kafka opened the door for more, until then reactionary, authors: Beckett, Robbe-Grillet, Ionesco, Sarraute, Butor, Artaud, Barthes, Derrida, Lévi-Strauss etc. Suddenly, much of this forbidden fruit was in bookshops, and everybody hastened to taste it. Critics—and far too many of them—became heavy addicts of the drug of rediscovered modernity. The cultural atmosphere of Prague underwent a dialectical change. A few years earlier, unless you told an absolutely comprehensible story with black-and-white characters, you were considered a political reactionary. Now, if you told a comprehensible story with realistically-drawn characters, you were a literary reactionary. Unless you sounded like Nathalie Sarraute or some unpalatable West German experimentalist, you were *passé*, outdated, uninteresting to the new, Kafkaesque literary establishment.

And where did I now stand? Oh, sure—these Marxist literary rediscoverers would say condescendingly—he *is* a good story-teller; in the traditional mode, that is. Quite funny, too. Certainly popular. And of course, he is *historically* important. After all, his first novel *was* a turning-point in the development of modern Czech fiction—

I was an item of literary history. But if you are a writer worth your salt you want to feel—and be recognized—as someone who has something to say not to history, but to your *contemporaries*. It is nice to have Ph.D. theses written about your turning-point novel. It is nicer to see that novel, in cheap paperback, on display at railway bookstalls.

In the days of the anti-realist witch-hunt I did a lot of soul-searching. Was I, perhaps, guilty of neglecting the new liberalism in the arts? Of turning my back on experiment? I had never written a piece of fiction in order to please a tendency, or a literary movement; to start an intellectual fashion or toe a political party line. But shouldn't I try something in the manner of the, let's say, *nouveau roman*? Suppress my tendency to tell a good story well, possibly with a twist in its tail? Strive for a shapelessness which, allegedly, imitates life better than old Poe's structural concepts?

Then came the *annus mirabilis, annus horribilis* of 1968, and the sobered-up comrades tried to put the stupid clock of history back, with predictable results. The Orwellian boot of the Soviets that tramples on the human face forever, stepped on the face of my country, and brought about a *finis Bohemiae* as a land of Western culture. My place was no longer there.

And so we left, my wife and I, and settled in Canada, where my life-long devotion to the masters of American fiction paid off: I got a job at the University of Toronto, teaching American literature. Poe, Hawthorne, Twain, James, Hemingway, Fitzgerald, Faulkner, Lewis, Chandler, that remarkable procession of men who confronted a non-intellectual continent and produced their magnificent responses to its rawness. Within the limits of my capacities I tried to emulate them.

My wife founded, and through hard labour and perseverance built up, a publishing house, Sixty-Eight Publishers, which to date has brought out over 130 titles: books by contemporary Czech and Slovak fiction writers, poets, playwrights and essayists, living both in exile and at home, all banned in their own country—altogether about 600 such authors. In addition to that hardly imaginable workload, my wife has written two successful books of fiction, *Summer in Prague* and *Ashes, Ashes, All fall down,* and has become the darling of Czech and Slovak readers in exile and in Czechoslovakia, where her books and mine are smuggled in considerable quantities.

We found peace in this country, and that's all you need if you are a writer and have begun the downhill road of your life. You don't need the country of your birth any more; you don't even have to hear the everyday sounds of your native tongue. Against the background of an acquired language the fine qualities, the subtleties, the music and the charm of the words you write stand out; you become more aware of the uniqueness of that particular language—and every language has unique qualities. As a novelist I love, above all, to dwell in the world of my youth; but as a human being I know that that age, that landscape, even that community, are forever lost. I am not sentimental about a past that has disappeared. I loved my native town and the girls in it: but they are grandmothers now. I was quite fond of Prague in the sixties: but it does not exist any more. It's now the provincial captial of a Russian *gubernia*. You cannot enter the same river twice. You can't go home again.

And so it was on this continent of Poe, Twain and Faulkner that I set out to recapitulate my life in fiction. You can be a great poet at twenty, die at twenty-four and remain alive, because, for lyric poetry, all that is necessary are fresh, strong emotions and a sensitivity to words. But to be a ripe epic novelist you have to retain the freshness of emotions well into your declining years when you have accumulated a wealth of experience: the hundreds of real-life stories of which you were a part; the hundreds of sweet, funny characters, sad and obnoxious, that crossed your path; the decades of

167

Josef Škvorecký

historical upheavals, political somersaults; the wisdoms and stupidities of your age....

I was only forty-five years old when I left Czechoslovakia, and yet, within that short span, I had experienced all the existing political systems of twentieth-century Europe: liberal democracy until 1939; Nazism from 1939 to 1945; the uneasy democratic socialism of 1945 to 1948; Stalinism between 1948 and 1960; the liberalization of Communism from 1960 to 1967; the crazy attempt to square the circle in 1968; the Attila-the-Hun solution of the *Panzers* in August 1968; the colonization of *Regnum Bohemiae* which had begun before we left. All my compatriots went through this rigmarole. A writer does not and cannot write just about him- or herself. That fact has nothing to do with romantic, patriotic concepts of being a 'spokesperson for one's people'. It is the kernel of the fruit of writing. Some writers may *think* their only subject is themselves: if they are any good they are telling the history of their times and of their people in the form of a self-portrait. For the self-portrait has an open landscape in the background, with little human figures toiling and frolicking in it, as in a genre painting by a Dutch master. If all a writer manages is a picture of her- or himself against a blank curtain, then the writer is just a miserable scribbler who never grew out of puberty, no matter how much fucking is included.

I never intended to write satire, yet I ended up producing something that is indistinguishable from satire. I never thought of myself as a dissident writer, yet I was stripped of my citizenship because of literary dissent. I never dreamed of writing history, yet, perhaps, a stranger perusing my saga about the cynical tenor saxophonist would get a more or less continuous picture of the last four decades of Czechoslovakia's history.

What sort of writer am I really?

As Veronika, the sad heroine of *The Engineer of Human Souls,* put it: Let's leave it to the horses to figure out. They have bigger heads.

THE
SPECTATOR

"Reactionary Chic"
HARPERS & QUEEN

CHARLES MOORE · ALAN WATKINS · AUBERON WAUGH · PEREGRINE WORSTHORNE · NICHOLAS COLERIDGE · CHRISTOPHER HITCHENS · TIMOTHY GARTON ASH · MURRAY SAYLE · FRANK JOHNSON · ANDREW BROWN · PAUL JOHNSON · JOCK BRUCE-GARDYNE · CHRISTOPHER FILDES · COLIN WELCH · FERDINAND MOUNT · PETER QUENNELL · A.N. WILSON · ELIZABETH JENNINGS · ERIC CHRISTIANSEN · HARRIET WAUGH · ENOCH POWELL · JAMES HUGHES-ONSLOW · PETER ACKROYD · GAVIN STAMP · ALEXANDER CHANCELLOR · HARRY EYRES · P.J. KAVANAGH · TAKI · JEFFREY BERNARD · PETER LEVI

Don McCullin
A Life in
Photographs

Don McCullin

'I haven't turned down an invitation to war or revolution for twenty years. Why? Why, for instance, did I spend four years in Vietnam? I can feel the reason, but I can't articulate it.

My first war assignment was in Cyprus. I remember when I was asked if I wanted to do it: I was so excited I must have floated at least four feet above the floor. At last, after so many years, and after I'd photographed every minor labour dispute in every little town in Britain, I was being trusted. That trust changed me completely.

I was like some wild animal—a bull—finally let loose. I wanted the adventure; I wanted to be able to face up to fear and defy it. But I was also after something else: I wanted to show that I could be a great—no, the greatest—photographer around. I was determined to be fast enough and clever enough to carry myself into situations where a reporter with a camera wasn't meant to be. I thought I could get closer than anybody else; that I could show much more than anyone else. I was so determined that nothing could stop me. I took photographs while I was directly in the firing-line of snipers. I took photographs hobbling with a broken ankle down a street that was being strafed by a plane. I took photographs with broken ribs or a broken arm or with blood streaming down my legs. There was a time when if someone said, 'Look, Don. There's a cliff. Go and jump off the edge of it', I would have jumped. And I would have landed without breaking a limb.

I think I believed that I could make my photographs mean more than any others had previously. I didn't have any kind of criteria, but I knew that my pictures had to have a message. But what message? I couldn't have said—except, perhaps, that I wanted to break the hearts and spirits of secure people.

And then the criticism started.

"Do you know what your pictures are doing to people?" I was asked that all the time, but at first I had no idea how to answer. "Oh, come on," they'd say. "They're making Sunday mornings uncomfortable and miserable."

When I got out of the Air Force I had no qualifications. None. I was regarded as stupid. I had failed my 11-plus. I couldn't read properly: it was only later that I discovered I am dyslexic. I didn't even pass the RAF photography examination. I had failed the whole bloody thing. And I left feeling society had failed me.

I went back to Finsbury Park where I grew up, and it was there that I took the first pictures that were published. I used to photograph all the boys I went to school with, hanging around with them at weekends. There was no craft or skill involved. I just took photographs as innocently and as honestly as I could. When you do that, you can usually see that honesty in the photographs.

But I'm tired of talking about Finsbury Park. It's become a cliché: the hardships of growing up in a poor district. The roughness. 'Grooming' for confrontation.

Except, I wasn't being groomed. I was being fucked up. It was like being born with a stamp on your arm that never goes away. In England, you're born into a specific society and you accept its stamp. I slept in a bed in which I had to listen every night to my father's coughing, his death rattle. I went to school in the same shirt I wore the day before because it was the only shirt I had. Very early on, you learn on which side of the fence you live. And you can never climb over it. I've shown what I can do without qualifications. I've got out of Finsbury Park. But it doesn't matter what I've achieved, I still bear the stamp. It's like being born black. It doesn't matter what you do: every morning you wake up, you're still the same—black.

I was in Bradford, on some private business, and this woman, Norma Steel, came up to me and said, "Are you from t'press?" I said, "Yes, I suppose I am." "Right," she said, "come in 'ere. I want to show you this disgusting 'ouse." I went inside and she said to her son, "Tell the gentleman about the rats. They're as big as cats. That big." And she stretched out her hands. Very strange. I was keeping very quiet, just observing. The ceiling had fallen on to the floor, and there was a shit-bucket in the corner of the kitchen. In a beer can, she was boiling up water for her son's tea. The rest of the house was just like the kitchen. In the next room, she had a large, life-size cardboard cut-out of a very beautiful girl in a Father Christmas outfit, advertising Babycham. And then she said to the boy, "Now your mother's got to go over and visit this gentleman in Bingley, and you'll be staying with your aunt tonight." She was still whoring. Can you believe it? And this was about two or three dozen yards away from where the Ripper used to strike.

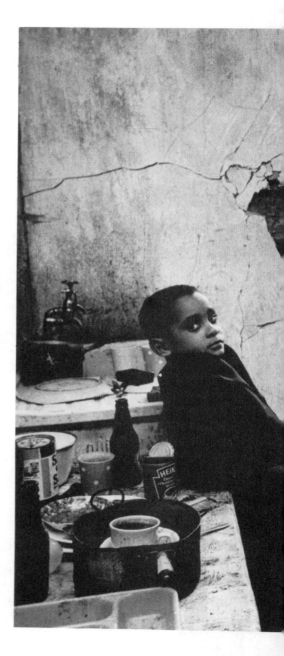

Don McCullin

T he Americans call photography an art. They have galleries, institutions, exhibitions. But what I'm doing is not art. How can I call it that? I'm stuck with a load of pictures of humanity —suffering, dying, bleeding. These pictures come from a witness. I've seen prisoners captured, stripped naked and blindfolded, trembling at the knees before someone gives the order to fire. I've seen men dragged out of cells in Saigon at dawn to a market square before throngs of people, and a fire engine standing by to hose away the blood after the execution. I can't detach the image my camera produces from the images in my mind. I can't separate my photographs from their subjects. How can I talk of these photographs as art objects? These are real people. I have inhaled their suffering.

Don McCullin

All my photography is confrontation. I did not happen to come across this man with his wife in his arms. I was not in their country by chance. I took this shot because I went there: to stick it up the nose of the person looking at this picture who has more of everything than the woman who was dying. I went to Bangladesh and was so humiliated and horrified and sickened by what I saw that I just kept shooting. I saw people dying in the mud, and parents crying over their dead children. I was so moved and so heartbroken that I couldn't possibly stop. Nobody, I thought, is going to get a free ride out of me. They're going to look at these people suffering.

This photograph is like a lot of others I take. I'm trying to shoot them so that you can't escape looking: they force themselves on you. If anything, I'm trying to photograph in the way that Goya painted or did his war sketches. I'm trying to bring in the surroundings, focussed by this terrible subject. I'm hoping to show the circumstances, the cause, the source, so that there's a story to the photograph. I sometimes think of pictures as 'pictures' in the old sense: as icons, with the impact of a religious image or a ritual tragedy. In this photograph, the man is rushing off to hospital with his wife, who has advanced cholera. It's hard to get away from it. It tells you too much. I'd like to think that it sticks in your mind the way an icon does, that it's remembered the way an icon is remembered.

180

Once, just before I got to Delhi railway station, I came across a large gathering of refugees from Tibet. They were lost and confused and, from an interpreter, I learned that they were also very hungry and tired. I asked if they'd had breakfast and he said no, so I bought some food for the whole lot of them. And then I asked this man if I could take a picture of him and his child.

He's a beautiful, dignified human being. He's handsome, prominent and proud, and happens to be on the wrong side of the ideological fence. He has that wonderful hat, and, with the child and the background, he seems to me to be almost Biblical. Again, one of those icons of the dispossessed.

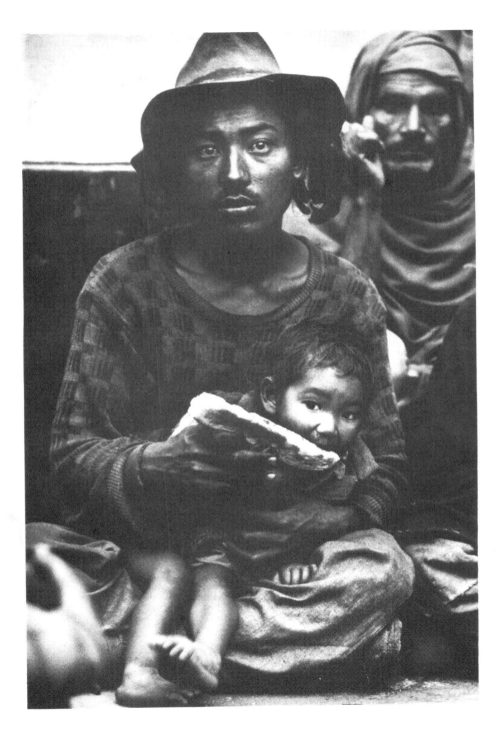

Don McCullin

The last time I went to Vietnam, I didn't see any of it. I had received a telegram—just a week after getting out of Phnom Penh before it fell—saying 'proceed to Saigon'. When I got to the airport, John Pilger asked if I'd go through passport control without him: he thought I was on some kind of blacklist. I was indeed immediately surrounded by 'white mice' (the name by which Vietnamese police were known, because of their white uniform, their speed and their diminutive stature). They were all over me and, after taking away my passport, said, 'You no come Vietnam, you no come here, you bad man.' I learned later that it was because of the photograph I'd taken showing the fall of Dang Hai, with the Vietnamese soldiers in panic, throwing away their shoes and rifles. Imagine—the Vietnamese government, one of the blackest régimes ever to be called a democracy, creating a blacklist. But it doesn't seem to make any difference who's in power. This year I applied for a visa to return to Vietnam, but the new government doesn't trust me either.

I've run into the same trouble throughout Africa too. When I arrived in Idi Amin's Uganda, I was arrested, incarcerated in the place where they used to kill prisoners with sledge hammers, and finally deported. And in Tel Aviv airport, I was stripped naked and arrested on the charge of possessing drugs. I have never taken drugs. Nor have I ever committed a crime.

I seem to be on everyone's blacklist. Even here. I did everything I could to get to the Falklands: I'd been at everyone else's bloody war, why shouldn't I be at this one? There was no one more qualified—and no one, therefore, that the government less wanted to see. After I contacted the Ministry of Defence, I was told that I would be given priority in getting on one of the boats. But I never heard from them again. The Imperial War Museum tried to send me, but they were stopped just when I thought I had a place secured. I even sent telexes to junior ministers. It was only later that I learned from a friend at the Ministry of Defence that my name had been spotted on the list of prospective journalists and had been immediately struck off.

A black American Marine just outside the gateway to the City of Hué. The Tet offensive. He looks just like an Olympic athlete, except that he's throwing not a javelin but a grenade. Within seconds of this photograph, a sniper blew off his hand. He returned with something that looked like a cauliflower. His whole hand had become a stump. I was there at the gateway for several days. The snipers kept killing whoever appeared there. Every day a new marine got killed. Every day a new guy appeared as a replacement.

Don McCullin

I was in Biafra and told a doctor there that I felt ill. He made me lie down for a couple of days and eventually looked in on me. I asked him to do me a favour. I'd seen a very sick boy and I wanted the doctor to come and look at him. When he came across the boy, the doctor said, "But this boy is mental." I said that that had nothing to do with it. He was starving, he was nearly dead. "That's true," the doctor said, "but he's not right in the head." I asked him again to look at the boy, but the doctor said there was nothing to be done and left. The boy was covered with tubercular sores and was holding up his trousers because they were falling down. People behind him were laughing at him.

When I began as a photographer, I believed that my work would suffer if I allowed it to become political. My work has turned out to be nothing but political. In fact, it's got to the point now where it is seen as being so political that I have to fight merely to take my pictures.

But what are my politics? I certainly take the side of the under-privileged. I could never say I was politically neutral. But whether I'm of the Right or the Left—I can't say. I feel I'm trapped by my background, my inability to retain facts, and my utter bewilderment when faced by political theory: I'm so defeated by it I don't even vote. I've tried, instead, to be a witness, an independent spectator, with the result that I can't get beyond the facts of what I've seen. I've experienced too much suffering. I feel, in my guts, at one with the victims. And I find there's integrity in that stance.

Photographers are just vehicles. They're taxis. You use a taxi to get you where you want to go. You use a photographer to show you something you want to see. I'm no different; except that I was showing people things they did *not* want to see.

I started thinking about the people I was taking the pictures for. I came to believe that, in a small way, I was creating a public, an awareness, and, at the same time, I was being created by it. I discovered that I had something to convey, something urgent that I had to get across. Why was it impossible for someone to contemplate the suffering of a man in Bangladesh? There *are* other things to worry about besides the agony of deciding what car to buy next or where to take a holiday. Isn't that what conscience is? A man is languishing in jail, and has been there for five years. And then I'm told, "Who gives a shit? You have no right to tell us about it."

I was astonished by people's anger. But why should I have to defend myself? Was I responsible for the deaths of the people I photographed? Did I injure them, torture them, starve them? Why am I the one being put on trial? I was just a taxi. I arrived where it was happening. And if I hadn't, someone else would have. And if someone else hadn't, the public would have remained in comfortable ignorance of what was taking place.

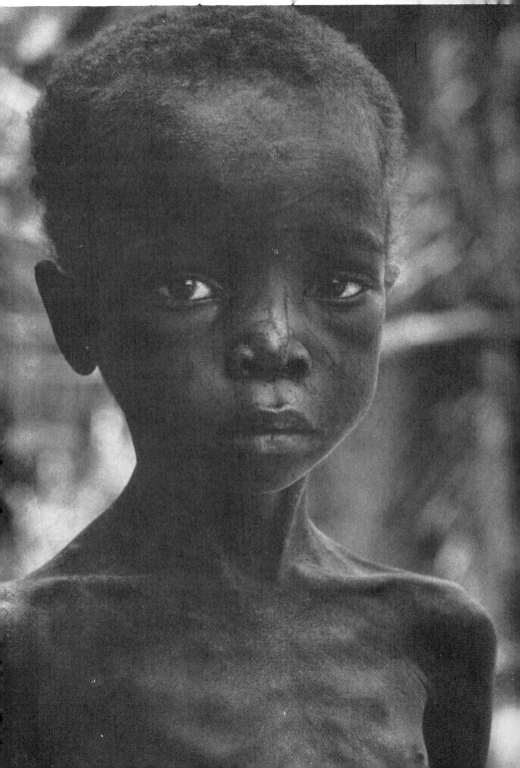

T hree blind women walking
past a group of guerrillas
during the last days of the
Smith régime in Rhodesia.

Don McCullin

I haven't given up war photography. I'm not only doing portraits and landscapes now. I'm just trying to sort myself out. I feel as though I'm an old Hollywood movie star who has to grow just a little older before he can discover his new role. I want to find out how I ought to be spending the next twenty-five years or so of my life.

I still work for the *Sunday Times,* but they don't use me. I stand around in the office, and don't know why I'm there. The paper has completely changed: it's not a newspaper, it's a consumer magazine, really no different from a mail-order catalogue. And what do I do, model safari suits? Cover some Women's Institute reception? Someone in the office said recently that I should think up new approaches to my work: "You ought to learn how to use strobe lighting, because we don't want to use any more of those photos of…" People are starting to reject, or at least turn their backs on, my sort. They seem happy with the way the press is developing. They certainly don't need me to show them nasty pictures. I should wise up: what is the point of killing yourself for a newspaper proprietor who wouldn't bat an eyelid on hearing you'd died?

I used to pride myself on being able to identify the sounds of different ammunition. I had to know who was throwing what and from what direction it was coming. But now I don't want to have to duck and weave and lie on my stomach just to take pictures. I want to be able to take them standing up. I'm not going to get butchered in a shop doorway in Beirut by some hysterical gunman. I can't face up to hotel rooms on my own, or taped music or a tannoy system announcing my flight. I want to drink a lot: it's a way of escaping.

I wonder if I've lost a certain kind of anger, if perhaps I'm just not angry any more? Perhaps I'm coming to terms, in a new way, with the business of being human.'

Don McCullin

Reinaldo Arenas
A Poet in Cuba

Reinaldo Arenas

In September 1958, I tried to join Fidel Castro's guerrillas. I was fourteen, the 'love child' of a family of poor peasants. But I was not really all that different from those around me: I knew what poverty meant, what real hunger was like, and I had experienced injustice and corruption at first-hand: in fact, just before I left, I came across a number of young men from the quarter where we lived: they had been strung up from the trees, lynched by Fulgencio Batista's henchmen because of their supposed connections with the 26th of July Movement, led by Castro from the Sierra Maestra. That was where I wanted to be; I had nothing to lose.

But the rebels didn't take me. They didn't take me in part because of my age, but mostly because I did not carry a weapon—a rifle or a machine-gun. That was what the guerrillas needed; they had more than enough men. I was in a difficult position: I could not go back home, because everyone now knew, thanks to my relatives' evident concern for my well-being, that I was a 'no-good rebel'. So I wandered the hills. From time to time, I spent a few weeks at the house of an aunt and uncle: they were also peasants and happy to shelter me as long as I did the jobs they hated.

With the fall of Batista's government—brought about more by panic and rumour than by confrontations with the guerrillas—I could come out of the hills, but I couldn't return either to the house where I grew up or to the village. I felt too much loathing. But things were going to be different now. There had been a revolution. I could escape the confines of poverty and the family.

And, at first, escape seemed possible. I got a scholarship from the Revolutionary Government to study agricultural economics. I was a young Communist ('young rebels', we called ourselves then), and in the following year I began a newly-established course on agrarian planning at the University of Havana. I was living in the capital's most luxurious hotel, the Havana Hilton no less, converted overnight into the Free Havana. My prospects—like those of many intelligent young people—seemed bright and full of potential. I was busy, reading constantly, and immersed in the complete works of Marx and Lenin (an official part of the course). I didn't have the time, the opportunity, or the capacity—the desire even—to understand that I was also witnessing the signs that a totalitarian state was in embryo. We had, after all, just overthrown a dictatorship. I had other concerns—from the poetic to the erotic. I was experiencing other revolutions.

But three years later, I was no longer a student at the university: I had been expelled, having shown that I had all the marks of a dubious morality and a dubious ideology. My friends began to disappear: they were said to be deviants—sexual deviants or political ones; it didn't much matter. They were interned in 'rehabilitation camps', where they were forced to work twelve hours a day and were not allowed beyond the guarded fence. In short, they were in concentration camps.

Some years before, a law had been passed: it made military service compulsory and prohibited anyone of military age (between fifteen and twenty-eight) from leaving the country. For me, military service would certainly have meant the 'rehabilitation camps'. And so, again, I did what I could to avoid the law and to survive. I moved house eleven times. I changed jobs as many times again. I was trying to disappear, to be invisible—to be as inconspicuous as possible. The police were already engaged—and very successfully too—in the 'round-up of anti-social elements'. Later on, there were other laws: one which prohibited people from moving house or changing jobs; and another, establishing the Census of Population and Housing as well as the National Identification Board, under which every Cuban was issued with an identity-card. On it was your number, your photo, and virtually your entire life history. It was an offence not to show your card at every one of the innumerable police checks. Being invisible became impossible.

I had not yet been to prison, and, intent on not being repressed, had written two novels, *Celestino antes del alba* (*Celestino, before Dawn*) and *El mundo alucinante* (*The Hallucinating World*). Both were smuggled out of Cuba and published in France, an act which later would also be considered a crime, if done without the consent of the State. Other laws and regulations followed: there were ration books; there was the National Revolutionary Militia which meant that we had to do night-guard duty after a full day's work—a day sometimes as long as twelve hours; there was the 'voluntary day of productive work', which involved spending weekends working on a State plantation in the country; and, finally, there was the

Committee for the Defence of the Revolution set up on every block of the city to watch every move and every aspect of our social, sexual and family life. The Defence of the Revolution also required us to do night-guard duty as well; we were also expected to pay monthly dues to support it.

In 1968, the year the Russians invaded Czechoslovakia, Fidel Castro gave a speech, in which he not only endorsed the invasion, but asked—and in the course of his speech, authorized—that, in similar circumstances, the Soviet Union should invade Cuba: it was a duty.

Virtually overnight, we were banned from the beaches, which were converted (Soviet-style) into Workers' Social Circles where, in order to bathe or just look at the sea and the horizon, we had to present our membership cards bearing the seal of our trade union and a stamp proving we had paid our monthly dues. All this merely to gain entry to a beach—where we would meet only the embittered faces of our comrades and enemies from work and those of the police, watching us. And, invariably, I suppose, the best beaches— the Miramar Yacht Club, the Comodoro, El Salado and the area of the Varadero known as the 'Dupont Development' (previously in the hands of the bourgeoisie)—were taken by the secret police, army officers, and Russian 'technicians'. We, the liberated workers, had a coastline of rocks. It must be remembered—if I seem to dwell on this—that Cuba is long and narrow and, most important, an island: life gains its meaning, its amplitude and brilliance, by the sea. To deny Cubans the sea is to deny them their past, their legends, their solace—the sense of the infinite.

And then, in 1971, eleven years after the Revolution, we lost even more: our artistic freedom. And it began with the Padilla case.

On 20 March 1971, the poet Heberto Padilla and his wife Belkis Cuza Malé were arrested and taken to one of the State Security prison cells. The place was notorious throughout Cuba for its horrors—each cell was about two metres square, soundproofed, with one bare lightbulb and a small hatch in an iron door at which the guard occasionally appeared. Padilla was sent there because Castro wanted a retraction: his work, critical of the State, was not only being published abroad but was attracting the admiration of young Cuban writers. Castro wanted Padilla humiliated, and he resorted to a method known for its effectiveness: torture. For thirty-seven days, Padilla was threatened with life imprisonment and with death. He was interned in a lunatic asylum, he was beaten, and he was tortured constantly. After thirty-seven days, Castro got what he wanted: a retraction and a repudiation of Padilla's closest friends. Including Lezama Lima—who had awarded Padilla the national poetry prize, for *Fuera del juego* (*Out of Play*) and Belkis Cuza Malé, Padilla's wife.

After the Padilla affair, the writer was seen in a different way: he was a worker—no different from any other—because 'he writes with his hands.' Magic realism, for instance, was now seen as a 'decrepit and picturesque vision fast being overtaken and left behind by the new social, scientific and revolutionary awareness.' What was most sinister about this new awareness—this 'superstalinization'—was the fine detail of its realization. The least significant details of our private lives swelled enormous dossiers. And, in the case of writers like Lezama Lima and Virgilio Peñera, after-dinner conversations were meticulously tape-recorded by the secret police. We had lost our freedom to write and to publish; now we lost the freedom to think out loud or have a private conversation with a friend. Above all, we lost—and Padilla was only the scapegoat—our dignity.

Cuban intellectuals were mocked. They were dismissed. They were asked to come face to face with police terror. They were, absolutely and justifiably, afraid. And they had only a few choices available to them: self-betrayal, cynicism, prison or suicide—exile was not a choice. Some committed suicide, among them the poet Marta Vignier and the novelist José Hernández. Some—like Nicolás Guillén, Roberto Fernández Retamar, Lisandro Otero and many others—betrayed themselves and became high-ranking servants of the State and thus of its system of repression. Some, less well-known, took a heroic stance and lost their lives—or a great part of their lives—in prison: Jorge Valls, Ángel Cuadra and Armando Valladares. The rest of them chose cynicism: the cynicism of silence, the cynicism of cowardice, the cynicism of waiting through a pregnant pause that could (and in some cases did) last a lifetime.

You survived as best you could: accepting, pretending to accept, applauding or simply not resisting the resolutions that condemned us as writers: condemned us to being invisible. Secretly, though, we persisted. We persisted in writing, and, at the risk of going to prison, we sometimes smuggled our writings out of the island. For there is a golden rule common to all writers under Communist regimes: a manuscript which has not yet crossed the frontier is a manuscript still to be written.

Lezama Lima continued to be paid his modest civil servant's salary as long as he did not open his mouth and, like Padilla and Virgilio Piñera, was prohibited from publishing and, as far as possible, from writing. I, like many others, had to take part in book-signings at the Cuban Writers' and Artists' Union, but I was not allowed to go over the proofs of the magazine of which I was supposedly editor. Clearly, my hands were contaminated and could have stained these texts written by Lieutenant Luis Pavón and José Antonio Portuondo, the Plekhanov and Zhdanov of Cuban Stalinism. How right they were to say that the 'intellectual works with his hands'.

A small group of friends still met secretly for readings and discussions, and managed to accumulate quite a number of unpublished texts. We even put together a magazine, *Ah, la marea* (*Ah, the tide!*) of which we produced six typewritten copies. We were our own public.

Virgilio Piñera, knowing he was a condemned man, dedicated his time to writing, rewriting and revising everything, even his previously published works. He worked like someone—and so it proved to be—drawing up his last testament. A testament which, naturally, found its way straight to Castro's insatiable police. José Lezama Lima found consolation in work as well. Every time we met, he cited the example of Racine who, while writing a defence of the Sun King and editing the *History of France*, was also, in the shadows, writing *The Secret History of Jansenism*. Perhaps in our modest way, we were a little like Racine, and, in admiring and pitying him, we pitied ourselves. Lezama also often quoted Antonio Pérez: 'Only the strongest stomachs can digest poison.' Lezama and Virgilio both had strong stomachs and swallowed a lot of poison— all that they could—but that poison finally destroyed them. Their work was cut short and their early writings have been altered and distorted. Now both these persecuted authors, censored and mutilated by the system, are seen as its passionate defenders. In this, perfect totalitarian systems have always been in the vanguard: they modify not only the past and the future, but they also abolish the present.

I knew that I could survive only by writing. I finished several books of poems, a volume of short stories, two novels, including *Otra vez el mar* (*Once more the Sea*) a work which, having been put in the hands of my then best friend, Señor Aurelio Cortés, was delivered immediately into those of the police, and so had to be rewritten several times.* I was lucky enough to be able to smuggle nearly all these manuscripts out of Cuba.

By 1974, I had published several books abroad that had been banned in Cuba. And with the introduction of two new laws—one directed against 'Delinquency and Ideological Diversionism' and the other meant to protect 'Family, Youth and the National Patrimony'—I, like others, was finally ready for prison. For years, I had been under the close watch of the State secret police and the secret police I lived with—my relatives. My room was searched, I was pursued, beaten up and humiliated in every sense of the word. And, finally, I was arrested. I was kept in a temporary cell before being sent to a top security prison—*El Morro*—but I managed to escape. For forty-five days I was free. I was thirty years old, and had never experienced a freedom of this sort—the ephemeral freedom of a fugitive. I composed and sent a document to France addressed to the UN, to UNESCO, and to the International Red Cross, summarizing some of my vicissitudes and humiliations. I was then recaptured, and taken to the notorious (because so horrific) State Security Prison. Its cells were in a former Jesuit monastery, the windows of which had been bricked up.

---

*Parts of this book were translated and published under the title 'Coming down from the Mountains' in *Granta* 13: 'After the Revolution'.

Reinaldo Arenas

I have never been a hero—I am not the stuff of which they are made: I signed anything they put in front of me. Whether I signed or refused to sign the papers—documents and documents that amounted to an exhaustive *mea culpa*, a passionate repentance of my whole life—was a matter of indifference to my conscience. How could I take them seriously? Could anyone reading the statement I had sent to Paris really believe that a fortnight later, writing from a State Security prison cell, I could declare that I was enchanted with my life in Cuba? Was that pantomime the reality or was there another, more profound reality, to which I could perhaps, if I lived, bear witness one day? By taking the whole drama seriously didn't I run the risk of making it seem important and even relevant? Or are all these questions merely the justifications of a coward?

For many years now life in Cuba has operated on at least two levels. There is the official one, a long-running performance of assemblies, voluntary work, political circles, unending speeches, applause, parades and the reading of the State newspapers—the only ones published. Then there is real life: our secret resentments, our dreams, our longing for revenge, our grudges, our loves, our rages. To sign a recantation before a torturer—who will, if we refuse, destroy us—is the most terrible weapon we have. I do not even think I need historical corroboration. In the document sent to the outside world I had in any event already stated, with the foresight totalitarian systems engender, that what I wrote was the truth even if later I might be forced to deny it. Others have had and will have more heroic courage than mine. But no divinity ever visited me in my cell, only the guard on duty with his hackneyed, sinister jibes and questions. I was, you see, a confessed homosexual in a society structured around an overdeveloped supermachismo that was wholeheartedly supported by the State's discriminatory laws. I was fair game for abuse. And to save myself I had to rely on my limited resources of guile. I was crafty and contriving and cynical, and found myself therefore once more in the open prison two years later, and, after four years, out of the open prison which the island has become.

During that time I passed from being a non-person to being a
non-writer. I could not live; I survived. I kept a photo of myself as
a youth. I framed it, placed it in the middle of the room, and every
now and then I would put some flowers before it, as one does for the
dead. This impressed my visitors, most of whom were policemen
often disguised as criminals, who viewed my intellectual and
physical death with great enthusiasm. But secretly I knew that
somewhere someone was waiting for me: the things most dear to
me, the pages I had written clandestinely, were safe. Of course, a
lieutenant (the one looking after my case) visited me nearly every
week. To this person, who obviously rejoiced in being a member of
the Holy Castro Inquisition, I had to tell my whole life story, inform
him of every step taken, every action. So as to avoid getting my
friends in trouble, I put a notice on my door: 'Visits are appreciated
but not received.' If I evaded or failed to mention anything
(however insignificant) the officious lieutenant always picked me up
on it and made a great fuss: the tap-tap of a typewriter was an enemy
to be silenced; a letter sent abroad was a proof of infidelity; the
praising of a Western writer was a betrayal.

In May 1980, when I at last found myself on a boat, leaving the
loved and hated shores of my island, taking with me only the clothes
I was wearing, I knew that the monumental charade I had sustained
for more than twenty years had finally brought its reward: I was
going to a place where I could shout. And before making my final
exit I closed with an act worthy, I think, of a comic opera. Just as we
were leaving, we had to sign a confession (yet another) in which we
declared that we were truly immoral people, unworthy of living in
an 'enlightened' society. I wrote a frenzied and pathetic diatribe
against myself, addressing the whole lament to none other than
'Comrade' Fidel Castro. The immigration official and the State
Security agent smiled at me in satisfaction.

Translated from the Spanish by Margaret Jull Costa

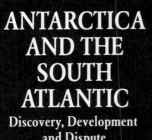

For the Others

CHRISTIAN MCEWEN
THE BUSINESS OF
MOURNING

One of us is missing.
One or maybe two.
I count us on the fingers of one hand.

I was the eldest of six children. Please God, bless Mama and Papa and Katie and James and Helena and John and Isabella and me. It was important to me that we were six. It was important to all of us. 'How many children are there in *your* family?' We were competitive about it, slightly superior.

Somebody is missing.
Which of us is gone?

James is gone, and Katie. James shot himself in June, and in September Kate was drowned.

The news that someone is dead is a tiny tragedy all of its own. It is devastating when you hear it, and it stays potent for a long time afterwards. I do not cry about my father any more, but if I want to miss him (and I sometimes do) I tell myself he's dead in the words my mother used, three and a half years ago.
'Darling, Papa has died—'
In the same way I tell myself the news of James and Katie.
'It's not good—James has killed himself.'
'Another horrible tragedy. Your mother's on the phone.'
For a single moment I believe they're dead. Then my attention skitters back to normal. There are six of us, and I'm the eldest. It is in the nature of things that I should die first. Kate is twenty-five. James is twenty-two. I am twenty-seven and there is nothing to worry about.

When my father died, Kate looked for him all over the house. She went into his study calling for him, 'Papa—' He had a heart attack, and died at fifty-three. Kate was twenty-five. James was twenty-two.

It is the end of the third week in June, and I have just arrived back from the States, where I've been living for the past four years. James's funeral is the day after tomorrow, and James is nowhere to be found.

I want to look for him, but I don't know where to start. He was wild this year, crazy, maverick, out of control. Everybody tells me so. He has painted a gigantic mural on the kitchen wall. There are bullet holes through the windows of the flat.

Two and a half months later, Kate is drowned. I do not look for her. Her body is in Africa, and I am on the phone to British Airways. We talk, flatly, about the carriage of human remains.

When a grownup dies, a grandmother or a grandfather, a parent even, or a friend, it is a single death, a relatively simple thing. When a child dies, or someone you have known as a child, it's not so simple. I knew James and Kate for all their lives. I am who I am, in part because they were who they were. For twenty years we divided the world between us. I don't know how to talk about this. I feel I've lost so many people, and some of them are me.

The day before Kate's funeral, my cousin Sam gives me a massage. I am very frightened. I drive with Mama to the hospital to see the body.

After Mama had gone, I knelt down beside the coffin and looked at Katie for a long time. The bruising shone dull grey across her nose, like the smudge of a BB pencil. There was another, blacker bruise on the left side of her face, and a dark mark on her left cheek, and also on her chin. I touched her all over and I talked to her a little, very softly. Her skin still had that Katie softness, very very cold—

James killed himself. There is no doubt about that. He locked himself in John's bedroom and he lay down on the bed. He wedged the shotgun between his legs, reached down with his long arms, and pulled the trigger.

And Katie? Katie drowned. But no one knows the circumstances of her death. She disappeared early one Thursday morning, and was found next day by the police, washed up above the high-tide mark, ten minutes from the house where she'd been staying. What did she do the day before she died? The Kenyan authorities do not care to investigate.

Christian McEwen

For a while there are rumours that she'd been attacked, that she'd taken an overdose, that she too had committed suicide.

For a while there are a hundred stories on the go.

It is June, it is July, it is August and September. Isabella has twelve packets of photographs. We look at them for James, and then we look at them for Katie: blurred faces, fat orange wallets. We look at pictures and we go on talking.

James on heroin, James manic, James stampeding around London and New York, doing deals and picking people up. James denouncing Mama to the papers. I thought I knew those stories. I thought I knew them all. But everyone I talk to has a different version.

James was a junkie. He needed to get settled. If he'd only had a girlfriend. If Papa were alive.

I ask more questions and I listen to more answers. If I listen long enough will I believe he's dead?

I take James's diary and I read it from cover to cover. He was a good writer, better than any of us, and I hear him teasing as I turn the pages. I sit on the tops of buses and I try to make space for him inside my head: to become a little of what he was—funny, loving, generous. The desperation and the gossip drop away. Then Kate is dead, and everything begins again.

James and I were in the States together. We wrote letters to each other, often. I loved him as a grownup friend, not simply as a brother. With Katie, things are different. I knew her best when we were in our teens. Since then, we've gone our separate ways. She was the beautiful one, I was the tomboy. She was the artist, I was the academic. Without quite realizing it, we were defined in opposition to each other. Now she is dead, and I don't know who she was, or how to mourn.

I visit Katie's lovers and her friends. I hear their stories too. Kate and housing crises, Kate and painting, Kate and problems with her business deals. Sometimes I think there are no happy stories. James

212

and Kate: two miserable people. Then I meet other friends, hear different stories, and they're alive again. They're both alive and well.

When I went with Mama to the hospital to see Kate's body, I thought I'd learn something. Whatever happened after that, I'd know that she was dead. But all I did was add a dead face to the crowd of living ones: Katie faces in the photographs and drawings, Katie faces from this summer, and all through our growing up.

After Katie dies I dream I am to blame. I don't know how exactly, but I feel very uneasy. Then a parcel arrives from Papa: lots and lots of sheets of paper, a long long letter—and I know it isn't my fault after all.

Faces, faces, and a shaky sense of guilt. Everybody had it, fumbling, as if guilt were somehow a relief, easier to admit to than those blazing absences. So many conversations started with, 'If only—'. Running through them was an almost messianic regret: 'I should have saved them—'

It is difficult to acknowledge that people have their own lives, their own deaths, their own integrity. You cannot save them. After James died Katie had a dream in which she said to him, in the words we all were thinking, 'I just wish you hadn't done it—'

James looked over at her, teasing, scornful, utterly successful. 'I *know* you do,' he said.

We wished all summer that James hadn't done it. We wished all autumn that Kate hadn't drowned. At the same time we fought to understand that they were dead, to school ourselves to that, to know it well.

'It's not good, James has killed himself—'

'Another horrible tragedy—'

I write to everyone I know, as though by that repeated telling I could tell myself, thoroughly once and for all. But James and Kate come back again, they will not go away. I see them in the pub and on the street. They're not here at this moment, not right now. But they'll be in. James is visiting some friends of his, and Kate, she's working, over at the flat.

You try to tell yourself, 'They won't come back,' and still, you cannot know it. Your body knows it, in its tears and restlessness, its absolute exhaustion. The rest of you takes time to understand. You do the washing up, you go on coping. You drink and talk. You cry, sometimes you scream.

Only much later does all this come into focus: as a time without perspective, a strange lost time without a future. I remember being genuinely surprised when someone asked me to a party. I had forgotten there would ever be parties again.

Friends help, and so do all those letters of condolence. Friends know about ordinary life. They know about parties. They can remind you that the pain won't last forever, that now *is* extraordinary, and things will change.

In the meantime, there is mourning, which is a complicated business. From the outside it looks simple—you're in pain, you miss someone, you cry. But mourning isn't simple in that way. Whatever you do or feel, whether you go to pieces or you cope, you always have the sense that you're pretending. If you are brave, then really you are showing off. If you scream, it means you want attention.

I thought about all this, and wondered why. In part it is to do with other people, shifting expectations. You 'ought' to be brave. You 'ought' to express your feelings. The rules are contradictory. But mourning is complicated, even without pressure from outside. Sometimes you can't do it, even if you want to. Sometimes you do it intolerably well, and are overwhelmed with feelings—fear and anger, jealousy and hate, and a whole range of things which hardly seem to qualify as feelings—muddle, numbness, even boredom.

But even at its worst, no grief is constant. It does let up sometimes, and when it does, there can be moments of extraordinary clarity, of real happiness.

In the week between Kate's death and her funeral, some friends of hers came up to stay in Scotland. We played football, we danced, we went for walks and climbed trees. We picked mushrooms and made a huge cauldron of mushroom soup. These were distractions, it is true. But they were also celebrations, tributes to the ordinary, acknowledgements of the spaces that exist: the gaps inside the pain.

From the outside, James's death and Kate's are labelled 'tragic'. We, the family, the survivors, are to be pitied.

I do not want that pity, or that version of events. I do not want a story of James's life which brings him 'inevitably' to suicide, a story which starts from Katie's drowning and works backwards into fate. 'She was too talented, too beautiful to live. She was a Botticelli angel, born for Paradise—'

Kate was not an angel. She was a human being like the rest of us. She drowned. It was an accident. The currents pulled her down.

All summer I fight to keep things separate and difficult, to resist the 'therefores' and 'of courses'.

James killed himself. That was a choice he made. He might have made other choices. Yes, he might.

Kate has been dead for nearly two months, James for just over four. It is Halloween, it is Guy Fawkes Day, and the intolerable present has heaved itself back into place. The summer is over, that strange hot summer. It has come to an end. I still cower against the future and its unknown blows, but for the moment it is nice to be inside, to be sitting at a desk again, protected, somehow, by the winter and the cold.

Meanwhile the summer's legacy is still not sorted out. There are death duties to pay because of James. There are old debts, old difficulties that Katie left. This month my mother is moving house, leaving the upstairs bedroom where James shot himself. She has already collected and distributed his things. At some point in the future she will drive down south for Katie's.

In my head are pictures of them: James and Katie. One dead face and many living ones. They are little children and I look down on the curly tops of their heads. They are great big people far taller than I am. I stare at them, and up beyond them into the sky, where in a dream I saw them both, their faces made of clouds.

They have left me their letters and a few bits of clothes. They have left me their friends, an enormous number. And they have left me alone, as they've left each of us alone. I look up, and I look down. There is a gap below me, where they used to be.

JAROSLAV SEIFERT
SKATING WITH
LENIN

Jaroslav Seifert

We skated with Lenin

When Lenin came to Prague in 1912 he stayed in the Zizkov Quarter: first at the Hotel Myska and then at the Golden Wheel Inn. He must have had a rotten view from his windows, because the inn overlooks the monstrous Zizkov gasworks. I remember them well. Our flat was in the same block as the Golden Wheel, whose landlord was a family friend, maybe even a distant relative. I used to go there for our beer, and he always poured generous measures.

According to the memoirs of Lenin's friend Onufriyev, Lenin liked to go skating at a nearby rink, especially on winter evenings. In those days there was only one skating-rink in our neighbourhood: the one by the Czechia football ground a few streets past the present-day Prague Central Station. And directly opposite was the Villa Teresa, which was to become the first Soviet Embassy.

This was also the skating-rink that I and my friends used to go to. We, too, went mainly in the evenings—afternoons were spent at school or over homework.

The rink even had music. Sometimes from a hoarse gramophone, sometimes from a barrel organ. Tea could be bought in the changing rooms. We liked skating in a 'snake'. Several boys would link arms, and then the ones in front pulled, knees slightly bent, while the ones in the back, squatting, would be dragged along. The snake weaved its way across the rink, bumping into prim girls dancing in elegant pairs. The girls, shrieking, would leap for safety into the heaps of snow along the edge of the rink. Which was just what we wanted.

In the winter of 1912 a small man in a Persian lamb-skin hat was also skating there. Little did he know that one day his bust would grace the entrance hall of the villa opposite, and would stare across his old skating-rink on to a Prague wreathed in dirty fumes from the railway station. And that is how Dr Alexander—or Dr Maier, which is what Lenin was called when he was in Prague—entered our lives.

Some ten years later we used to meet by his bust at the Villa Teresa, greeted by dear old Antonov-Ovseenko in his Red Army uniform.

It did happen, didn't it? Tell me, my friends from the streets of Zizkov, we did spend most of our winter evenings at the Czechia skating-rink, didn't we? Come on, say something!

But I forget. All this was over sixty years ago. Far too long ago. And they may not be among the living.

The Birth of a Poet

I have a little granddaughter. I love her, naturally enough. She loves drawing. At first she was happy with an ordinary pencil. Then her mother discovered that drawing was her favourite occupation and bought her coloured chalks and crayons. Lots of them! So now she carries these tools in a shoe box, and every now and then I try to sharpen them all. But with little success.

'Grandpa, draw me a princess!'

Reluctantly I pick up a yellow crayon and start with a golden crown. I make the dots of an ellipse for the teeth, like the open jaws of a shark. She immediately snatches the pencil away.

'Not like that! You've got to start with the head!'

Her little fingers move over the paper and a moment later a startled princess in a pink dress loaded with coloured lace is staring at us.

'Draw me an elephant!'

Clumsily I draw a monstrous heap of meat on four pillars, decorated in front by a sort of fire-hose and in the back by a happy pig's tail. This too fails to please. A moment later there is another elephant on the paper, delightful and inimitable in its naivety.

An aunt of hers is worried that she might want to become a painter. A disaster, I agree. But I am sure that it will not happen. I too kept covering pieces of paper in drawings when I was a boy. When my parents gave me a painter's palette and a double-ended brush I was so happy that I can still remember the moment vividly. And the night I spent with the palette under my pillow was the happiest night of my childhood. I cannot remember a more beautiful present. Sometimes it takes so little to make people happy. So why is there so little happiness in life?

I spent hours drawing and painting. And then I forgot my passion.

When I went into the first form of my *gymnasium*, the school had just opened a new building in Libusin Street. The first sight of the art room took my breath away. It was a beautiful room full of wonderful light and modern drawing tables. It reminded me of the studio of a painter I knew. I was enchanted and my old passion for painting returned.

We were taught first by a relative of the painter Kremlicka and then by Professor Marek. He looked just like Maurois, both in his face and figure. He was a splendid man, charming, a superb draughtsman and a real connoisseur of art. He was always telling us something interesting. He wrote art reviews and designed book jackets and title pages.

And so I found myself trying to become an artist by attempting to master drawing. Professor Marek had an encouraging saying: any fool can learn to draw decently. Since I did not think of myself as a fool—quite the opposite, in fact—I felt there was hope for me. Once I learned to draw, things would get easier. I was sure I would make a painter.

But I did not. And this is why. When we got to the fourth or fifth form, Professor Marek told us to make up a still life from objects brought from home. My class brought apples, oranges, lemons, vases with roses, boxes, candlesticks—that sort of thing. But I felt that an empty beer bottle, a glass of beer, a slice of bread and a sausage were objects more appropriate in a work of art by a proletarian from Zizkov. I arranged my still life on the drawing table. And then I waited, like the others, for the Professor's approval.

He took one look and said sharply: 'For God's sake, Seifert, take that sausage away immediately! There's no way I'm going to allow you to paint *that!*'

It took a moment or two before I understood why. I was shocked.

And that was how I decided that I would rather write poetry.

First Love

The boy I sat next to at school told me that there was a little street in the Mala Strana Quarter called Dead Men's Street, and that in this street there were several houses of ill repute. The girls were, apparently, kept under lock and key, and their clients were supposed to be mainly Hungarian soldiers (this was during the last months of the First World War.) The ladies, he said, sat on the laps of the soldiers, who could kiss them whenever they liked.

The very next day I headed for Mala Strana Quarter. It was quite a way to walk from home. My heart was beating madly. A couple of stalls left over from the morning market stood in the Mala Strana Square. One of them belonged to a butcher. Several exquisite white lambs—with pink ribbons tied round their slit necks—hung from the hooks. For a while I stood and hesitated. Then I set out for Dead Men's Street. Somehow I knew which one it was. The street sign said Bretislavova, but I later found out that no one used that name. It was called Dead Men's Street because once upon a time it had been on the route of funeral processions to a cemetery at the top of the hill. It kept this name long after the cemetery had ceased to exist. It was short and narrow.

And not a soul to be seen. I walked up and down the street, gazing into the windows of the houses as I passed. Not a single grubby curtain moved. Early afternoon was clearly not the time for amours. Perhaps the girls were having an afternoon nap. At the top of the hill I turned back, disappointed. As I reached the bottom of the street I suddenly heard a light knock on one of the windows. I looked. The curtains opened and there was a girl with plaited dark hair that fell on her shoulders. I was rooted to the spot.

When she saw my petrified glance, she smiled and said something. I couldn't hear her. I leaped to the other side of the street, but couldn't resist looking at the window again. The girl was very pretty, or so it seemed to me, and her smile was kind. When she saw how nervous I was, she opened her blouse, suddenly, with one movement of her hand. The shock made me alternately pale and then bright red. I stared at the girl's naked breasts with horror. She was smiling at me. I staggered. After no more than two seconds, the girl buttoned her blouse up, beckoned to me and closed the curtain. I beat an inglorious retreat.

I thought that this was love. The unhappy girl from Dead Men's Street swimming in my tears. The miserable brothel should have repelled me but I was drawn by the irresistible vision of the girl. I had the feeling that the girl and I had been promised to each other. Forever. I was certain that only real love could be this strong.

But I could not summon up the courage to enter the doorway of her house. I spend days wandering about the street; I played truant from school—but I never saw the girl again. Her window was dumb and blind. In my imagination, I saw her ill, with me sitting on her bed holding her hand. But I did not have the courage to enter. I cursed my timidity, but every time I made a strong resolution to go in, my feet would carry me straight past the doorway.

The poor girl, who may not have even been beautiful, accompanied me everywhere. A silent companion of my thoughts, she was with me day and night, and her breasts, painfully mauled by greedy male hands, shone at me through the darkness. In my excited dreams, I placed coronets of flowers on her head. She would look surprised. Her skirt was creased and grubby at the hem. But none of that mattered. If it did, what sort of a poet would I be then? And what sort of lover?

Driven by desire I finally resolved to take those fatal steps. All I need is the courage to grasp the doorhandle, I said to myself, and after that it will be easy. With this I headed for the house. In the doorway I found a strange old woman. Her toothless mouth whispered something salacious about pretty young girls waiting for me inside. I extricated myself and rushed off.

I did not go back for several days. And then I swore again that I would overcome my fear and cowardice. As I turned the corner of Dead Men's Street I saw a fat rat on the pavement outside the house. It was dragging something filthy in its teeth. It saw me, stopped and looked at me with its pink eyes. And then it jumped over the stone steps, through the door and into the hallway I was about to enter. I felt sick. I turned away and never came back.

For a long time after I felt certain that I would never again see something as magical and surprising as the sight which met my eyes in a dusty window in Dead Men's Street.

What a fool I was! How often I remember that adventure with a sigh, amazed that I could have been so wrong. So very wrong!

A Slice of Salami

Some time in the early twenties, I was asked to write a poem for the May Day issue of the literary magazine *Proletkult*. It was a rush job and took no time at all. Stanislav Neumann, who had commissioned the poem, read it without a word. He just puffed rather hard at his pipe and smiled. I knew why, but I still wanted to have the poem published. It was called 'Glorious Day' and it was terrible.

In my poem—well, that's too good a word—in my 'rhymes' I settled two scores: first, with the bourgeoisie. And then I turned on members of both our Socialist parties.

In those days three separate groups marched in the May Day parade through Wenceslas Square: the Communists, the Social Democrats and the National Socialists. It was a sort of flexing of political muscle. And the next day the papers argued about the number of demonstrators in each group. They always gave two figures: one according to the police, the other to the respective parties. The figures never tallied.

My poem sang joyfully:

We want a new world, the world of our desiring,
For life is beautiful and the flowers smell lovely,
The earth breathes out a new moisture of joy,
And we, the proletariat, are longing for it.

So far so good. Of course it was all old hat, without originality or charm, but it was ideologically correct, so no one disapproved. The trouble came from my emotional conclusion:

We who have fasted our whole life
Will want to sit down one day,
Free of care, to a groaning table
And listen to music as beautiful
As the vibrations of angelic wings.

I seem to remember that life was quite tough in those days, especially in our house. After the war, my father was often without a job and our plates were seldom full. And that is what made me sing my shameless praises of the basest materialism:

We too want to eat roast pork with sauerkraut
And stuffed veal or goulash for dinner.

I ought to add—both in my defence and as an illustration of Neumann's kindness—that he understood my plight. He was a good man and I think he liked me. Whenever he saw my hungry Zizkov face, he used to take me for a meal at the Hotel Palace, a treat he could not always afford. He liked mutton, which was a taste he acquired when serving on the Southern Front, but veal was his favourite. Especially veal kidneys and *ossobuco*. We used to order one dish of *ossobuco* for the two of us, and even so we could not manage to finish it all. And with potato salad it was absolutely delicious. I was in transports of delight as I savoured each mouthful of the dishes which are now so familiar. I included them in my poem, together with the contents of the shop-window at Koloman's, the most expensive grocery in our neighbourhood:

We, too, want to drink bottles of Burgundy
And eat jellied eels,
And we feel a strong and unshakeable faith
That one day we, too, will sit down in peace
To a table with whole cheeses on it.
For our pain and poverty,
We want to be rewarded by the best which
An over-generous earth can offer:
Smoked salmon, salami, caviar . . . .

And so on. The first letters of protest came from readers in whose name I had *not* spoken: the bourgeoisie. I was young and all the fuss pleased me. So much interest in my poem! Even if it was negative. *Épater le bourgeois* was one of the slogans we used with the greatest enthusiasm.

But it was not only the bourgeoisie who got upset. I was summoned to the office of Smeral, the leader of the Communist Party and editor of the Party newspaper. He told me, kindly but firmly, that my poem was silly and harmful to the workers' cause. I knew that, but it was too late.

But that was only the start. Even Neumann was critical. It wasn't my poem which horrified him— after all, he had been the first to publish it—but the postscript to a book of my verse in which it was reprinted. The book was called *Nothing but Love* and the postscript was written by Karel Teige:

Nothing but Love does not belong to any tradition other than its own, the tradition created by today's youth and today's revolution. It moves materially through the proletarian world. From which it has acquired a new spirit and a new courage. It does not contain lies or illusions about the workers. It removes the pathetic nimbus of political martyrdom given to the proletariat to the bourgeoisie and pseudo-socialist poets. It puts the worker in his true light. It sings his most primitive physical desires, which are equal to sacred nectar and sacred ambrosia in their worldly manifestations.

Under the banner of the avant-garde, Teige allowed himself to be carried away in praise of my verse. He was to become Neumann's most implacable opponent, and Neumann tried to reason with his views in *Proletarian Art,* a chapter of which was dedicated to my poems. He said he was disappointed with my second book of verse and hoped that 'in the next book the author will hear not only the call of the followers of Circe but also that of the virgins. Judging by his "brave" poem "Glorious Day", Seifert understands the need for this, but only in the most primitive form, and is capable of developing his ideas only as an epicurean.'

Half a century later the young Moravian writer, Jiri Rambousek, returned to the affair: 'Seifert's concept of the revolution, as expressed in "Glorious Day", is very relevant. It has been interpreted as the expression of the poet's selfish desire for bourgeois pleasures. In fact it is the honest and healthy admission of youth that it cannot be satisfied with promises of future pie-in-the-sky'.

This must be the last word on that awful poem.

The French say: What a lot of fuss over an omelette! And I say: What a lot of fuss over a piece of salami!

A Night at the Coal Market

There are two landing-stages on the River Vltava that are tied to the bank with chains. The largest one is for the big steamers which dock with ceremony and dignity; the little one is for the pleasure boats which land at frequent intervals, hooting. The boats are usually very full, but the steamers have two decks with plenty of space.

It is a Sunday in June. The sun is hot and Prague is emptying quickly. Some of the side-streets are reminiscent of the emptiness of a small country town. All Prague has taken to the woods or the river.

I join one of the big steamers and stand on the deck, looking at Prague Castle and the National Theatre drift past as we approach Podoli. There used to be a landing here too. But that was long ago. Now the shore is covered by thousands of bodies blissfully basking in the sun: old and young, some good-looking and some less so. The boat passes this human nakedness and carries on to Zbraslav, leaving all those still bodies behind to enjoy the luxury of immobility.

Which brings back a terrible memory.

There is an American movie called *The Nuremberg Trials* with Spencer Tracy, Burt Lancaster, and the amazing Marlene Dietrich who, still beautiful at the age of seventy, has a role which is unsympathetic, but very truthfully played. In the movie, the public prosecutor shows film seized in German concentration camps. It is horrifying. Hundreds of stiff, densely packed corpses of prisoners tortured to death are buried by bulldozers in shallow furrows covered by soil. The bodies fall into their grave, slowly, one after another.

And there's not a tear.

At times it seems to me incredible that after such experiences—and, after all, they are quite recent—we can be standing by the bar, drinking our drinks, joking with the girls behind the counter, smiling happily. Can our lives—and there were thousands of *our* people among those corpses—have stepped over those terrible events in order to go on, as if nothing had happened? I am not talking of those who are younger. But maybe it is necessary. Maybe we could not live otherwise. So let us not remember.

But how can we forget!

Just a moment ago, there were thousands of human bodies lying in front of me. They were alive, of course, and the people were happy. They did not think of death at all. Why should they? But quietly, invisibly, the bulldozer approaches. It digs shallow graves for us, which it will cover with soil and forgetting.

Maybe this is something different. Someone may cry and sigh over us for a moment. But then too the silence.

I will not say more.

A Conversation on a Terrace in Marienbad

It was a hot September afternoon. The promenade was still quite empty, the musicians had not yet arrived. Just as I was about to get a drink, I heard the jubilant words: 'So here you are! We've been looking for you for days!'

Skrivanek, I thought. In the sanatorium yesterday, they told me that a Mr Skrivanek had been looking for me. An old friend from my school-days, they said. I could not remember him. After all, it's been nearly seventy years since I sat behind the desk of our Zizkov school.

I looked a bit surprised, but I said: 'You're Skrivanek!'

He was. He looked at his wife, pleased: 'See. I told you he'd recognize me! We used to sit next to each other at school.'

I was beginning to remember the small and hard-working boy I sat next to at school. I never had much to do with him. That was all I could remember.

They dragged me off to the terrace of their hotel. He ordered vanilla ice for his wife. When I raised my glass and she bent her head over a plate decorated with the flags of Marienbad and of the Papal State, I had a chance to take a close look at her. She looked nice. She was younger than her husband, and pretty. She obviously had an independent mind and I liked that.

To break the silence and avoid having my memory tested I asked him what he'd been doing all these years.

'I am a lawyer,' he began, and paused significantly. 'But I'd better begin at the beginning.' And he slowly went from his days in Zizkov to his move to Pilsen and then back to Prague. After graduation his father helped him get a job in a big company, where he worked in a large office. That's how he began his career.

My eyes were on the other side of the street. In front of the house opposite us was a pond with a pair of swans and some brightly

227

coloured ducks. The ducks threw themselves hungrily at any food thrown to them by passers-by. But the swans moved slowly and nonchalantly, ignoring anything that fell out of their reach.

My schoolmate continued his slow and detailed account of his life. When he was given an office on the first floor with a good view, he had obviously reached the pinnacle of his life. He became the head of a department and an office boy changed the flowers on his desk every day.

From the hotel terrace I had a good view of people's faces. All were full of the cares of the spa, mainly pleasant ones. Occasionally my glance would rest on the face of his silent wife. She was only half-listening. She knew his story well.

I too was only half-listening. But I still heard him describe his problems during the German occupation. He got demoted and his place was taken by a fat German woman in glasses. His German was good, so the Germans would occasionally ask his help. But that did not do anything for his career.

As the wind blew towards us over the roofs, it brought snatches of music from the promenade, like wisps of sugar spun from a pink cone.

After the war, things got easier. Not only for him, I thought. He got his first-floor office and his fresh flowers back—only briefly, alas.

My friend stopped to look round for the waiter. In that brief moment, I lightly stroked the hands of his wife under the table. That sort of thing was allowed in Marienbad. At first I was a little afraid of her reaction. She blushed, but then her eyes and mouth lit up with a small smile and she looked me straight in the eyes.

We had already paid and got up to go when Skrivanek turned to me and said, as if in passing: 'And what have you been doing with yourself all this time?'

'To tell the truth,' I said, 'nothing, really.'

'Nothing? There you are!' he said, quite satisfied.

Translated from the Czech by J. R. Dorrell

How to make a year last 13 months!

Buy a subscription to **The Times Literary Supplement** for a friend or relative as a gift and take advantage of our special offer of a 13-month subscription (56 issues) for the price of 12. Simply complete the coupon below and send it with your cheque or postal order made payable to Times Newspapers Limited.

If more than one subscription is required, please enter details on a separate sheet of paper. Offer applies to U.K. only. Details of overseas subscriptions are available on request from the address below.

TLS

The Times Literary Supplement

ADAM MARS-JONES
WEANING

Head a-wobble

The breast approached him, and he entered it. Drinking, he was milk.

He was lavishly suckled. He lived on his mother's left hip, facing where she faced, so that her right arm was free. He could sleep even with his head a-wobble to the rhythm of her pestle, as she prepared food. Awake, he had only to cry, he need only swim with his arms, to be lifted to suck.

She would turn her nipple upward, and lift him down on to it. He learned to draw milk up into his mouth.

As he grew up he would drink, and likewise urinate, without embarrassment. Snacks, so long as they were light and informal, were liquids: casual and seemly.

When he was two months old and skilled at the getting of milk, his mother gave him solid food. She gave him his bath, then held his head in the crook of her elbow; she filled his mouth with a thick paste of bananas and rice. She piled more on top, so he must either eat or choke. When he tried to cry, she adjusted the pile of food in his mouth, and poked food downwards into his mouth with a finger.

Eating and defecating, as he grew up, were sources of shame. He would sit sideways at table, hunched up, facing the back of his neighbour, and throw the food far back into his mouth. His hand would stay near his mouth, covering it as fully as possible.

Rhythm

During his sixth month, his mother's attention began to break up. She would focus on him for a moment, and tickle his lips with the nipple; but she looked away the moment he began to suck. She withdrew her interest, taking it back to herself, leaving nothing for him. She gave him to other women to suckle. He was no longer guaranteed by her gaze, and his feeding lost its rhythm, became untender and frantic.

She broke the sequences. She set him in his bath, and teasingly thrust her finger between his lips; in delight he bit at her hand, which she left with him while she looked in another direction. Once she made as if to leave him with another woman, saying loudly, 'I'm off home! I'll leave you here!' but by the time he was fully crying she was absorbed in another conversation.

Darkness and definition

Like all the other mothers, she was weaning herself, before she had even weaned her baby, from motherhood in its chronic form. She reclaimed the privacy which had preceded her pregnancy (though this was not her first child). She began to borrow other women's babies, holding them over his head or giving them the breast. His eyes, as he cried, took on darkness and definition.

Sometimes, if he threw a tantrum, she would hand him the borrowed baby. But just as he was going to throw his arms round her neck, she took up the baby again, or started a conversation with a neighbour.

He learned, like the other children, to grasp firmly at the other nipple while he was nursing; claiming his fragile monopoly.

Fighting cock

Of course she had always handled his penis, flicking it lightly from side to side to dry him after urination, exclaiming quite loudly, 'Handsome! Handsome!' When he started to walk he hung on to it, for balance or steering, himself.

But now she would tease it and ruffle it, pull it and even stretch it. She would grasp his penis and give it a quick tug, as if pulling it off, while in fact letting it slip through her fingers. Or she would pass her hand repeatedly upwards over the area, pressing his penis upwards with each sweep of the hand; or she would ruffle it with repeated little flicks. She treated his penis as if it was a toy, or a musical instrument, or the neck of a fighting cock that needed to be angered for a bout.

Adam Mars-Jones

If he responded, she soon lost interest; if he ignored her, the teasing became sharp and almost cruel. He learned to keep out of range, skirting her at a little distance until she installed him at the nipple.

His time at the breast was running out, but here he was still a god, however minor, to be placated. Here he could still control events by sheer appetite: he nursed so fiercely that he split the nipple. He had the satisfaction of being cuffed by his mother, of forcing her to that act of sustained attention; and he had the privilege of being denied the fugitive sips that other children were allowed, in the months that followed their exile.

Parasol

Many years later, in a field one early morning, he came across a parody of the breast he had forgotten so sheerly. It was six inches across, and a fleshy grey in colour; it had a definite nipple, with a puckered areola around it at a convincing distance. It was held up by a stalk perhaps seven inches tall. The original had nourished him unstintingly. This replica, he decided, was poisonous: so intensely poisonous that it would be unwise even to touch it.

He took off his belt and looped it round the stem at its base, then gave a quick tug. The fungus toppled, disclosing an underside of frilled velvet spokes. He used his belt as a sling to carry it home, holding it awkwardly at some distance from his body.

His parents were well informed about the fungus. It was, apparently, a parasol mushroom, sizeable but not record-breaking (they could measure a foot across the cap), harmless and indeed delicious. Why not butter it, salt it, pepper it, and put it under the grill?

He found, all the same, that he was very unwilling to be its eater; not from motives of squeamishness, but from a horror that was almost religious. Luckily it became damp and discoloured, after a few days, and could be thrown away without embarrassment.

NOTES FROM ABROAD

On the Orwell Trail
Bernard Crick

Thank you, Mr Chairman, for your kind words. I'm delighted, I really am, to be making my first visit to Grand Rapids, and, no, I can never tire of talking about Orwell.

God but am I tired and saddlesore. What a year. I just kept on talking through all that media razzmatazz and ideological bodysnatching. For mental self-protection I tried to vary my standard '*Nineteen Eighty-Four* in 1984' lecture with an occasional 'Little Eric and the Bodysnatchers' or 'The Other Orwell'; but market forces went for the standard product—thirty-one times in this country alone. And in North America: Grand Rapids, Akron, Chicago, Cleveland, Ann Arbor, Montreal, Boston, New York—all in January. Then back in the spring for Albion, Michigan; Syracuse, New York; Portland, Maine; Rosemont, Pennsylvania; Wake Forest, Guilford, Charlotte, Wilmington Beach, Greenboro, Laurinburg, Chapel Hill, Raleigh—all in North Carolina. Boulder, Denver, Fort Collins, Pueblo, Colorado Springs, Grand Junction—all in Colorado. Then the great Library of Congress Orwell experts' shoot-out in Washington and the Institute of Humanities at NYU to end, forgetting, or not forgetting, as the case may be, half a dozen High Schools along the trail.

Tired and saddlesore. Now there is only one more Orwell conference in Vancouver where I'll do 'Orwell's Socialism', a more academic version of Sheffield Town Hall back in March (the second Marx Memorial Lecture); and one more special lecture, 'Orwell and Englishness' at Bangor, North Wales. But the gods punished me only yesterday. A seven-hour train journey from Edinburgh to Cardiff was two hours late, in time to see the last of the Historical Association fading down the lane. And to think that in April I had driven myself through a blizzard across the Rockies from Colorado Springs to get to Grand Junction in time. British Rail is the pits.

I must admit to feeling a little nervous here at Albion College when I see so crowded a hall and so many of you clutching, or pleasantly sharing a text. I feel like that proverbial lion thrown into a den of Daniels.

O n the trail in the States, it could make such a difference if the audience actually had a copy of the text. *Nineteen Eighty-Four* acted as a catalyst for discussion of any high matters that were worrying people, but was it *Nineteen Eighty-Four* or 1984? Some questions revealed that it was not only dear Julia who fell asleep during Goldstein's testimony. I began to realize that even the virtuous who had read the text could be completely defeated or brain-washed by the media's preoccupation.

T he year began briskly. On 2 January, *The Times* reported: 'Mrs Margaret Thatcher in a buoyant New Year message to the Conservative Party yesterday said that George Orwell was wrong and she promised that 1984 would be a year of hope and liberty.' I checked my lecture script against my notes in a motel somewhere in North Carolina in April and found that I had been smuggling in the word 'prosperity' after 'hope'. I amended. But it was bad enough. Her speech-writers—all educated Oxford men, nary a girl—should have known a satire from a prophecy. But at least they didn't claim Orwell for themselves. In the same paper, on New Year's Eve, Neil Kinnock had already tried to restore Orwell to socialism: it *was* a satire and mainly from a *democratic Socialist* point of view (someone had schooled Neil that Orwell always used the holy phrase with a lower-case *d* and an upper-case *S*), for which Conor Cruise O'Brien gave Kinnock a drubbing on 8 January in the *Observer.* O'Brien had already had a go at me in a full-page blast-off on 18 December. In my 'otherwise admirable' biography, I had been so obtuse as to say that *Nineteen Eighty-Four* was anti-totalitarian in general, whereas it was obviously about 'something which can only be Communism, as it developed in the Soviet Union.... If *Nineteen Eighty-Four* is even partially any kind of satire on our Western way of life, I'm a Chinaman.' Amazing how old street-fighters stop moving and lower their guards: 'If *Nineteen Eighty-Four* is even partially any kind...' I often read that passage on the more intellectual campuses, and they rolled in the aisles. But it isn't in the least funny if you don't know about O'Brien and his Left-Right late development. I can *just* see that, if you had grown up in the darkest mid-West, or in a Communist cell totally isolated from the rest of British society, and knew nothing about Orwell's other writings, you *could*, I admit, read the texts of *Animal Farm* and *Nineteen Eighty-Four* as purely an attack on the Soviet Union, and not even partially as any kind of satire on our Western way of life.

The worst atrocity was in the *Daily Mail*, which printed doctored extracts from the book throughout the first week in January. The guardian of the text is the literary agent Mark Hamilton, head of A.M. Heath Ltd, who is in the tricky position of being both agent to the estate (which now benefits the adopted son Richard Blair) and Sonia Orwell's literary executor. His decisions are usually better than this: each *Mail* page had a box by Professor John Vincent pointing out the anti-Soviet and anti-socialist implications of each altered extract, in case the *Mail's* readers were very, very thick. Hitherto, I'd only thought them thick. And not merely a grossly shortened text, but a simplified diction too: real Newspeak sub-editing. Nothing remained, for instance, of Goldstein's remarks about the useless manufacture of atomic bombs and the institutionalizing of the 'cold war' (the earliest use of the phrase I know is Orwell's in 'You and the Atom Bomb' of 1945): a device, Goldstein explains, to burn off 'surplus value', frustrate equality and maintain hierarchy. Nor were the *Mail* readers given the passage that spells out all that went on in sweet Julia's section of Minitrue:

> Lower down there was a whole chain of separate departments dealing with proletarian literature, music, drama and entertainment generally. Here were produced rubbishy newspapers containing almost nothing except sport, crime and astrology, sensational five-cent novelettes, films oozing with sex, and sentimental songs which were composed entirely by mechanical means on a special kind of kaleidoscope called a versificator. There was even a whole section...engaged in producing the lowest kind of pornography.

I share Orwell's view that the masses are controlled—or that people are massified—by prolefeed. We've no idea whether that is what they 'really want', for that is all they are *given*. A large part of his book is a great cry of rage that the Education Acts, the Reform Bills and cheap printing should have resulted in—the popular press. The disparity between formal literacy and the content of print does chill the bones: and that it should be done to Orwell himself!

*T*elevision and radio did better. I did scores of interviews in November and December: with the French, Swiss, Swedish, Dutch, American, German, Spanish (and Catalan), Australian and Japanese. In television and radio, words can be left out, but they cannot be deliberately written to suit editorial policy. But the producers usually cut when I said that the date 1984 was just a joke on George Orwell's part. On the whole, though, I was able to get them off the psuedo-question, 'Is 1984 going to be anything like Orwell prophesied?' and on to the, I think, better one: 'Of the things he was attacking in 1948, what should still worry us today?' What a difference it made when, not so often, the interviewers *had read the book*. The best moment was when a great Japanese literary journalist, who had come over specially, had trouble with his English; the hired cameraman had filmed me the week before for the Swiss, and had gone away and read the book: and so he asked the questions. Such small extramural triumphs are rare but worth whole seminars.

I didn't see the ninety-minute life, *The Road to 1984*, with James Fox as Orwell, produced for Granada Television by David Wheatley. But I read the script. Everything violent, sadistic, deathwishywashy, with flashbacks within flashbacks till the mind boggled, as I'm told the eye did too. No sign of the gentle, pastoral Orwell. I was sent the script because someone anonymous and friendly in the organization thought that I might be interested to see that every quotation from Orwell's own words could be found in my book. A massively simple research effort on someone's part. As was *Time* magazine's. *Time* boasted of putting a Reporter-Researcher on the project, their London correspondents interviewing Orwell's old friends and colleagues, before 'Senior Staff Writer Gray pondered the Orwell legacy.' Now either this tip-top *Time* team didn't get beyond Dillon's Bookshop or everyone they interviewed used the identical words they had used for me some years before. But there's no copyright in research, and they could have gone to the sources and reached exactly the same conclusions. That is possible. I used to find that some distinguished literary men prepared for being interviewed by me for the biography by closely rereading their old interview and articles. How wise not to trust their memories. Most people's memories are a compost of what they recall about a famous friend at the time and what they have subsequently read. 'I knew Orwell, Professor, ever since we both came back from Spain at the beginning of the thirties,' said Stephen Spender.

BBC Arena's five programmes, 'Orwell Remembered', produced by Nigel Williams, were well received and got in just before the invasion of Grenada and the turn of the year. But I was a bit disappointed: Nigel Williams had come to me two years before with a lot of interesting talk about the unreliability of memory (from my 'Introduction' to the *Life*), and wanting to do a programme that didn't sin by confusing the photographic authenticity of old people's remembrances with truth, but would instead cross-cut and juxtapose conflicting viewpoints and testimony. But it didn't really work out except in the Spanish war sequence. Elsewhere it proved too difficult. Old people talking were so compelling as images that the quest for truth soon went out of the window. Still, 'Orwell Remembered' was fascinating visually, even though it was inexcusable for Nigel Williams to read his well-chosen Orwell passages himself. Williams has the would-be classless, flat-vowelled, modern South London accent, invented by Paul Scofield, popularized by Peter Hall in Pinter productions, and affected since 1968 by the sixth forms of London Public Schools to show their classlessness and annoy their parents and teachers. Orwell plainly spoke in an upper-class military accent, the inflectionless tone of people who have had to read without comment reports about trivialities, massacres and monumental cock-ups regardless.

I'm sure there was a comic if morally rather impressive disjunction between the military tone of Orwell's voice and many of the radical things he said (and an alienation effect indeed, positively forcing the reader/listener to think): 'We cannot win the war without introducing Socialism, nor establish Socialism without winning the war.' Strange that we don't have any recording of his voice, when he worked for the war-time BBC writing scripts even after *Animal Farm* had made him internationally famous. Probably the truth is that his BBC colleagues regarded 'Old George' as one of the boys, and what a joke that one of his books had become a bestseller. Hope for everyone! Most unsuccessful authors deeply believe that it is all luck what isn't influence. But Ronald Pickup in 'Orwell on Jura'—a brilliantly successful, gentle and elegaic low-cost film from BBC Scotland, written by Alan Painter, produced by Norman McCandlish, directed by John Glennister—got the voice exactly. And the mannerisms and character. Old Orwell friends who saw it, and the two nieces and the nephews portrayed in it, were awed at the exactness of the impersonation. What a first rate actor can do! I think he got Orwell's character better than I did (but then, I don't think biographies should be about 'character'—Dr Johnson misled us and still more did Boswell). My only contribution was the simple suggestion that they listen to tapes of Avril Blair reminiscing about her brother.

'Mr Chairman, I know the lecture has been on Nineteen Eighty-Four *as a work of fiction, and the lecturer has made his point. But nevertheless would he mind telling us why, despite Orwell's own express prohibition in his will, did he write a biography at all?'*

'Well, thank you for asking that. It may relieve the gloom and boredom. I found that no problem [not quite true]. That was a problem for his widow, Sonia. When I first heard of his wish that no biography should be written, years before Sonia approached me or I thought of doing a life at all, I remember thinking, "that's either a very arrogant or a very modest fellow." I imagine that he thought biography meant what Lytton Strachey had made it mean: the reduction of a public achievement to some private "hidden wound". Some reviewers thought the worse of me

that I didn't find one, or else they didn't notice that I had. But I think that that's a pretty odd way to approach giving a clear account of someone's actual life. "Inspector, I've discovered that he had a very unhappy infancy." "Cut the shit, Sergeant, I want the record not the explanation!"'

I may have had a second drink before that lecture, or on the other hand, the second drink may have been wearing off, leaving me tired and irritable. I could see the year coming a mile off and realized that I was getting sucked back into Orwell and away from my romantic hope of being totally absorbed in a work on British-Irish relations. But I decided to lie back and enjoy it.

There's an apocryphal story that Sir Alan Bullock set 1 May 1963 as an arbitrary cut-off date for his life of Hitler, and if on 2 May evidence was discovered from captured archives that Hitler had Jewish parents on both sides, it would have to wait for the second edition. In my book, I had a deadline thrust on me. But I never reckoned on the afterbirth. And when the 'Great Year' began, I just lost control and my First of May became New Year's Day 1985. I couldn't resist Barcelona or Jerusalem, or Holland and South Germany for the British Council. Old students, whose careers seemed to hinge on my coming to the school, multiplied. I was asked to the Council of Europe's three days on '1984 and the Future', but was pledged to Pennsylvania at the time. I was not asked in September to the American Freedom Foundation's Orwell Conference at Peterhouse, where the princes of the radical Right gathered like Mormons to rewrite history and re-baptize the departed soul of Orwell as Rightist. They claimed that many old friends of Orwell attended. I could offer a list of those who didn't. Saint Malcolm Muggeridge did, who is of the opinion that had Orwell lived he would be a Conservative and a Catholic; and his closer old friend, Tosco Fyvel, who is convinced, he told the *Hampstead and Highgate Express,* that had Orwell lived he, like Fyvel, would have joined the SDP. I find it (sorry, Tosco) an odd kind of friendship that amends the views of a dead friend.

Some friends said, 'Bernard, you were clever to get your book out in 1980, then in paperback in time for the Great Year.' Again hindsight. I got it out then because a contract was signed in 1973 between Mrs Orwell and myself. I demanded unrestricted access to everything *and* an unrestricted right to quote from copyright anything he wrote, even if she didn't like the result; and the right to take the manuscript elsewhere if the publisher to the Orwell estate, Secker & Warburg, turned it down. And she countered, very sensibly, by saying that I must deliver within five years a publishable manuscript. When I delivered it, she had, predictably, changed her mind about the whole commission. The first version was not publishable, but Tom Rosenthal, then head of Secker & Warburg, pretended it was—held out desperately, as if at Verdun, against Sonia's attacks, and gave me time to regroup and rewrite helped by excellent readers. Harcourt, Brace Jovanovich in New York did not hold out; indeed Jovanovich himself needed little urging to drop it since on reading it he discovered that Orwell was a socialist, or that I persisted in foolishly thinking so. He lost a BIG non-returnable advance; I admire a man of principle. But by then Rosenthal was too shattered to celebrate Jovanovich's benediction. Sonia gave Rosenthal no peace. But she wasn't in a good position: she had actually lost the contract, her agent had never even seen it, and she had to ring me up to get a copy to take advice on how to break it; so the threat wasn't as serious as it sounded. And my small solicitor (Mr Peter Kingshill of Gray's Inn) had done his work well. It withstood the scrutiny of the big boys. 'It makes a change from conveyancing and divorces.'

Sonia was, I would say to questioners, really very magnificent and scatty. She read one review I wrote in the *New Statesman* (8 October 1971) of a volume of essays on Orwell edited by her friend Miriam Gross. I praised the book, called him a giant with warts; but ended by saying that 'the time may not be far off when there can be a full biography and a proper critical appraisal, not the strident attacks or warm justifications which dominated the Orwell market before these present essays.' I noted that she had asked Saint Muggeridge to do it, but that he had backed off:

A thousand pities that, with her obvious fears of enemies,

Orwell's widow presented the biography to such an Impossibly Busy Person and entrusted mainly to herself the Secker and Warburg so-called *Collected Essays, Journalism and Letters of George Orwell:* the best one can say is that it is a good amateur job, but incomplete, and is now an obstacle to a genuine collected works. Perhaps the excellence of the present essays may convince her that it is wrong to defend her late husband's reputation, papers and writings so jealously.

She rang up Tom Rosenthal and said, 'That's the man, who is he?' Never so cast-up and cast-down in one sentence. Sonia didn't know me, even though I was then writing signed articles monthly on the leader page of the *Observer,* being once one of David Astor's promising 'young men' (touching forty, still some promise left); Sonia, instead, had been reading the literary pages line by line to see if her protégés were being puffed, or to plan punishments for their detractors. She spent her fortune entertaining the great or fattening young lions in the hope they would grow into big, mainly male cubs of the kind towards whom Orwell (to his discredit) was not particularly tolerant—the 'pansy poets' and 'the nancy boys of literature' (usually from Cambridge). David Plante bit the hand that fed him in his portrait of Sonia in *Difficult Women*—witty, 'insightful' as they say, but nasty.

Of course she was impressed by the genius of my review. But I think it was a mixture of my luck and her guile. The luck, for me (since I instantly wanted to do it), was that that very week she had realized she could not stop Stansky and Abrahams' *The Unknown Orwell* from appearing, albeit she stopped them from quoting anything. Her guile was that I think she knew no more of me than that I was a professor of politics who could plainly write in English and not socialsciencese; so by choosing me, first, she would disappoint all her friends, those who had candidates or wanted to do it themselves (but that none could say she had acted irresponsibly—a professor, after all); second, by the same token she wouldn't actually lose any friends; and third, she probably believed I'd write a pretty flat, boring, wholly political account and not go too deep into anyone's motives, hers or his.

She was a strange mixture of sophistication and simplicity. And a very tough lady, but also a vacillating one, capable of great indecision as well as wild decisiveness. Tom Rosenthal wanted a press release announcing that there was at last to be an authorized biography. But I rang him up two days before and the morning before our deadline. Virtually the same conversation: 'Tom, she hasn't signed the contract. I'm going to say to the first journalist who gets hold of me that there's been an awful misunderstanding, that she hasn't met the only conditions which I think are possible for a scholarly biography with a living widow.' 'Don't worry, I'll talk to her.' I went to bed that night at about 11.30. My then wife said to me, 'Are you very upset?' I said that I was terribly disappointed but not upset. I knew what I needed to know. If she wouldn't sign, the whole project was impossible. 'I don't want to waste five years of my life and then have colossal quarrels and end up with a manuscript I cannot publish. I wasted two years with that damned Rowntree toleration project because nothing was put on paper.' Then as in a fairy story or a Le Carré novel, the bell rang and there was a taxi driver who had brought the signed contract from Chelsea to Hampstead. A little note was attached: 'I've signed your bloody piece of paper. Let's have lunch some time.'

The contract with Secker & Warburg had a secret clause. I insisted on deeding the British volume rights to a charitable trust to help young writers of the kind that Orwell would have helped had he lived. I told David Astor of this and he promised, being one of Orwell's friends, to match my first year's contribution. Rosenthal was very worried. He saw beyond my philanthropy. My philanthropy was genuine enough. I disliked the idea of making a lot of money out of a socialist; Sonia had already told me that she had torn up three or four thousand pounds of IOUs from 'poor writers' on Orwell's death; and I disliked the fact that after that good act she had made no charitable use whatsoever of her growing fortune. But my scheme was also intended to blackmail the widow. I would approach her shortly' before publication—say, the day before—tell her that my fund with some support from others was about to go public, and invite her to head the subscription list. But never try blackmail. By the time the book was being printed, she was dying from cancer, and obsessed with dislike of the book and with self-reproach for breaking Orwell's expressed wish. And she and I had not spoken for eighteen months. It all went very sad and sour.

I delayed the announcement of the trust for a decent two years, and the trustees have now made the third annual award to a poor writer.

So that's the tale of how I got on to the Orwell trail.

'Where would George Orwell have stood had he been alive today?'

'He would have stood with difficulty on either one or two sticks, being eighty-one. God knows. It is difficult enough to explain what did happen, quite impossible to explain what did not happen. I know that the good Mr Norman Podhoretz has written an article called 'If Orwell Were Alive Today' in Harper's Magazine *in January 1983, and that he says that Orwell would now certainly be a neo-conservative. He says that I only make him a socialist because I am a socialist. And I suppose ditto for Mr Michael Foot who is convinced that if his old* Tribune *colleague were still alive today and walking with him on Hampstead Heath he would still be an old style* Tribune *socialist. Foot may reach this conclusion for very much the same reasons as Podhoretz: an ideological perspective, comrades. But it does by chance coincide with the only possible scholarly rule: to locate somebody at their last known address on this earth. I wonder what Professor Zwerdling thinks?'*

'That sounds good to me, Bernard. Could I have a question, one on the text?'

American academic conferences on Orwell—there have been none in Britain (except for a University of London Extra-mural Department summer school)—tended to produce too many papers prepared in advance, over-long and remorselessly read: all written for publication, somewhere—perhaps. The art of the stimulating lecture is in decline. Idiot questions from the audience are usually ignored. and the discussion period is often token. But being used to extramural and political platforms, I'd usually take the questions and make something of them, or use them as an excuse to say something else that at least makes the questioner sit down feeling less of an idiot.

None of the campuses was in the least like those in Kingsley Amis, Malcolm Bradbury and David Lodge novels. As regards sex, I was never out of the sight of people called Deans, often 'Deans of Chapel'; and as regards booze, they've certainly cut down in the last decade. I remember as a young man first lecturing in the States and being tongue-tied by alcohol at free-flowing parties afterwards, frequently even before. Now so many people are munching fibre and drinking spring-water out of sterilized bottles. But it may be that a ghost is haunting the trail, particularly in departments of English Literature: the ghost of Dylan Thomas. Some plainly think that they killed him. I think he killed himself. Sensibly most American academic hosts now try and size up their guest a little, sometimes even ask him, before giving him the California wine equivalent of the old Martini treatment. The Martini is now almost as archaic as the cinema organ, the Atlantic liner, the kibbutzim and the LSE.

At Rosemont College, the good teaching sisters of the Holy Child of Jesus voted me an awfully good sport to stay the whole weekend. I thought that that was what I was being paid for, not just an in-and-out job; besides, some of the other papers were interesting, and the audience was fascinating. Indeed in most conferences, the bigshots tended to come in, give their paper and go. One moment there was Christopher Lasch, and the next even the grin was gone. After his talk, an old friend Sheldon Wolin, perhaps the best, hard punching light heavy-weight political philosopher, looked wistfully at me as if he wanted to talk, even suggested that I rode out to the airport in his cab. I stuck with the troops. Or, for the hour or so that they did stay, the bigshots would only talk to me or to each other. I suppose they have had enough of students all the time, and are bit uncertain how to handle odd members of the public. Orwell certainly attracts odd members of the public.

The very mixed nature of the audiences in the United States made one of my points for me. Even though these audiences were very different from the 'common man' for whom Orwell thought he was writing—the old Wellsian public library-using lower middle class—many of the non-university Americans who attended the campus lectures represented some kind of equivalent. They were not worried, unlike our dandy princes of the *New Left Review,* about Orwell's incorrect theoretical stance, or lack of one: they loved him for the irreverence of his radicalism, especially those who had got past—yes, perhaps in some way the stumbling blocks of—*Nineteen Eighty-Four* and *Animal Farm,* into the essays and the better of the earlier books. And many people turned up only having read, or heard of, *Nineteen Eighty-Four* to talk about war and peace. Several conferences almost turned into 'nuclear freeze' rallies, and the old militant Right did not picket. Perhaps it took 'em by surprise. Such discussions got far away from the text, but I had a private feeling that Orwell would have relished them. Satire is, after all, essentially negative, meant to discredit some established position and open up new thought and new perspectives. I don't say that the new thoughts would have been his thoughts, but he triggers them off. His books are very good for adult political education, much better than the humourless polysyllabic didacticism of many fellow socialists.

I certainly saw in the large numbers of non-university people who came to the campus Orwell occasions an America that is not represented by the President, however large his recent election margin. Many people were deeply worried by the nuclear arms race and the growth of state surveillance. On every occasion there was plenty of evidence that the Podhoretz body-snatching had not worked. Most people laughed at it. An almost definitive refutation was written by Gordon Beadle in the winter number of *Dissent* for 1984. Mark you, Podhoretz is a clever man. There's no street fighter more cunning than an old Trot turned radical right. The aforementioned January 1983 article in *Harper's* was not mistiming or jumping the gun, but was just the inevitable dreary preliminary, written with a minimal reference to the facts, to the cheerful, vulgar mass version that appeared later in the January 1984 *Reader's Digest:* Orwell as unequivocally a friend of free enterprise and an enemy of all socialism. But I doubt if such rubbish does anything more than titillate the saved-already, or please Mr Podhoretz's rich friends.

Some of the ambiguities have arisen because almost from the beginning people typecast Orwell as a simple, straightforward man who happened to write simple, straightforward books. It should be obvious that Nineteen Eighty-Four *is anything but straightforward: it is a highly complex text. So it is then thought that Orwell was over-reaching himself, or was in a kind of inspired depression. I simply assume, however, that Orwell was a highly self-conscious literary artist who deliberately achieved the effects he did achieve.*

In the end Orwell fully succeeded in his deepest ambition, to be a popular novelist. Indeed he is almost all that is left of our common culture, as regards the printed word rather than the broadcast media: he is still read for pleasure and instruction by an audience almost as wide as once read Dickens, Mark Twain and H.G. Wells, writers on whom he modelled himself. The plain style he developed was to reach the common man, not fellow intellectuals.

The further I got down the trail the more I realized that the references to Dickens and Wells did not mean much to the non-Eng. Lit. members of the audience—the majority. Thus I slipped in Mark Twain. But as it stands, that is a bit of half-thought-out word-processing, for Orwell did not model himself on Twain. He was rather like Twain, both in the audience he addressed and as a pessimistic humorist: 'God damn the Jews,' said the Yankee, 'they are as bad as the rest of us.' And I'd never been able to make much of Orwell's unsuccessful request in 1934 to Chatto and Windus to write a short life of Mark Twain. It needs more thought. I'm good at throwing up ideas in lectures, a bit lazy about following them up. So many, so many.

I was saying all this, and more, about Orwell's 'I' often being a literary device. I couldn't care less whether he shot an actual elephant or saw an actual hanging. In the biography I cast some doubt on both incidents. Sonia's amanuensis scrawled in my manuscript's margin, 'He said he shot a bloody elephant, why doubt his word!!!' It is not that his achievement would actually be greater if it was proven to be a fiction, then to be classified under 'Stories, short' rather than 'Elephants, shooting of'; but simply that the achievement is, in any case, a stylistic and, I think, a moral one (David Lodge has written so well on the stylistic achievement in his *The Modes of Modern Writing*). And here I had trouble with general audiences. Devoted Orwellians demanded that I should not shake their faith by doubting anything Orwell said. I would reply that I had greater faith than they in his ability as a creative writer. But he does figure in a kind of secular cult of 'the honest and straightforward man'. I didn't want to feed that, however worthy its adepts.

Then I learned something on the trail, hearing a lecture by Hugh Kenner on 'The Politics of the Plain Style'. Kenner's politics are not mine. But I found his argument very convincing. He locates Orwell's style in Defoe more than Swift, and he points out that plain style is as much a rhetorical device, to inspire trust, as is high style, to inspire respect. And the divide between fact and fiction is crossed freely by both men. *The Story of Robinson Crusoe, by Himself* said the original title page. Originally many people were confused, and it took some time to realize that the book was by Defoe, the Grub Street hack. And his *Journal of the Plague Year* is vivid with accurate and true detail, but Defoe was five at the time, so the 'I' was a storyteller's eye—though one who had obviously 'interviewed' or talked at length to many adult eye-witnesses of the horror.

The great trick of satire, Kenner said, is to create confusion about the genre. I had already been quoting Abraham Lincoln's remark that 'Honest Abe is very useful to Abraham Lincoln' as a way of confusing the too literally-minded common Orwellians: Lincoln, another god of the political cult of the common man, could be highly self-conscious about his projected image, and it fitted him well. As did Orwell fit Blair.

One trouble with Orwell's common style and populist stance is that they embarrass some academic literary critics. They are more comfortable with either the traditional novel or the modern, post-futurist one. They don't know what standards to apply to Orwell, and in Britain are still not sure that he is 'in the canon'. There has been a notable holding-off from any critical reappraisal of Orwell or reviews of books about him in both the *Times Literary Supplement* and the *London Review of Books*. Odd. Also, British literary editors are, I suspect, offended by the 'Is this 1984?' razzmatazz of the media. There's still a good deal of the 'Literature' with a capital *L* around, and if the mob get hold of the wrong end of the stick then the stick is polluted. As a political philosopher I've never handled a clean stick in my life.

The contrary was true in America. Some pretentious rubbish has been written, but also much very good criticism, either already published or in the pipeline from some of the conferences. American journals and universities actually like the interdisciplinary nature, as they see it, of Orwell's achievement. In Britain, it is an embarrassment when so much intellectual activity in universities is either demarcation disputes, or the marking of territory with ritual droppings. Some Eng. Lit. teachers made me quite (but quietly) angry by complimenting me publicly on the fact that I could read a text closely and write English. This was often plain arrogance, but in Britain it was also curricular isolation. They haven't got a clue what goes on in other subjects and pick up nothing, unlike their counterparts in the States, from their over-specialized students.

At the end of the day I prefer American middle-brow civic earnestness to our habitual extremes of indifferent high intellectualism or the cynical provision of prolefeed: the dismembering of the common man and the common reader. Orwell proves, on the demand side, that more common men can be common readers than literary editors imagine. But on the supply side, I'm puzzled. The frequent question, 'Are there any people writing like Orwell today, and if not, why not?' always stumped me. No pat answer. I could only go off into a reflective ramble.

'Orwellian' conveys gloom and pessimism; but 'Orwell-like' conveys simplicity, straightforwardness and a love of both nature and naturalness. For a man who prided himself on simplicity of expression, the varying interpretations of Nineteen Eighty-Four *both now and at the time of publication are extraordinary.*

In England the non-university Orwell evenings—especially a memorable Adult Education weekend in Higham Hall near Cockermouth—attracted the already convinced Orwellians. They were rather like old Wellsians, all radical in sympathies, but loving and exemplifying the non-political values: home-brewers and country lovers to a man and a woman, not the urban intellectual socialists who politicize everything. But they were all-too uncritical of him, and mostly pretty cool about *Nineteen Eighty-Four*. Even if they saw it was satire, they didn't like its savage tone. They didn't like 'that sort of book'. 'What sort of book?' 'Too modern and violent.' Many different worlds exist side by side. Both literary and political culture are pluralistic. In America popular audiences were inclined to read *Nineteen Eighty-Four* very literally, almost to forget it was a novel. And when I said 'Swiftian', as the original jackets had said, it didn't always ring a bell. It probably didn't even back then in 1949 to all common readers. I had to work on that.

Swift in Gulliver's Travels *lashed the follies of mankind, almost as if he despaired of them: the darkness was part of a grim or black humour. And Swift worked by gross and savage caricature—like some of our 'sick' cartoonists today. We do not believe that there are giants in a place called Brobdingnag, but we do believe that mankind can be monstrously cruel and also careless: some of the power-hungry like tramping on us, others do it by accident because they simply do not notice people of our size. We do not believe that there are dwarves in a place called Lilliput, but we do believe that mankind can be small, petty, pompous and parochial. Orwell similarly works by gross and comic—if your stomach is strong—exaggeration to mock the power-hungry of all kinds, whether totalitarian or domestic.*

*T*hat became in a sense the key passage in my little defence of *Nineteen Eighty-Four* as a thoughtful novel against '1984' as a media event, an event that confused rather than focused real public worries. By dismissing, like the Prime Minister, a literal-minded reading of the text, the inference was drawn that everything in the garden is still lovely—for those of us still in jobs and with a deep shelter. Podhoretz and O'Brien (the Chinaman, not the Oceanian Inner Party member) play the same game: if Orwell was an anti-Soviet communist, as indeed he was, then he must be really, truly, at heart, for unrestricted free-enterprise, tax cuts and greater military expenditure. Most of us dwell somewhere in between—as he himself often said.

Nevertheless, so many miss its satire. Perhaps it was too difficult to write a novel on two levels which would appeal equally to the common reader and the intellectual.

> He gazed up at the enormous face. Forty years it had taken him to learn what kind of smile was hidden beneath the dark moustache. O cruel, needless misunderstanding! O stubborn, self-willed exile from the loving breast! Two gin-scented tears trickled down the side of his nose. But it was all right, everything was all right, the stuggle was finished. He had won the victory over himself. He loved Big Brother.

*O*rwell had scrawled a random sentence in his last notebook: 'The big cannibal critics that lurk in the deeper waters of American quarterly reviews.' Ever so many of them have gone on about the despair, pessimism, even nihilism in this last passage of the novel; and most ordinary readers agree. Leave aside that it is *not* the last passage (the last passage tells us about the failure to translate the classics of English literature into Newspeak, and shows us that Newspeak had been abandoned). Just read that passage slowly, sorry. It is so familiar. I would sometimes read it twice, once in a tragic, serious voice, once in Mr Polly's kind of voice. Could Orwell possibly, had he meant to be pessimistic, have written such an awful, grotesque, inflated passage? 'O cruel, needless misunderstanding. O stubborn, self-willed exile from the loving breast.' This is deliberately the language of bad romantic popular novels. Then the early-Wellsian, ludicrous 'gin-scented tears', followed by two sentences lifted straight out of the stock language of street-corner evangelicalism and the temperance movement: 'the struggle was finished' and 'the victory over myself'. This is not pessimism, it is mockery. Big Brothers can break little brothers, but then look what they get: not Aryan man, Soviet man, still less *citoyen,* but a broken pathetic little drunk. They can break, but they cannot make. Hannah Arendt is right.

An old Southern story someone told me helped get the point across. The well-fed, clean-uniformed Federal cavalryman rides down and catches a filthy, limping rebel foot-soldier with a broken musket. 'Johnnie Reb, I got yer.' 'Yep, and a hell of a git you've got.'

Laughter is a great enemy of tyranny. Historians and social scientists have concerned themselves with two modes of controlling absolute power: the first is to put power against power—checks and balances, defence, even rebellion; the second is reason, persuasion, some might add prayer; but there is a third, much practised by both writers and ordinary people who have to live under tyranny, or even under elected governments whose policies they detest but cannot change; and this third dimension is often ignored by historians and social scientists, or only studied by students of literature as a genre, not for its content or social force—satire. Orwell mocks the power-hungry and offers Nineteen Eighty-Four *as both a mocking text and a weapon in all such struggles.*

But as one climbs down from the podium (I hope I can re-adjust to a fixed desk), the real world is still there and one almost looks forward to 1985. But these are just notes towards an interpretation of the Orwell phenomenon, which he would have hated.

Notes on Contributors

Norman Lewis's most recent book is *Voices from the Old Sea*, a section from which originally appeared in *Granta* 10: 'Travel Writing'. **Raymond Carver**'s fiction has appeared in *Granta*s 4, 8 and 12. In the new year Picador publish his *Collected Stories,* and Collins *Fires,* a new selection of poems and fiction. **Beryl Bainbridge** is the author of eleven novels, the latest being *Watson's Apology.* **Michael Ignatieff** lives in London. In October Chatto and Windus published his *The Needs of Strangers.* **Doris Lessing** contributed to *Granta* 13. Her new novel *The Terrorist* comes from Jonathan Cape in the spring. **Vladimir Rybakov**'s first novel *The Burden* was published in October. A second, *The Brand,* is currently being translated. **Breyten Breytenbach**'s account of his political imprisonment in South Africa, *The True Confessions of an Albino Terrorist,* was published in October. An extract appeared in *Granta* 12. **Todd McEwen** is the author of one novel, *Fisher's Hornpipe,* and two stories, 'Evensong' (*Granta* 8) and 'They tell me you are Big' (*Granta* 10). **Eddie Limonov**'s autobiographical novel, *It's Me, Eddie,* is published by Picador. He lives in Paris. **William Boyd**'s most recent novel is *Stars and Bars.* He contributed to *Granta* 7. **Josef Škvorecký**'s 'Miracles' was published in *Granta* 13. His new novel *The Engineer of Human Souls* comes from Chatto and Windus in February. **Don McCullin**'s photographs of El Salvador appeared in *Granta* 9. Collins publish a collection of his work in their series 'The Great Photographers'. **Reinaldo Arenas**'s novel *Once More, the Ocean* is published by Viking later this year. An extract appeared in *Granta* 13. He now lives in New York. **Christian McEwen** lives and works in London. The poet **Jaroslav Seifert** was awarded the 1984 Nobel Prize for Literature. Born in 1901, he is the first Czech winner of the prize, and was one of the original members of the Charter 77 human rights movement. London Magazine Editions publish his *Umbrella from Piccadilly,* poems about London and Prague. **Adam Mars-Jones** recently edited *Mae West is Dead,* an anthology of gay writing. He contributed to *Granta* 7, and is currently working on a novel. **Bernard Crick** is Professor of Politics at Birkbeck College, London. His other books include *In Defence of Politics.*

For reasons of space letters have been deferred until the next issue.